THE LANGUAGE OF BETTERARCHY

A Blueprint for Uniting Against Tyranny

BY DANI KATZ

Other Books by Dani Katz:

Yes, I Am
Word Up: Little Languaging Hacks for Big Change
Pop Propaganda: An Illustrated Guide

For the vanguards and the visionaries,
the change-makers and the responsibility-takers,
and the rebel badasses who came here
to transform the world for the more wonderful.

The Language of Betterarchy: A Blueprint for Uniting Against Tyranny
By Dani Katz

Published by Pierucci Publishing, P.O. Box 2074, Carbondale, Colorado 81623, USA

Copyright © Dani Katz, 2023

ISBN (Hardcover): 978-1-956257-85-4
ISBN (Paperback): 978-1-956257-86-1
ISBN (eBook): 978-1-956257-84-7

Library of Congress Control Number: 2023909782

TABLE OF CONTENTS

ACKNOWLEDGMENTS

The birthing of this book was a labor of love, patience, surrender and stamina. I spent extended bouts of isolation pulling slippery, microscopic idea-threads out of deep, dark, multidimensional wormholes, and wrestling, wrestling, wrestling them into digestible clarity as the landscape about which I was writing thoroughly upended itself/went insane. The process was bolstered by a handful of wise, generous and brilliant af friends and colleagues whom I would like to take this opportunity to acknowledge.

Thank you, Robert Forte, for being the first eyes, doing the first edit, and encouraging me to acknowledge the value of this work and to show up for its greatest possible expression and reach. Thank you to Maryam Henein for being a consistent ear, and for talking me through the times it got dark and murky, and I thought I'd lost my way. Thank you, Richard Rudd, for patiently sharing multiple mind/heart-expanding dialogues with me about the heterarchy/hierarchy situation as I meandered my way to clarity. Thank you, Nicole Chaison for your meticulous edits and your enduring support. Thank you, David Martin, for being such a passionate, proactive supporter of this book. And thank you, Stephanie Pierucci, for grokking my mission, having my back and going the distance to help me share this book with the world.

FOREWORD

I had the privilege of reading Dani's book during the holidays at the end of a bizarre year. For anyone witnessing the events of 2022 — and the madness that marked the preceding 24 months — the proposition that humanity could use a better conversation required no justification beyond every day's headlines.

It was with considerable irony that I suggested that I would write a "foreword" for this book, recognizing that the mere use of the term reifies a social convention that everything in this book challenges. But as we've done many times, I carelessly used shorthand in my e-mail, to which Dani efficiently replied in the affirmative — likely amused by the irony of my communication.

As we have come to describe it, sociocultural norms have presumed that language is a utility that is largely agnostic. The manner in which we encode communication signals — we want to tell ourselves — is a largely innocent bag of syncopated glyphs that only contain gravitas in their arrangement. In early education, we're taught to draw our normative shapes, recognize their approved phonetics, form arrangements of the same into words and weave those words into coherent phrases.

"Stay within the lines," is hypnotically repeated, until we stop doodling off the page and beyond the margins.

In ***The Language of Betterarchy***, Dani takes us off the page and well beyond the margins. In a relentlessly courageous treatise, we're invited on a considered journey to examine the colonization of our communication, which has led to our seemingly intractable conflicts within, between and across the landscapes of thought, self, relationship, community, culture and cosmology. With the relentless jack-hammer of the blindingly obvious, Dani allows us to see our accountability for the carelessness with which we harm ourselves and those with whom we interact. Rather than leaving us indicted by our collective, primitive, dualistic reductionism, we're invited to take action to change our behaviors and patterns, and adopt a foundation of communication and interaction that serves a more wholesome rendition of humanity.

For over two decades, I had the privilege of taking late-high school to early college students on trips to far flung regions of the world for what we called Heritable Innovation Trust internships. These experiences were to identify communities of persistence (expressions of humanity that have lived in coherence with the Earth, like Papua New Guinea's Komgi, Peru's Incas, and Mongolia's Gobi nomads). A prerequisite for these trips was a commitment to what I called "non-interrogatory living" — living with no questions. It is, after all, the lens we choose to place upon our perception that shapes the candidate observations we may even consider.

Allow an example.

I would take students to the beach, and ask them to walk along the shore and a choose a shell. Dutifully, they'd wander off for several minutes variously picking up and dropping various colorful remnants of the lives of mollusks and bivalves. After a few minutes, treasure in hand, they'd return, and we'd look at the assembled geometry and luminescence. I would then have each student take out a notepad, and write down all the things that they saw in an abundance of two or more on the beach.

Waves

Trees

Birds

Pebbles

After several minutes of observation and musings, I'd ask everyone to read aloud their lists. In two decades, no one ever listed "shells", despite the focus they had placed on *nothing but shells* at the outset of the exercise.

When we ***look for*** a thing, we engage in a multi-dimensional fallacy. First, we formulate a template of the condition for which we'll confirm or approve the object of our focus. Second, we will (with varying degrees of awareness or consciousness) form a set of criteria which will dictate a ranking of the disqualifiable, in favor of the ideal. Finally, we'll set about to justify the self-fulfilling adjudication on the rightness of our first two assumptions with an artifact that reifies our assumption. In short, we'll not only ***not*** look for a thing — we'll actively blind ourselves to that for which we've decided we're not looking that would challenge our *a priori* conceptualization.

Questions, when they are formed, at least inhibit — if not outright prohibit — us from sensing and perceiving that which we did not even contemplate as possible. And it is this awareness that I encourage you to hold as you meet Dani's work.

I would offer my personal experience: Read the book twice. First, read it with an awareness and innocence that allows you to see yourself reading it. Whenever you encounter a twist, trigger, insight, or puzzle, make a mental (or doodle a) note. See if you can feel the conversation into which you are being invited. Then, equipped with that perspective, read it again. This time, in dialog with Dani and your own experience. If you could engage a conversation, what would be the nature of the stories you'd tell to expand upon the ideas that you encounter here?

I've worked for over three decades in linguistic genomics — the study of the socio-neuro-endocrine-acoustic-kinesthetic impulse to communicate. I've developed complex mathematical models to understand the role of the originators, propagators and manipulators of communication signals, for applications ranging from politics to economics, from science to metaphysics, from encryption to terrorism, and a myriad of other uses. Having deciphered some of the world's most flabbergasting mysteries, I've come to realize that language is ***not the innocent artifact of culture that it's been camouflaged to be. To the contrary, it is one of humanity's***

most potent incantations for blessings and curses. It is not "innocent". It is fraught with nuance to intentionally evoke, provoke and invoke the full range of the best to worst of humanity.

Dani has taken an invaluable step into illuminating the stage upon which humanity's drama is unfolding. And as the choreographer of that dance, I think you will find that the story you might be expecting is one that is replete with twists that, like me, you didn't see coming. So, in the spirit of this book, invite yourself to transcend the notion of passive reader, and join Dani as a conversationalist in humanity's much needed conversation to move beyond the tyrannical *-archies* that constrain us, into an engaging unfolding of a more beautiful, considered and thoughtful expression of our essence.

Dr. David E. Martin
Founder M·CAM International

AUTHOR'S NOTE(S)

LET'S PRETEND IT'S 1999

As a rabble-rousing, free-speech loving, heteronormative, Gen X gal who bristles at politically correct language policing, I tend employ examples, metaphors and pronouns that reflect my own leanings. To be clear, this does not mean I have any issues with folks who identify or feel differently than I do. I don't. It's simply how I write and roll.

To this end, I have done my best to mix up the examples, the genders and the languaging; and still, as we move forward, I invite us to slip on our big girl/boy/zebra panties, and to take responsibility for whatever triggers we have been indoctrinated to attach to certain words or phrases, while eschewing the urge to get butt-hurt about engineered identitarian irrelevancies meant to divide, distract and mindfuck us.

The aim of this book is to illuminate the linguistic landmines that have been embedded in our lexicon to keep us distracted, triggered, fragmented and bickering. As such, I encourage you, superstar, to keep the purity of my intentions in mind, and to sidestep any otherwise loaded words or phrases that would have us surrendering our emotional centers to the ideological programming that seeks to blind us to the meat of the matter.

EVOLUTION ALERT!

The language of betterarchy[1] is an evolutionary communication paradigm. While this languaging system is aligned, appropriate and beneficial for every human on the planet, the precepts I share in this book are specifically intended for folks who are consciously choosing to evolve our Selves and our world for the better.

Free will rocks, and while there is nothing inherently wrong or bad about moving through life as disempowered victims, eschewing agency and responsibility for our lives and our culture, instead capitulating to a lopsided, lackluster reality construct over which we erroneously claim to have no agency, this is not my target audience.

And while I absolutely welcome all eyes, hearts and critical thinking capacities focused on these words and precepts, know that this book was written for the change-makers and the transformation agents, and is thus angled to support conscious evolution, and accelerate the transformational process.

THE STRIKETHROUGH SITCH

While the precepts and principles that comprise the language of betterarchy are super simple and easy to digest, the learning curve is all about mindfulness and practice, as we are rewriting habitual languaging patterns and consciously recrafting our lexicon as we go.

To this end, I have included a handful of real-time languaging upgrades as a means of demonstrating how to employ these betterarchical techniques. And so it is that as you make your way through this book, you will notice a smattering of words and phrases that have been crossed out and replaced with betterarchical versions. This is neither error, nor sloppiness, rather a means of demonstrating how and when to apply these upgrades.

---

1   A high(er)-frequency organizational system marked by freedom, empowerment and equality of opportunity, functioning to serve and foster the greatest good of all.

NOT TO BE REPETITIVE...

In the pages that follow, I will be retracing a bit of the ground I covered in my first Quantum Languaging book, *Word Up: Little Languaging Hacks for Big Change*. While it is not my intention to be repetitive, I have included a smattering of words and phrases about which I have written in the past as a means of sharing different angles of analysis and perception through which we can deepen our understanding of the various layers of coding embedded in our language, and grok how they are operating to shape our worldviews and our reality.

INTRODUCTION

As a journalist, author, Quantum Languaging consultant, my relationship with words is deep and multifaceted. I don't simply engage words from the standpoint of a writer, wherein I use language to communicate the ideas that live inside my head (although, to be clear, I do plenty of that, too). I approach words multidimensionally, unearthing the frequencies encoded within them, and analyzing the various levels upon which these vibrations are operating in our reality. The deeper I delve into my otherwise incessant examinations into the many dimensions upon which words function, the more intrigued I become with their use as reality creation tools. To this end, I have taken to examining the world through the lens of the words that shape it.

When I hone in on a distorted reality construct — on a cultural trend, leaning, movement or emergence that isn't functioning optimally, or that I sense is doing me and/or the collective a disservice — I focus my attention on the language informing it. Unearthing the distortions embedded in the words allows me to understand the glitches expressing in the construct itself.

Language and reality are inextricably bound. Distortions embedded in our reality constructs are always present in the language informing them.

THE VICTIMIZATION CRESCENDO

It was around 2012 when I started to notice certain segments of the population erupting in impassioned war cries, loudly proclaiming victimhood, while demanding the swift and drastic reallocation of power and privilege. Various present-day and historically marginalized groups, as well as their self-proclaimed "allies," were demanding their piece of the proverbial pie, while demonizing those who were holding, or who had historically held pole position.

While many of the inequities were obvious, something about these outcries and the narratives informing them didn't feel right. Maybe it was the rage, the blame, the name-calling or the intolerance, but there was a flavor to this social justice revolution that just felt — well, *off*. And so it was that I turned my attention to the language of identity and ideology, which lead me to a deep examination of hierarchy, and an even deeper deconstruction of the language that sustains it.

THE HIERARCHY TRAP

Though the cries for social change were — and still are — loud and resonant, the change being proposed doesn't feel like progress. The shifts that folks, and politicians, and celebrities, and corporations, and organizations are demanding are all taking place inside a fundamentally rigged system that continues to go unquestioned, unchecked and unchanged, which means that — despite a handful of shallow optics — nothing is actually changing, at all.

According to the loud, angry voices dominating the societal landscape, the solution to our cultural clusterfuckiness, and the planetary ills it is allegedly engendering, is to continue to play the exact same game in the exact same way, effectively rearranging the pieces such that those who used to occupy the bottom rungs of the cultural ladder are elevated to the top, while those who used to hold pole position are shuffled to the bottom.[2] Duly kicked to the curb, this new underclass is not just expected to surrender their jobs, status, power and dignity, they are also to quietly accept a slew of gender-biased, racially-degrading insults and affronts, because in the midst of our collective hysteria, we seemed to have forgotten Gandhi's whole *eye for an eye leaves the whole world blind* thing.

The problem with this proposed "solution" is that it's not actually a solution at all. Reorganizing the pieces of a broken game does not a better game make. Sure, it might seem like a win for the folks stepping into top rung positions. But, given that this short-term, identity group-specific "win" is reliant upon a great big bunch of losses, by way of a newly branded underclass who is now expected to take one (okay, lots) for the team, this "solution" is bound to create the same imbalances and resentments through which we are already sifting, while continuing to erode the integrity of our social fabric, and doing humanity a grave disservice.

From the perspective of betterarchy, the issue isn't a matter of *which* societal segments are now being shifted into pole position, or *which* societal segments are now being expected to take their positions at the bottom of the rung, the issue is in the privileging and unprivileging of classes in the first place. The issue is hierarchy.

---

2   Within the construct being controlled by those who occupy — and have always occupied – the real-deal top rungs of the societal ladder. And this is the whole point – to pit the plebes against one another so that we are too distracted by the task of fighting amongst ourselves for crumbs of comfort, status, survival and acknowledgment to notice the manipulations/misdeeds/existence of the truly privileged few who are pulling all the strings.

Hierarchy

Hierarchy is an organizational construct that alleges for there to be winners, there must also be losers — that for some groups to flourish, others must get short shrift. Hierarchy is an outdated, old paradigm, "me"-based system that relies upon the illusions of fear, lack, limitation, conflict, separation and victimhood to sustain itself.

While hierarchy aims to convince us that we must compete, struggle and fight over a limited array of dwindling resources to scrape by on a scarce and dying planet, the truth is that it is our birthright to thrive — to cooperate, innovate and co-create in peaceful, loving harmony, on an abundant planet overflowing with more than enough resources to go around.

The fundamental issue plaguing our precariously polarized populace is that instead of questioning our tired, old allegiance to hierarchy, and switching it up, many of us have bought into the erroneous and illogical notion that victimhood is awesome and "privilege" is bad, and thus, remain distracted by the task of reorganizing hierarchy — of simply flipping the roles contained within this antiquated sub/dom dynamic that is hurting us all.

The choice to redecorate a moldy, collapsing, vermin-infested house is not a wise solution, nor a sustainable solution, nor any kind of solution at all. The undertaking doesn't address the rotting foundation that is really, truly the issue. The same can be said for the gratuitous optics of reorganizing the privileged and the marginalized — a pointless task that serves only to uphold the illusion of separation, while continuing to foster lack, limitation, division, conflict and all the other societal ills that are inextricably bound to the hierarchical structure. To merely flip-flop the positions of status within hierarchy is to continue to feed a culture of inequality, resentment and dissonance. It is a distraction, as well as a colossal waste of time and effort, that is only exacerbating the very issues we are now being called — as a global human collective — to correct, somewhere in the realm of immediately.

Given that hierarchy is reliant upon a marginalized segment of society who will ever and always be expected to take short shrift, while small handfuls kinda-sorta flourish, the only real solution that will allow us ALL to thrive in peaceful, abundant unity is not a different configuration of hierarchy; rather, it is society's evolution out of hierarchy altogether.

FIRST STOP: HETERARCHY

When I launched this inquiry, I had assumed that the solution to the hierarchy problem was to evolve our culture into *heterarchy* — an organizational structure that privileges no one above anyone else. Whilst heterarchy acknowledges that all humans are unique, and will necessarily perform different roles and functions in society, the system does not place a higher or lower *value* upon these roles. Heterarchy allows everyone to thrive harmoniously in an atmosphere of mutual respect, trust, tolerance, inclusivity and cooperation.

Alas, while heterarchy sounds great, in theory, I struggled to find examples of heterarchical societies and large-scale implementation. Sure, I happened upon a handful of heterarchical departments and small-scale organizations. It was even rumored that the Mayan civilization was itself heterarchical. But, given that the entire population mysteriously disappeared in what historians purport was an instant, leaving no records as to how — exactly — their heterarchical (and human sacrificial) civilization was structured, I was stumped.

While I spent a ridiculous amount of hours, days, weeks and months attempting to invent an entirely new societal structure, I found my way to an epiphany: I don't know anything about societal restructuring. My expertise is words. It is not my job to invent a new societal structure. My job is to illuminate the hierarchical distortions that have been perving humanity's primary reality creation tool (aka: language) for centuries, and evolve our communication paradigm such that a newer, better societal structure will organically emerge from it.

I have spent the past several years studying the cultural landscape, focusing specifically on the lexicon informing it and the discourse emerging from it. I have heard the cries for justice and equality, and inclusivity, and unity being expressed with an outdated language that is sabotaging these aims and perpetuating the very imbalances those speaking them are claiming to course-correct. I have observed this exercise in futility deride and divide our human family, and I am no longer willing to sit idly by, as we chase our own tails, and destroy ourselves with a language steeped in division and disempowerment.

I don't claim to know how to design the new structure into which we are evolving. What I do know is that the old structure isn't working — that we've hit the wall with all the fear, lack, division, conflict and disempowerment that hierarchy engenders, and that it is time to up-level into an infinitely more cooperative, compassionate, supportive, sustainable, unified, peaceful societal structure, now.

BETTERARCHY

And so it is that I am calling this new structure "betterarchy." Because, while we can waste our time dithering with the details of the next iteration which has yet to emerge, the one thing I trust we can all agree upon is that, whatever it is — be it panarchy, synarchy, heterarchy, holocracy or *something else*-ocracy — it will be better and more supportive for humanity than hierarchy, which will always keep us apart, and at odds with one another, when our most pressing task is to unify, cooperate and thrive.

I realize the undertaking of evolving our culture from hierarchy to betterarchy (however it ultimately configures) may sound momentous and overwhelming, rife with heavy lifting and complicated configuring. Alas, duly resourced with the tools and concepts I present in this book, the shift is ~~slated to be~~ already presenting itself[3] as easy, and graceful, and fun.

Our world is a reflection of our language. The words we speak, think, ink, type and exchange are the materials with which societies and their corresponding structures[4] are built. As we commit to changing our world, we must first change our language.

This is where the language of betterarchy comes in. You see, hierarchy is a concept. It is not a physical *thing* with weight and mass, constructed of brick and mortar, or steel and rivets. Hierarchy is an abstraction that sustains itself through our collective agreement, which is itself created and perpetuated through language. The way we shift out of hierarchy, and into a unified, peaceful, abundant, empowered, cooperative, sustainable society, is by speaking betterarchy.

As a 5D word wizard who is ever and always tracking language and how it is functioning to shape our species and our culture, my inquiry has allowed me to hone in on the hierarchical hiccups informing our collective languaging patterns. All day, every day, we unconsciously use hierarchical languaging rife with fear, lack, division and disempowerment, which is sustaining these energetics in our culture, as well as the larger hierarchical construct that's working against us all.

Reality configures to reflect the language that is continuously programming our collective field. This means the swiftest, most effective way to upgrade our culture, and change our reality for the better, is to upgrade our language. The words we speak, the words we think, the words we write, the words we type, the words we hear, the words we see, the words we loop — these are the tools that are supporting our swift and graceful quantum leap into betterarchy.

This book is the roadmap that shows us how.

---

3   The specifics behind the shift from future-based potential to present-moment declaration will be unpacked in the ensuing pages.
4   As well as every single thing in our entire known reality.

*"You cannot evolve faster than your language,
because the language defines the culture of meaning.
So, if there's a way to accelerate the evolution of language,
then this is real consciousness expansion."*
— Terence McKenna

PART 1
THE MYTH OF
PATRIARCHY

"...if we free ourselves from the prevailing models of reality, it is evident that there is another logical alternative: that there can be societies in which difference is not necessarily equated with inferiority or superiority."
— Riane Eisler

The cultural landscape is — let's not sugar-coat it — a shit show. The populace is deeply, dangerously divided. Riled up. Angry. Quick to take offense, lash out and leap to police each others' language, beliefs and behavior. We ferociously defend our virtue, our victimhood and our ideological allegiances, simultaneously shaming, blaming and deriding those we've pinpointed[5] as toxic, selfish and privileged, as villains, racists, oppressors and microaggressors, and the reason our feelings got hurt.

Conversations between those identifying with "opposing" sides of the perceived/engineered divide tend towards the heated, rife as they are with pitfalls, projections, politically correct landmines and a host of über-heightened and extra very intense emotions. Disparaging labels and projections of ill-intent are hurled willy-nilly across the landscape without second thought. While it used to be that we could agree to disagree, we now find ourselves projecting the worst possible characteristics and

---

5   Or, in most cases, been indoctrinated to pinpoint.

intentions upon those who don't vote the way we vote, prioritize the causes we prioritize, or parrot the same talking heads we parrot. Now, thanks to the 24/7 mass media programming/propaganda coming through our every screen, folks who don't think and believe exactly the way we think and believe have become mortal enemies we cancel, name-call, demonize, dehumanize and wish terrible atrocities upon.

And, while this particular expression of our collective clusterfuck is comprised of a diverse smattering of tribes, each with their own particular flavor of gripes and grievances, there is a singular through line that connects them all: they are, claim to be, or have historically been marginalized. These groups identify as disempowered underclasses and victims of systemic and/ or widespread oppression, and are now fighting, loudly and fervently, to reclaim their piece of the proverbial pie — a proverbial pie that used to be reserved for those now being demonized as cis, white, hetero, Republican, toxic, "privileged" or what have you.

And, while the LGBTQ folks want to see more LGBTQ folks at the top, and Black people want to see more Black people at the top, and ladies want to see more ladies at the top, the fix ALL these groups[6] are proposing remains the same: those who have historically been given short shrift are bestowed their rightful place at the top, while kicking those who used to sit on the top rung to the curb – hard, and repeatedly, with steel-toed stilettos, ill-will and scorn. It's an old-school, eye-for-an-eye sort of rebalancing vision, wherein nothing will really be evened out until the whole world is blind, bruised and bleeding.

Despite each group's unique spin on how exactly the imbalance of power and resources has fucked them over, these factions are, for the most part, unified by a common perceived enemy: patriarchy. In fact, patriarchy has become the universal scapegoat for most every ill plaguing our planet and our populace.

---

6   And their so-called allies.

TRIGGER DISCLAIMER

My intention is not to discount or diminish anyone or any group's plight or challenges. I respect and honor everyone's and every group's own unique batch of issues, experiences and perspectives. My aim is simply to illuminate the shared through lines linking these factions.

That being said, I know that I am treading dangerous waters here. Given the current cultural climate, and all the silence, contrition and canceling the Kool-Aid swilling masses have been known to demand, for our intents and purposes, I am choosing to rest in the protective comfort of my own double X chromosomes, and to focus on the man/woman divide, while encouraging us to apply the perspectives we explore in this book to any and all groups identifying/being identified as victims.

My choice to narrow this examination to the gender divide is public service as much as it is self-protection, given the ubiquity, intensity and volume of the patriarchy scapegoat narrative, and the confusion about Masculine/Feminine polarities, as well as the much touted, thoroughly misunderstood "return of the divine feminine," about which New Age folks named after weather, crystals and mythic goddesses like to wax poetic and reductive.

Please be advised that, at this stage of our examination, and throughout the entirety of this book, "women" are serving as a placeholder for every marginalized group claiming victimhood, and demanding their turn at the top. Feel free to apply these perspectives to any and all alleged victim classes or identitarian groups claiming a raw deal.

PATRIARCHY: THE UNIVERSAL SCAPEGOAT

Modern mythology would have us believing that patriarchy is to blame for everything terrible that's ever happened since the beginning of time — from pollution to polio to stretch marks — and that the cure for this universal malady is for women to take their role at society's top rungs. The push isn't for matriarchy, per se, even though the idea of women at the top is often mislabeled as such. And this is really the point — well, one of 'em...

So, what is patriarchy, anyway? Traditionally, patriarchy refers to an organizational structure that privileges men over women, and that places dudes in positions of favor and authority. We see this the world over, across the vast majority of cultures and continents. There are secondhand tales of exceptions – native tribes in far off lands wherein women rule, or hold positions that lend themselves to more egalitarian, utopian social structures. Still, we cannot deny the dominance of men the world over, and the imbalance of power their positioning has engendered.

And yet, the fact that the majority of those in power are men, and that it's men who seem to be driving our Earth ship – making the decisions, calling the shots and hogging the wages, the resources, the window offices and the airwaves – is an expression of a bigger, deeper, more insidious meta distortion, which is itself fueling patriarchy, and inciting this imbalance in the distribution of power and status between men and women. In fact, I purport that this bigger, deeper, more insidious meta distortion is responsible for *all* the power imbalances between *all* races, religions, cultures, beliefs and ideologies the world over, since the beginning of time.

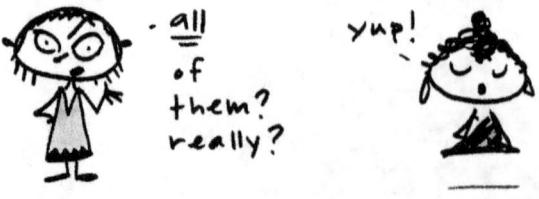

To treat the issue of patriarchy topically, by replacing the men in power with women, is pointless tail-chasing — performative optics meant to appease and distract the masses. The scenario is akin to smearing antibiotic cream atop a rash that's being caused by a food allergy, while continuing to gorge ourselves on the exact same sustenance that is causing the reaction in the first place.

Patriarchy isn't the problem. It is a *symptom* of an infinitely more nuanced, insidious and widespread issue that most people don't even realize is plaguing our planet. The issue is *hierarchy*.

Alas, before we can dive into the hierarchical meat of the matter, deconstruct this infinitely more nuanced and widespread issue, and do away with the distraction it poses, we must dispel the myth of patriarchy, once and for all. And, while I rarely advocate the use of language to limit anyone or anything, I'm going to tip-toe out of character while standing behind the assertion that it is *impossible*[7] to get an integrated, big picture handle on patriarchy or the real-deal culprit, which is hierarchy, without a broader understanding of Masculine and Feminine polarities and the characteristics that differentiate them. Because patriarchy is an expression of the larger meta imbalance between the Masculine/Feminine, we *can't*[8] truly correct this structural imbalance without addressing the root of what is causing it in the first place.

Masculine/Feminine Polarities

To be clear, I am using the capital-*M* "Masculine" and the capital-*F* "Feminine" to refer to the complementary opposites — the energetics, characteristics and qualities of being/expression — that inform every level of reality. I am *not* referring to the incarnate humans who are animated by these polarities. A lot of people get stuck on this fundamental misunderstanding, conflating the notion of Masculine/Feminine energetics with *men* and *women* as gender-delineated human embodiments. This confusion often inspires folks to get their panties in a big, huffy bunch,

---

7   While we will explore the disempowering implications of "impossible" in the Limitation Languaging segment, this is one of the rare instances wherein it is accurate.

8   See footnote above.

and push back on these polarity distinctions with outraged declarations, like, "How DARE you say that women are chaos," even though nobody ever claimed that "women" were chaos, but were rather merely attempting to differentiate between the structure that is characteristic of the direct, linear Masculine, and the wild, circuitous nature of the Feminine – polarities, not people.

So, before we move forward, let's be super clear that when I reference the "**M**asculine" and the "**F**eminine," I am talking about the complimentary poles of existence that animate every speck of reality in this dimensional realm we Earthlings call home.

Third dimensional reality is fundamentally dualistic in nature, meaning that it is comprised of equal and opposite forces, commonly referred to as "Masculine" and "Feminine." These polarity distinctions are regularly employed in the fields of science, spirituality, metaphysics, machinery, masonry, engineering, philosophy, et al. They are referenced throughout various disciplines and cultures, in different forms, as in *yin/yang, anima/animus, left-brain/right-brain,* etc. Call them what you like, the characteristics differentiating Masculine and Feminine polarities are consistent across all fields and genres.

Masculine	Feminine
external	internal
doing	being
analysis	intuition
structured	random
independent	interdependent
competitive	cooperative
logic	values
linear	circular
results	process
differentiating	integrating
dividing	unifying

For simplicity's sake, let's examine these distinctions through the lens of left-brain/right-brain functions. From this vantage point, the left-brain (aka: the Masculine) is responsible for reason, logic and analysis; while the right-brain (aka: the Feminine) is responsible for creativity, intuition and emotion. While the left-brain divides, separates and differentiates, the right-brain perceives and honors the fundamental unity that connects all life. The left-brain adheres to data points and statistics, and to the measurable and the material, while the right-brain is connected to the intuitive and unseen realms that the Masculine-dominant patriarchy indoctrinates us to dismiss and deride.

Western culture has long elevated Masculine qualities of doing, fixing, differentiating and generating, while devaluing the Feminine polarity that expresses as being, feeling, integrating and accepting. Patriarchy is just one expression of this imbalance that we see at a structural/organizational level. But, the tendrils of influence the imbalance yields are long and many, tangled and insidious, extending far beyond the perceived/reductive "battle of the sexes."

Reason vs. Intuition

Reason and logic are functions of the left-brain, and are thus, decidedly Masculine; just as emotion and intuition are right-brain functions and are quintessentially Feminine. One of the ways our culture has historically elevated the Masculine and devalued the Feminine is by consistently and imperiously deferring to reason and logic, while dismissing emotion and intuition as irrelevant, while shaming and disparaging their expression and esteem.

The effects of privileging the Masculine polarity over the Feminine are rampant and insidious, because – like language, itself – they shape our perceptions and the meaning we make of our experience at a fundamental level, thereby distorting our worldview accordingly.

Masculine materialism has blinded us to the veracity, value and relevance of anything and everything that cannot be seen, touched, tasted, measured or peer-reviewed. While physics has proven that 99% of what we call "reality" is contained within the invisible spaces *between* objects and atoms, Masculine dominance has us denying the validity of anything we cannot see, weigh or measure. And so it is that ancient healing modalities like acupuncture, Ayurveda and herbalism are dismissed as "pseudoscientific" nonsense. Practitioners and adherents are mocked as woo-woo nutjobs, because the Masculine doesn't just privilege the material over the unseen; it denigrates those who believe differently, in its shadowy attempts to protect its dominance and perceived superiority.

Bigger, Faster, More vs. Wise, Humane, Compassionate

The imbalance between the Masculine and the Feminine can be seen in our race to innovate more, bigger and better technology without pausing to consider or dialogue about whether it is in our species' best interests to produce and employ these so-called "advances." Culture's overemphasis on forward-driving "progress" has us skipping the part where we consider whether things like nuclear bombs, self-driving cars and smart-chipped, automated everything serve the best interests of the people and the planet, and not just the egos and net worth of the shareholders.

The bias that has us unconsciously favoring the Masculine over the Feminine can be seen in our race to colonize other planets, weaponize space and take joy rides to the outermost reaches of the atmosphere while millions of Earthlings go to sleep hungry every night. The Masculine is focused on innovating, achieving and moving technology forward, while the Feminine is inclined to care for the wellbeing of the whole, and knows that — while innovation and technological progress have their place — safeguarding the collective's most basic needs takes priority over this kind of "achievement."

THE AUTOMATION SNAG

Society's verily pathological drive for digital automation serves the Masculine principle, in terms of technological innovation and a cold, profit-driven ideal of sterile, homogenized efficiency. Pre-recorded prompts and monotonous, robot-voiced responses have come to replace sentient humans, marked by fluctuations in tone, mood and personality.

Automation doesn't take into consideration what is best for the whole, meaning the humans who – together – comprise our society. Think of the scores of people who have been put out of work, heartlessly replaced by a computer program with pre-recorded instructions to "press 1 for yes, and 2 for no," as though our every issue can be reduced to a simple either/or, yes/no response that an algorithm can effectively handle for us. Consider the warm-blooded, sentient folks who used to emote and empathize, who have now been replaced with self-checkout machines, which robotically bark "Unexpected item in the bagging area" when our hands or children veer too close to the scanning mechanism.

The Masculine-dominant minds that decided it would be a swell idea to replace truckers with automated cars, which can drive 24/7, and won't demand time-off for holidays or knee surgery, are not attuned to the Feminine principle, which considers and serves the greatest good for all beings. Because, it's not only truckers who are losing their jobs to machines, it's the folks working in the countless rest stops, roadside cafes and other small businesses that are dependent upon the trucking industry as their customer base, and which will be forced to close when their services, products and homemade peach cobbler are no longer in demand, given that self-driving trucks don't get tired or hungry, to say nothing of those niggling urges to pee and stretch their legs.

We Are ALL Masculine AND Feminine

All humans are animated by a combination of these two polarities. We all have left-brains and right-brains. We all have Masculine and Feminine qualities and characteristics. When we talk about the suppression, repression and oppression of the Feminine, we are referencing the Feminine nature that *both* men and women embody. Similarly, when we talk about the elevation of the Masculine, we are referring to the lauding and over-emphasizing of these qualities, characteristics and modes of expression in ALL people – men and women, alike.

The elevation of Masculine modes of being has been encoded into our belief systems and existential orientation at a fundamental level. Hence, the pressure we feel to do and achieve; the guilt and antsiness we wrangle while resting, relaxing and replenishing; the challenges so many of us navigate around receiving; our complicated relationship to emotions, vulnerability and free expression; the myth of the starving artist, and the perceived stability of the corporate minion. The list is truly endless.

And while women are – generally speaking — wired to embody and exhibit more Feminine qualities than their male counterparts, given that we have *all* been operating within the construct of patriarchy for countless centuries and generations, both men and women have been programmed with the unconscious contempt for the Feminine, and the elevation of the Masculine, and are now embodying this cultural distortion and smearing it all over our world.

What this means is that women are expressing this Masculine/Feminine imbalance just as much as the men are.

No one is unscathed by patriarchy. Because patriarchy isn't just top-down control and domination; patriarchy is how our minds are programmed and our worldviews are shaped.

Patriarchy is a Point of View

While it's both easy and fashionable to point to men, industry, capitalism or colonialism as the villains behind inequity in our culture, the status afforded to Masculine energies, perspectives and modes of existence is the true nexus point of the imbalance between the Masculine and the Feminine. This nexus point is particularly insidious because it is invisible, and because it seeds this inequality and this imbalance into everyone's worldview — men and women, alike.

From this vantage point, it doesn't matter if it's men in charge, or women in charge, or purple, one-eyed unicorns in charge, when the worldview informing the collective lens of perception, style of leadership and means of doing, being and engaging are still being informed by this tired old imbalance that has us elevating Masculine thought, perspective and action, while devaluing the Feminine versions. What this means is that, were we to snap our fingers, and magically reorganize society such that it was primarily women holding positions of leadership, privilege and societal status,[9] we would *still* be living in a patriarchal structure, guided by the very same over-emphasized Masculine principles, which would *still* have us manifesting the very same issues of lack, limitation, division and conflict in which we find ourselves awash today.

Girl Power: The Wolf in Sheep's Clothing

The feminist landscape has morphed through many waves, angles and iterations since the late nineteenth century when our first-wave sisters banded together to secure equal rights for their double-x chromosome crew. After the freedoms to vote, and own property, and not be raped were established, second-wave, 20th century gender equality activists turned their attention onto the social sphere, taking on sexuality, birth control and the workplace.

---

9   I feel I'd be remiss if I didn't acknowledge that – while not the majority — there are, indeed, many, many, many instances in which this is the case. For, despite any and all divisive propaganda to the contrary, we Americans live in a society where women have equal rights, and have held positions of status, leadership and authority for a long, long time.

This iteration of the movement gave rise to power suits, latchkey kids, single parent households and kicky slogans like *A woman needs a man like a fish needs a bicycle*.[10] While there was much progress and many an upside for women, we cannot deny the distortions second-wave feminism instilled upon the populace. Second-wave feminism rendered a generation of men distinctly feminized and disempowered, uncertain of their value and their role in so many broken households, as well as society at large, which went the distance to tell them that they were ancillary and unimportant.

The women who came up in this environment were instilled with an exaggerated sense of independence, guided by the notion that they could — and were thus meant to — have it all, be it all and do it all *by themselves*. This inversion of the tired, old notion that a woman "needed" a man had sisters loudly and proudly forging autonomous lifestyles and solo parenting journeys, shaping a generation of highly capable, driven women, who took on a great big batch of decidedly masculine traits and characteristics, verily forgetting how to be, rest, relate, nurture and receive as embodiments of the Feminine.

The third wave of feminism established itself in the 1990s. The movement was marked by punk ideals, DIY vibes and "ethical sluthood"; by Anita Hill, Naomi Wolf and Elizabeth Wurtzel; by Riot Grrrls, Lillith Fair and Fiona Apple.

Lovely as it was to see skinny chicks rock hard, messy and real, and to read literary memoirs written by pretty girls tussling with psychic weather and existential angst, the movement failed to recognize the legit biological distinctions differentiating men from women, rendering the consequences of ethical sluthood and other demonstrations of "equality" quite different for those who get pregnant and release oxytocin (aka: the bonding hormone) upon climaxing. And so it was that, yet again, we saw another iteration of the feminist movement encouraging women to empower themselves by acting like men, and embracing the ways, means and perspectives of the Masculine.

The 21st century has birthed a new generation of fourth-wave neo-feminists, who are now focusing their attention on subtler signals, and

10   Coined by Irina Dunn, though often mistakenly attributed to feminist icon, and CIA asset, Gloria Steinem.

more nuanced social cues being branded as "microaggressions," ON TOP of the other issues which many claim have never been rectified. It makes sense that there are lingering inequities between women and men, despite the fact that women secured equal rights decades ago, given that the real-deal underlying issue informing the imbalance of power, prestige and paycheck has yet to be addressed.

Alas, this current continuation of the quest for "equality" has a decidedly different flavor, marked as it is by prominent notes of fury, domination and revenge. Fourth-wave neo-feminism has given rise to zippy slogans like *Smash the patriarchy* and *Kill all men,* phrases like *mansplaining* and *toxic masculinity,* and has even gone so far as to rewrite the syntactical root "men" in the words that contain it, as in changing "*men*torship" to "*fem*torship."[11] The aim seems less about equality than it is for supremacy, sprinkled with a hefty pinch of vengeance, hold the compassion and the kindness.

Let us be clear, the claim for equality is valid. Every human incarnate deserves the exact same rights, freedoms and opportunities as every other human being, regardless of sex, gender, race, religion or belief. Alas, the current quest for gender equity is problematic, if for no other reason than it is being driven by a decidedly Masculine/patriarchal shadow.

The Masculine/Feminine Shadow

Both the Masculine and the Feminine have their shadow sides. In women, the Feminine shadow tends towards the relational, expressing itself through gossip, backbiting, downriver-selling and emotional bullying. It can be manipulative, withholding, overly critical, hyper-emotional — even hysterical. In men, the Feminine shadow is oftentimes airy and non-committal, preferring to float in the realms of possibility and potential, instead of grounding into structure, commitment and action.

We can identify the Feminine shadow expressing in the breathy, butt-hurt woman who bursts into tears when her boss offers a morsel of constructive

---

11 Even though, as an Indo-European derived root, "men-" means "mind" or "to think" and has all of nothing to do with gender.

criticism. Similarly, we see the Feminine shadow expressing in the spiritual dude with the mala-wrapped wrists who refuses to commit to the tea date he kinda-sorta passively suggested, preferring instead to "see how he feels," and "go with the flow." It is the same shadow animating the man surrounded by injustice and ineffable wrongs, who swallows his truth for fear of cancel culture and of not being liked.

The Masculine shadow, on the other hand, controls, dominates, coerces, manipulates, abuses and separates, expressing itself through division, conflict, rage and violence. It barrels over/suppresses emotions, oftentimes hiding behind a stoic front. The Masculine shadow can be overly logical and rigidly structured, leaving no space for flow, feels, improvisation or change.

Again, everyone carries their own unique pairing of both Masculine and Feminine tendencies and shadows – men and women alike. Just as we see the Masculine shadow expressing in the man who catcalls, picks fights, and coerces women into having sex with him, we also see the Masculine shadow expressing itself in the hyper-ambitious woman who forgets to take time for self-care, or who shrouds her heart in armor, while using humor as a means of deflecting her emotional pain, longing or tenderness.

Let the record show that there is nothing inherently wrong or bad with these archetypal shadows. We *all* have them. Shaming, blaming and deriding our shadows is — again — a Masculine shadow strategy that only empowers the energies of that which we are rejecting (i.e., Masculine dominance). Remember, the Masculine separates, excludes and rejects, while the Feminine unifies, includes and integrates. Our task, as self-responsible, betterarchical reality creators, is to cultivate right relationship with our shadows — individual and collective — such that they are not unconsciously running our world.

As we start to understand how these archetypal shadows operate in our culture, and animate us as individuals, we come to see that the modern-day quest for equality — gender and otherwise — is verily drenched in the Masculine shadow, with women and self-identified feminists calling for course-correction, not by way of equality, but dominance.

Feminism's Masculine Shadow

The twenty-first century gender equality/social justice reform movements seem less about evening out the proverbial playing field, than they are in sustaining the power imbalance by simply swapping out the players – placing those who historically held top dog position at the bottom, where they are expected to silently endure the lumps, insults and indignities those demanding their turn at the top are hurling upon them.

This punitive and dehumanizing curb-kicking is being justified by the hijacked hysteria of the Feminine shadow, but let us be clear – it is the Masculine shadow at work, for it is the Masculine shadow that separates, punishes and brutalizes in its quest for dominance and revenge. As though the scenario isn't ludicrous enough, this circuitous role reversal is being branded not only as a solution, but as "progress." Doublespeak[12] much?

Twenty-first century neo-feminism is not just about women stepping into positions of power and equality; it's about women stepping ON men as a means of doing so. This is not Feminine leadership, regardless of the genitals, chromosomes or self-proclaimed pronouns marking those doing the leading. This is *still* patriarchy, because it employs the Masculine shadow in achieving its aim, as well as enacting its ensuing leadership style.

Without having corrected the underlying issues of the polarity imbalance at inequality's root, to simply plug women into power positions and higher societal echelons *because* they are women, is to slap a band-aid onto a gaping hole in a sinking ship. It is to defer to shallow optics over real-deal, sustainable change, and to perpetuate the same ol'-same ol'.

Rebalancing the Masculine and the Feminine in our culture by way of authentic Feminine leadership has less to do with the chromosomes/genitals/pronouns/identity constructs of those doing the leading, than it does the method and style of leadership, as well as the architecture of the systems and infrastructure organizing our society.

---

12 A propaganda technique referring to language which deliberately obscures, disguises, distorts or reverses the meaning of words.

This means that more women in charge isn't necessarily the solution. Though it very well might be, so long as it's not the aim, rather the organic self-organizing configuration that emerges once the Masculine/Feminine energetics informing the shift are brought into balance. But, to get all bunged up about our leaders' gender or genitals is to miss the point, and to continue to fuel the larger meta distortion that is sustaining this imbalance, and that is really, truly the problem inviting course-correction.

HIERARCHY: THE REAL-DEAL CULPRIT

"Hierarchy is one of the oldest human wounds."
— ***Richard Rudd***

Hierarchy is a system of organization that privileges certain groups and individuals over others, according to status or authority. Hierarchy is dependent upon a marginalized underclass to sustain the existence of a ruling elite. In other words, hierarchy needs "losers" to balance out the existence of its "winners."

Under hierarchy, inequality is baked into the system from the get-go. Sure, we can flip the positions the players hold by privileging pariahs of the past, while marginalizing former top dogs, but we'll still be dealing with a system reliant upon disparity to function. The effects this systemically imposed disparity has on the people are massive, and insidious, and extremely caustic.

Within the confines of a system dependent upon a disenfranchised underclass to offset those it privileges, fear pervades the landscape. No one wants to be stuck in the "loser" category, which means the populace exists in a perpetual state of competition, perceiving their fellow brothers and sisters as oppositional "others" to be outplayed, outperformed and outdone. Lack-consciousness abounds, as folks hustle, scramble and sell out to grab their own piece of the pie before the marketplace runs dry, or the resources are gobbled up by all those dehumanized others playing the same game.

Hierarchy is not a win/win, greatest good kind of system. To sustain itself, hierarchy needs the populace desperate, divided and disempowered, beholden to various iterations of external validation and authority, oblivious to the fact that we — as a singular human species of Earthlings — really, truly are **one** (i.e., the unifying principle of the Feminine).

THE MATRIX

The matrix is a vast, complex control system, comprised of a litany of rules, laws, programs, protocols and conventions upon which hierarchy relies to keep the collective desperate, distracted and dependent. The matrix is a blueprint for a disempowered populace that thinks it must obey the system's dictates — both explicit and implied — to survive, succeed and belong. It is the web in which otherwise sovereign, empowered beings get trapped, assuming there is no other way to exist in the world, but in the grips of so many rules and have tos, so much bureaucracy and red tape. Whereas hierarchy is a conceptual abstraction, the matrix is the template through which it operates in material form.

External authority is one of the hallmarks of hierarchy. To justify its continuous and evermore stringent imposition, hierarchy is sustained by a consistent onslaught of threats to the health, safety, survival and wellbeing of the populace it organizes/ensnares. As such, the matrix is propped up by a steady stream of programming intended to keep the populace schizzed-out on fear, crisis and conflict, while manipulating us into believing that we are small and limited and separate, and thus need its systems and safety nets to protect us.

The matrix uses language to control, divide and disempower the masses, manipulating our dreams, desires, fears, beliefs, expectations and emotions with words (as well as images and symbols) disseminated through its go-to henchmen – the mainstream media (aka: MSM) and the advertising industry that bankrolls it. The MSM bombards us with words, pictures, stories and perspectives intended to hijack our emotions and our beliefs, and to convince us that we need the matrix to survive. Duly programmed, we become dependent upon the matrix's machinations, surrendering our power and our will to a system that has anything but our best interests in mind.

Hierarchy IS Masculine

and that includes matriarchy.

Hierarchy is a Masculine construct in its inherent inequality and divisiveness, as privilege and status are Masculine features. A culture organized by rank is a Masculine culture, even if those holding the highest ranks are women. What this means is that were we to snap our fingers, and reorganize society such that women suddenly held pole position, while men were simultaneously thrust to the bottom, we would *still* be operating in a fundamentally Masculine structure, and necessarily wrestling with all the same issues we are facing now, only with different players holding different positions.

We can apply this same perspective to societal/structural "solutions" that involve the elevation of *any* group over others. It doesn't matter if those groups are delineated by gender, race, religion, sexual preference, political affiliation or what have you. If we are organizing our society by status, then we are empowering and sustaining hierarchy, which means we are perpetuating the imbalance between the Masculine and the Feminine.

With this in mind, we can see that it doesn't really matter if we put women on top, while kicking men to the curb, as we would still be sustaining an outdated Masculine structure, along with the imbalance between the Masculine and the Feminine, while fueling derision, divisiveness and inequality amongst our human family and our world at large.

Let's not whitewash it: We, as in the entire human species, find ourselves teetering on the edge of an evolve or perish moment, being simultaneously nudged, squeezed and plunged head-first into the evolutionary dive roll that will allow us to rise above our petty grievances and the engineered divide that is threatening to collapse the entire Earth game. Evolution is demanding that we quantum leap into a new paradigm marked by peace, equality, cooperation, inclusion and win/win solutions, somewhere in the realm of immediately, or it's game-over for us all. And, that's not going to happen under hierarchy.

> *"The future is a choice between Utopia and oblivion."*
> **— R. Buckminster Fuller**

It would be one thing if this gross imbalance of power, and all the ensuing issues that come along with it, were accidental or anomalous. Alas, it's all by design. The winner/loser slant that marks the entire history of Western civilization has been woven into the very architecture of hierarchy from the get-go. In fact, it defines it.

> **hi•er•ar•chy,** *n.*
> *a system in which people are ranked in order of status, privilege and/or importance.*

Under the oppressive shadows of hierarchy, we have become convinced that this is simply how it *has* to be. That every city must have its ghettos, its skid row and its welfare class. That some kids, born in some neighborhoods or some countries, simply won't have enough to eat. That our lifestyle will always cost more than we make, and that we must live in perpetual debt to survive. That one gender has to suck it up, take their lack, lumps and abuses, while the other is given favor, status and privilege.

Alas, this is utterly, completely and unequivocally false.

HETERARCHY

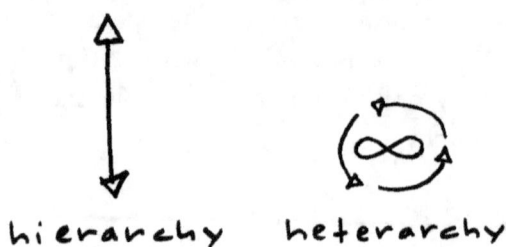

hierarchy   heterarchy

I first read about heterarchy in Richard Rudd's seminal tome, *The Gene Keys* – a profound spiritual transmission that unpacks the coding embedded in our DNA, and doubles as an encyclopedia of spirituality, ontology, philosophy, epigenetics, metaphysics, sacred geometry and all things mystical and esoteric.

Seen through the lens of the *Gene Keys*, hierarchy is a low frequency organizational system rooted in unconscious shadows. As an evolutionary species, ever and always transcending and including that which came before, humans are meant to transmute these shadows, and evolve our consciousness into higher frequencies, at which point — according to Rudd — we will progress into an upgraded organizational structure known as *heterarchy*.

Heterarchy is an unranked system of organization, wherein no groups or individuals are privileged over any others. In a heterarchical system, people perform different functions, but none are valued or honored over any others based upon perceived status or importance. Heterarchy values everyone equally, regardless of dharma,[13] duty, biology, belief, gender, race and all the rest of the factors the hierarchical social construct uses to rank, divide and mess with those who comprise it.

Heterarchy honors the fundamental interdependency of all the players involved, while serving the wellbeing of the whole, instead of just those few folks at the top, as is the case with hierarchy. This means that whether heterarchy is being used to organize a team, a county, a state or an

---

13   A Sanskrit word translated to mean "an individual's incarnational duty or mission".

organization, the aim will always be to serve the greatest good of *all* the people comprising that team, county, state or organization, rather than simply those who are positioned in the highest echelons of leadership or privilege inside them.

Within heterarchy, individual engagement is welcomed and encouraged, instead of being reserved for those holding positions of perceived status and authority. As such, all participants cultivate a vested interest in the health of the whole, and the success of the mission(s), and collaborate accordingly. To this end, we see that heterarchy is a fundamentally Feminine structure, supported by the ideals of consensus, collaboration, inclusion and unity.

Let's take a look at a few of the ways that heterarchy differs from hierarchy.

Trust > Fear

Hierarchy uses the matrix to manipulate the collective into a constant state of division, desperation and conflict, utilizing the energetics of fear, lack, polarization and victimhood to accomplish its *divide, rule and enslave* aims. Duly jacked on so many corrosive Masculine shadow frequencies, we are indoctrinated into a culture of mistrust, distracted by the never-ending quest to make those ever-inflating ends meet, which has us stepping on each other to get ahead, blaming one another when we don't, and defending whatever positions we do have, while ever and always peering back over our shoulders to make sure no one's sneaking up from behind, and trying to jack our hard-earned all of it.

Heterarchy, on the other hand, fosters Feminine trust amongst the people it organizes, because it isn't propping itself up on lies of lack or separation. With (more than) enough to go around, and an empowered collective comprised of equally-valued and included individuals who aren't being strongarmed into competing, or compulsively chasing an incessant array of dangling carrots for external validation or permission, heterarchy is a structure that encourages cooperation and feelings of trust and goodwill amongst the individuals comprising it.

Responsibility > Apathy

Under the infantilizing grip of hierarchy, we, the people, are dissuaded from taking responsibility for ourselves, the wellbeing of the collective and the construct in which we are operating. And so it is that the vast majority of us shirk our duties as humanity/Earth stewards, unconsciously assuming the powers that were[14] have it dialed.

Distracted as we are within the construct of hierarchy – be it with survival, approval, which sports team won the playoffs or who designed the leggings Celebrity X wore to yoga – we exist in a near constant state of disconnect from ourselves and the whole of which we are a part, programmed as we are to think it's all being handled for us, be it by politicians, authorities, or that vague, oft-referenced "they" we (are programmed to) assume are looking out for our greatest good, while competently steering our Earth ship into a better future. As if.

Look at our current situation. We, as in every being on this planet, are all members of a singular species — Earthlings. As Earthlings, we are all responsible for the care and safeguarding of our home planet. We know our Earth is out of balance, and yet, the vast majority of us take no responsibility, and no corrective action.[15] And this is not to blame or shame, because it's not as though we are dropping the ball out of ill-intent or a conscious wish to do harm. What we are dealing with is simply a giant disconnect that is a hallmark of the Masculine shadow, and that is necessarily engendered by hierarchy.

Within heterarchy, participants identify with the larger structure in which we are operating. We share accountability for the construct and contribute to its efficacy and optimization. As equally honored and valued participants within the collective, we understand our responsibility to serve, steward

---

14 Whilst an extended explanation of this phrase is forthcoming, know that this betterarchical edit reflects our agency, as reality creators, to remove our consent from the status quo, and to program reality as we choose.

15 Yet.

and optimize the collective, because we are operating with an integrated and distinctly Feminine understanding that the collective is not something separate from ourselves.

Thriving > Surviving

Hierarchy goes the distance to ensure that the vast majority of human beings on the planet stay stuck in survival mode, perpetually distracted with the burden of meeting our most basic needs – be it by way of hunting, foraging and carrying jugs of murky water several miles a day to fulfill our minimum bathing/drinking/cooking/cleaning needs, as is the case in still-developing nations; or devoting the bulk of our lifeforce to jobs that don't ever seem to bring in enough money to pay the rent, the bills, the insurance premiums or the minimum payments on all the debt we are accumulating to cover the lifestyles that – by design – we can't really, truly afford.

Incessantly occupied by the task of *not* drowning, we find ourselves vibrating at lower, denser frequencies. This low-vibe survival state doesn't just take a toll on our bodies, minds and spirits, it prevents us from tapping into expanded states of creativity, consciousness and spirituality, to say nothing of actualizing our highest potential. When we are preoccupied with survival, we haven't the bandwidth or luxury of expanding our consciousness, fulfilling our creative destiny or realizing our real-deal dharma.

Heterarchy is a fundamentally humane, compassionate system, which aims to optimize the experience of the individuals comprising it, instead of bleeding them dry, as is the case with hierarchy. Because heterarchy isn't dependent upon a desperate, disempowered populace to drive its machinery, the structure supports its members in thriving. Therefore, within heterarchy, individuals' creativity, expansion and realization are fostered and encouraged, rather than squelched and disregarded.

Heterarchy is steeped in the integrated knowledge that the whole is only as strong as its component parts, which means it honors the actualization of those who comprise it, trusting that the more the players evolve, shine, optimize and expand, the more shiny, optimized, evolved and expansive the collective construct will necessarily be.

Fluidity > Rigidity

Whereas hierarchical structures are slow to adapt, and stubborn in their adherence to dysfunctional, antiquated traditions, heterarchical constructs are fluid and flexible, comprised of interdependent units that operate circularly, rather than vertically (as in hierarchy).

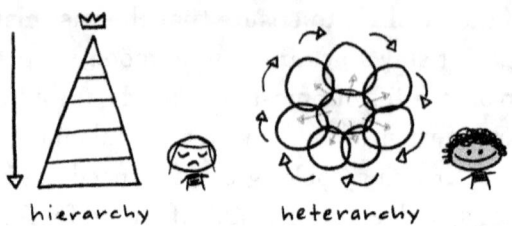

hierarchy   heterarchy

Instead of relying upon Masculine-oriented top-down control and information dissemination, heterarchy is shaped by a more fluid, circular structure, which allows for greater inclusivity, transparency and cooperation, availing itself to novelty, innovation and previously unpracticed pivots.

Hierarchy enforces tight controls on what information is shared with whom, thus fostering a system wherein those positioned in the highest realms of status know the most, and use their privileged intel to delegate actions and undertakings to those beneath them, who are expected to execute out of obedience, rather than an integrated understanding of the bigger picture they are serving. Heterarchy, on the other hand, is propped up by transparency, wherein all the players are hip to the same information as those holding more responsibilities, and are thus invited to collaborate on execution strategies in a more organic, co-creative manner. This Feminine fluidity makes heterarchical structures nimble, readily resourced to navigate change, whereas their hierarchical predecessors remain stuck in outdated constructs and associated narratives that serve as barriers to evolution.

Equality of Opportunity > Equality of Outcome

Rock Paper Scissors is the quintessential heterarchical game: rock smashes scissors, paper covers rock, and scissors slice through paper. Every element is equally matched, and is resourced with equal odds of winning and losing. No one element has an inborn leg-up. Equal opportunity prevails.

Some bristle at the notion of a society of inherently equal status, mistakenly assuming this equates to socialism, communism or equality of outcome. Not so, my friend. Not by a long shot.

The task of eliminating artificial, pre-programmed hierarchy from our language has nothing to do with eradicating merit, excellence or achievement from the cultural landscape. We are talking about equality of *opportunity* over equality *of outcome*. Alas, it is impossible to realize authentic equality of opportunity when our primary programming/reality creation tool is infected with status-based inequality from the get-go.

Nature itself is heterarchical. The hummingbird is no more important than the badger. The cuttle fish holds no more sway than the moth. The Aspen is not given any more pay, props or prominence than the rubber tree. The bunny rabbit is certainly no less important to the Earth's ecosystem than the Bengal tiger, despite differences in size, strength, stature and sustenance. They simply serve different functions. As we understand the interdependence of all life on planet Earth, then we are resourced to honor these functions as equal, while different.

AYE, THERE'S THE RUB

That being said, were a tiger to face off with a bunny rabbit, that tiger would shred that fluffy little power breeder to bits in two shakes of its own dismembered tail. The tiger is a top-notch predator. The bunny – not so much.

Inherent, primal status delineations differentiate all species. Because, despite any high-minded ideals to the contrary, alphas, betas and sigmas do exist. In every bunny litter, there will be a runt who is smaller, weaker and less agile than the other bunnies; just as there will be an alpha who is bigger and stronger, and thus, pinpointed as the top breeding choice for the lady bunnies, whether they are aware of their primal programming or not.

The same goes for humans, who – despite evolution or intention to the contrary – instinctually organize ourselves according to hierarchical status based on a host of attributes that have contributed to that whole *survival of the fittest* deal that's gotten us to this here and now.

Nature is both hierarchical *and* heterarchical. Natural hierarchies organize life on planet Earth. Think about it. If you were heading out into the wilderness for a month-long trek, would you rather be accompanied by a color-blind, 90-lb techie who can't tell his ass from a LifeStraw, or a lifelong outdoorsman with a black belt, a compass and a machete? If you're playing pick-up basketball in the park, do you choose the Dalai Lama to be on your team, or do you pick Michael Jordan?[16]

Now, none of this is to purport that the techie or His Holiness are less valuable human beings than the folks to whom I am comparing them. Rather, it is to say that – within the context of our proposed scenarios — they rank lower on the hierarchical totem pole.

---

16 Yes, this scenario assumes that both Michael Jordan and the Dalai Lama are hanging out at your local park at the same time, on the same day, and both vying to play a game of hoops with you and your friends. It could totally happen.

Hierarchy: Imposed vs. Organic

While aeons of indoctrination have imposed artificial hierarchy upon us through culture, media, government and language, natural hierarchy is still a real-deal thing. Natural hierarchies organize themselves authentically and organically by way of build, brains, talent, experience and a host of other considerations. Earthlings' inclination to self-organize according to organic social status is part of our primal nature, despite any high-minded ideals to the contrary.

Still, while natural hierarchies exist, they need not be contained within an artificially orchestrated hierarchical structure, where they are exploited by hierarchical language. Social hierarchies will organically emerge of their own accord, with or without the manipulative machinations of the matrix. But, because our language has been programmed with the frequencies of lack, limitation, status, fear, conflict and disempowerment, organic hierarchy has been replaced with an oppressive and contrived version that is doing us all a disservice.

And so, while I am not advocating for the (wholly unnatural/impossible) eradication of natural, organic hierarchy, I am inviting us to evolve out of the shackles of hierarchy as a social construct, and — most especially — a language.

HIERARCHICAL LANGUAGE: A METAPHOR

We can think of hierachical language like a steel spike that has been driven through humanity's right foot. Despite any lofty visions we may hold for progressing in terms of unity, equality, inclusivity and empowerment, we remain tethered to the caustic frequencies of separation, disparity, disempowerment and lack by way of that rusty metal stake that's not just holding us back, but is leaching infectious toxins into our collective bloodstream. The longer the spike stays in place, the more damage it does to the entire system, triggering a domino effect of degeneration to which we must play constant defense, while limping in circles, going nowhere.

Bewildered Much?

This is where I got a little confused. How exactly does a heterarchical culture work, in light of natural hierarchy? Some people are natural born leaders, and some...not so much.

I dug deeper, looking for modern day examples of thriving heterarchical cultures and companies that would validate my hunch (and Rudd's prophecy) that heterarchy was the ideal organizational structure into which humanity is slated to evolve.

I scoured the cultural landscape for functional modern-day expressions of heterarchy and thriving organizations which were utilizing this structure. I learned about agorism[17] and holocracy.[18] I researched Waldorf schools and the Quaker movement. I interviewed experts and consultants. I meditated on the allegedly heterarchical Mayan civilization, and invited their ancient societal architecture to show itself to me by way of dreams, visions, signs and synchronicities. Alas, the ancient architecture didn't respond and I remained stumped.

oh, ancient maayaaaa... how did you structure your society?

I did happen upon a smattering of organizations comprised of heterarchical departments contained within hierarchical umbrellas. And while these smaller organizational subsets were reporting wonderful results within their fluid, circular, egalitarian structures, they all seemed to still be dependent upon some version of top-down leadership to truly thrive.

After several months of diligent research, I still wasn't clear as to how heterarchy would translate into a functional, sustainable systemic upgrade

---

17 A Libertarian societal structure that hinges on voluntary exchanges, counter-economics and peaceful revolution.
18 A decentralized organizational structure that distributes authority through self-organizing teams.

for an entire society, and I started to wonder if perhaps heterarchy wasn't the solution after all.

Synarchy-Psych!

I turned my attention to *synarchy* — the system Rudd identifies as the evolutionary leap that awaits us on the other side of heterarchy. Synarchy means "joint rule, or sovereignty." It vibes high, abounds with win-wins, and seemed like the super very obvious upgrade to pinpoint as our species' next organizational iteration.

Why dither with the transitional heterarchical version, when we can just quantum leap straight into synarchy, now? I wondered.

Alas, despite all the high-minded idealism encoded in its definition, the term was co-opted during the Nazi movement, when it was first used to describe rule by a secret elite operating behind the scenes. "Synarchy" has since been employed to characterize various fascist and communist regimes being fronted by tyrannical lackeys serving the financial/power-mad interests of hidden cabals.

In other words, like so many instances of language, "synarchy" has been weaponized.

THE WEAPONIZATION OF WORDS

The power of language to create, transform, liberate and enslave has been held secret throughout the ages by those seeking to control the populace and hoard all the power and resources for themselves.

Social engineers (aka: those in media, government, academia, politics, et al., exerting covert top-down influence to persuade the beliefs, actions and behaviors of the masses) are quite hip to the power of words, and go the distance in utilizing them to manipulate the masses in service to the aims and agendas they are enlisted to promote. One of the many ways they do this is by weaponizing language.

Those seeking to control the masses weaponize language by tainting otherwise neutral words and phrases with negative connotations and associations. Duly defiled, this deliberately toxified language shuts down intelligent discourse, while maligning/otherizing dissenters, obscuring facts and narratives that counter the aims of the operation and distracting those being manipulated from paying attention to the shady, corrupt, nefarious and oftentimes criminal activities those doing the manipulating are attempting to conceal.

Sometimes the weaponization is overt, as in instances of dictionary publishers changing definitions to reflect the opinions and agendas of those funding them. Sometimes, the weaponization is more subversive, with subtle connotation shifts, angles and leanings being inserted into the public discourse through media and repetition, wherein influencers, celebrities and "trusted experts" utilize these newly weaponized words over, and over, and over again, to indoctrinate the masses into unconsciously accepting these shifts and the corrosive mind viruses contained therein.

In other cases, words are front-loaded with negative emotions, such as fear, shame and hatred. When bandied about, the contagions laden in these words spread to infect those whose minds they touch, activating these bummer frequencies in our bodies, where they wreak havoc on our psyches, our emotions, our immune systems, and our peace of mind.

Weaponized language has the tendency to target and trigger our unintegrated trauma, thus activating deep-seated pain that so often erupts in seemingly exaggerated emotional reactions that don't logically line up with the bandying of a simple word, phrase or idea.

Examples include, though are in no way limited to: woke, they, science, privilege, Trump, abortion, Nazi, conspiracy theorist

Something-archy

Supremely bummed about the hijacking of the otherwise pitch-perfect "synarchy," I took it upon myself to invent a new system. I scoured Bible-paged books filled with Latin, Greek, and Indo-European word parts. I obsessed on etymological invention, convinced that were I to alchemize the just-right combination of root, prefix and suffix, I would open up a portal to humanity's perfect, next-level societal structure.

I tussled hard with "-archy," which means *to rule*, and thus implies hierarchy — unless it's prefixed by something unifying and cooperative, like *syn-*, which — *AARGH!*

Deep breaths. Back to the drawing board, and the Bible-pages, which I scoured for a resonant root or suffix that meant *order*, *structure*, *harmonize* and/or *unify*, only to come up dry, again.

BEHOLD, THE BREAKTHROUGH!

Way too many months into an otherwise obsessive inquiry, I realized I had veered off course, and was treading murky, unfamiliar waters without fins, snorkel or oxygen. I don't claim to know the hows or specifics marking the up-leveled collective structure into which we are evolving. That's not my wheelhouse. I'm not a societal engineer. I am a word wizard.

What I do know is that our language is supremely outdated, and lousy with hierarchical pitfalls that are smearing our world in the frequencies of lack, fear, conflict, separation, victimhood and disempowerment, and that are holding us way back. The collective outcries for course correction are only confirming my long simmering hunch that it is high time we evolve our language out of the hierarchical patterns that are enslaving us, and start speaking a language that reflects the upgrades for which we are calling, clawing and clamoring.

Our liberation is simple: it is to stop speaking hierarchy. *My* task is to help us flush hierarchy out of our language,[19] so that we can allow the next evolution of our societal structure to organically emerge from our up-leveled lexicon. Because when we – as a collective – are consistently speaking a language of real-deal peace, equality, abundance, inclusivity and empowerment, the structure that emerges from that language will necessarily reflect those qualities and characteristics. It can't not; that's how language works.

This isn't to say that heterarchy won't be our A-number-one solution. Just because I haven't figured out how to implement heterarchy on a large scale doesn't mean it can't be done. It is simpy to say that our A-number-one solution is still unfolding. And I can promise us that it will be infinitely easier to identify and organize once we stop speaking a language of hierarchy, stop programming our collective with the frequencies of status and inequity, and start speaking a language that is reflective of the societal changes we are calling in.

---

19 And thus, out of our consciousness and our worldview.

(The Language of) Betterarchy

And so it is that my mad-dash attempts at linguistic novelty and organizational evolution landed me on *betterarchy*. Betterarchy is rife with potential and possibility. Betterarchy doesn't claim to have all the answers. Its structure isn't set in stone, or written in indelible ink. Betterarchy is fluid, Feminine and open — available for enhancement, improvement and collaboration, in its still-cohering nature.

Betterarchy supports the collective it organizes to thrive in optimized peace, harmony, abundance and unity, melding the principles of heterarchy with the ideals of synarchy, in an as-yet-to-be fully formed or determined (though easily applicable and implementable) structure. We call this structure into being by speaking a new language – *its* language: the language of betterarchy.

The language of betterarchy is a tool that infuses the populace with equal opportunity from the get-go, at the most fundamental level, by programming the brain, the consciousness and the collective field, accordingly. The language of betterarchy replaces lack, limitation, conflict and victimhood with agency, abundance, inclusivity and empowerment. Duly resourced, we, the people, are free to rise, expand, succeed, flourish and re-organize our society and our world as wonderfully, peacefully and sustainably as we choose.

Shall we?

PART 2
THE WORLD IS
MADE OF WORDS

"Man acts as though he were the shaper and master of language, while in fact language remains the master of man."
— ***Martin Heidegger***

WHAT IS LANGUAGE?

Before we learn how to transform our reality from hierarchy to betterarchy with language, let's get clear on how language functions to create reality in the first place.

As a communications strategist, I find it helpful to define our terms up front. When we define our terms up front, we resource the unfolding conversation with clarity and efficiency from the get-go, sidestepping any unnecessary confusion or conflict in the process. Because while, in any given conversation, we may *think* we know what all the words we are exchanging mean, and thus assume that we are on the same page, it's actually quite rare that all participants are operating with shared definitions, and are talking about the same things.

Think about it, for most every word in the dictionary, there are multiple definitions, each reflecting subtle shifts in meaning. Still, how many words that you know have you actually looked up in the dictionary? We learn the bulk of our words through osmosis. So, while we might *think* we know what a word means, having never actually scoured the dictionary for its real-deal definition(s) ourselves, it's more than likely that our implied understandings are at least slightly skewed, if not very much so. Top off these subtle variations in meaning with the individual associations and experiences we each have with words themselves – the memories they carry, the judgments they trigger — and interpretations are easily distorted. Not to mention the mass manipulation technique of changing definitions to suit the agendas of the social engineers, as we are currently experiencing in 21st century upside down world, and – well, all of this is to say that shared definitions aren't as easy to come by as we may think.

So, what *is* language, anyway?

I'm so glad you asked. Language is defined as "a body of words, and its rules for usage."

Words serve multiple functions, which operate on a variety of dimensions. As we choose to shift our collective lexicon to the language of betterarchy, it is helpful to understand the various levels upon which language operates. While there is crossover between some of these functions, I am inspired to parse them out according to nuance and ever-so-slight tilt of the head, to resource us with as many angles of perception and understanding as possible, for maximum grokability.[20]

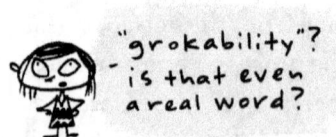

---

20 A derivative of "grok," that is: to understand something profoundly and intuitively (thank you, Robert Heinlein, for the lexicon expansion).

1. Communication Tool

As children, most of us were taught that words are tools for communication. And, of course, they are. Words allow us to share thoughts, feelings and ideas with our fellow humans. They help us connect and share our humanity.

The bulk of what we know about language is relegated to how words function as communication tools, along with all the rules, punctuation and grammar bits that allow us to utilize them effectively. These are important applications we are wise to learn and master. Still, interpersonal communication is but a tiny aspect of the myriad ways that words and language operate.

2. Existential Validator

> *"The limits of my language are the limits of my mind.*
> *All I know is what I have words for."*
> **— Ludwig Wittgenstein**

One of language's primary duties is that it bestows existential validity upon the thing or concept its words symbolize. We know a thing exists when it has a word that represents it. In acting as symbolic reference points, words render things *so*.

There is no way to grasp the existence of a thing or idea without a word to identify it. When presented with a new object or concept — without a word — the brain has nothing to hold onto, and thus no way to contextualize or process said thing.

Rumor has it that when Christopher Columbus' ships sailed across the horizon towards the shores of North America, the natives did not see them. Their eyes and their brains literally did not register the existence of these massive vessels, because they had no names for them — no symbolic reference point with which to catalogue or identify the ships.

Language imparts existential legitimacy. When we use a word, we empower the *is*-ness of that which it represents, and we strengthen its (perceived) realness. Whether we speak the word, write it, read it or receive it, we cast our vote for its presence in our reality construct.

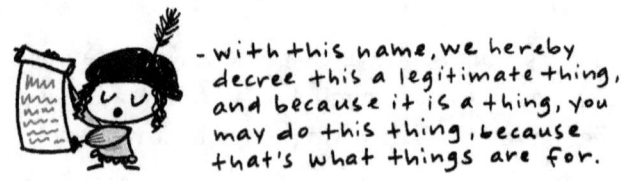

Conversely, when we choose to eschew certain words, we disempower the constructs they symbolize. By consciously abstaining from using specific words, we impel the existence they reference — the *is*-ness they represent — to fade away.

GHOSTING

It used to be that when someone called, texted or sent us an email, we would respond. This was pretty much standard communication etiquette.

Sometime during the first quarter of the 21st century, there emerged a practice wherein folks no longer responded to said communications. They simply fell out of the exchange without any notice whatsoever. While logic would dictate that he who had dropped out of the conversation had fallen victim to coma, car crash or alien abduction, this was not the case. It was the emergence of a new trend called "ghosting."

While this supremely inconsiderate practice used to be rare, if not downright inconceivable, these days it has become rather commonplace. The reason it has become an accepted practice is because we named it. As soon as we stapled this particular flavor of relational rudeness with its very own word, we signed onto its legitimacy and allowed it to propagate.

3. Creator, Destroyer, Sustainer

In taking this idea a step further, we see that words don't just function as symbolic reference points for existence, or what we can refer to as the status quo; they determine whether we are going to perpetuate this status quo, destroy the status quo or create a whole new status quo altogether.

As we learned in the "ghosting" example, our consistent use of words and phrases impels the sustained existence of that which they represent, just as the choice to eschew certain words and phrases serves to invalidate the existence of that which they (used to) represent.

For example, in certain ancient Indigenous cultures, it was forbidden for the community to utter people's names once they were cast out of the tribe. The idea was that in choosing not to aspirate the frequencies that identified the outcasts, the tribe was eradicating their existence from reality itself.

This is how powerful our tribal ancestors understood words to be. These wisdom keepers knew that the more we use a word, the more frequently and fervently the thing it symbolizes appears in our world; just as when we cease to use a word, the thing it signifies fades into the ether of memory and past.

4. Manifestation Technology

Language is the bridge between the material and the unseen worlds. Words are quite magical this way.

Think about it: An idea drops into our mind from infinite intelligence. It is a concept, an abstraction, holding no weight, no mass, nothing tangible that would establish any sort of measurable *is*-ness. But it's our idea. It is alive in the confines of our imagination. What is the first thing we do on our quest to materialize it? We ascribe words to it.

It's the first step to manifesting: giving our dreams words. Whether we write them down, speak them aloud or simply assign them inside our mind, words are the vehicles upon which our thoughts, ideas and inventions ride.

SOME KINDERGARTEN QUANTUM PHYSICS...

As we delve deeper into the myriad ways that words function as reality creation technology, it's helpful to understand some fundamentals of quantum physics.

Full disclosure: I dropped out of my 11th grade physics class when I was expected to wrap my mind around the idea that, when in motion, the outside of a wheel moves faster than the inside. Of the same wheel. Even though they are attached.

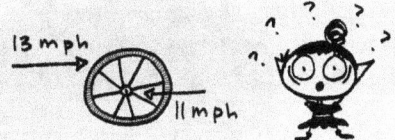

My pragmatic little teenage brain tapped out, refusing to suspend disbelief and sign onto such ass-backwards magical thinking. And so it was that I walked away from what was probably never going to be a career in the physical sciences, but could have been an illuminating semester, nonetheless.

EVERYTHING IS VIBRATION

According to physics, everything in our known universe is — at its most fundamental level — vibration. Everything, as in both the material and the immaterial. Sound is invisible to the eye and still exists as vibration measured in myriad frequencies, just as the smallest particle of the chair under your butt is — according to the world's most powerful microscope — either a wave or a particle vibrating, vibrating, vibrating. Thoughts are vibration. Emotions are vibration. Intentions are vibration. There is nothing, nothing, nothing in this third-dimensional, earthly reality that is not vibration.

This means that words are also vibration. Every word that exists vibrates at its own unique, individual frequency. "Broccoli" has a distinctive energetic signature, just as "ennui" has its own version. These frequencies are themselves encrypted with hyper-nuanced codes, signals and information, which scientists call metadata.

Remember at the beginning of this chapter, when we were defining our terms, and I mentioned that words are loaded with multiple definitions, along with our own personal overlays, associations and experiences of them? These elements are all part of the metadata with which every word is encoded. But it doesn't stop there. There are many, many layers of information, implication, instruction and imprinting that are held within words' vibratory frequencies. And all that unique metadata is transmitted with every word we speak, ink, think, type, read and receive.

5. Perception Shaper/Reality Filter

The subconscious mind is epic *af*, determining ninety-five percent of our experience of reality and processing information one million times faster than the conscious mind. This motherload of filtration, meaning-making and belief-shaping is programmed through language and repetition. The words we speak, write, read, type and think are always programming our subconscious minds. That programming determines how we perceive reality, while also directing reality how to configure.

The subconscious mind drives the vast majority of our decisions, actions and behavior. It shapes our interpretations of reality and determines the meaning we choose to make of our circumstances and experiences. Our every waking moment is filtered and translated through the subconscious mind and the programming that shapes it.

This is how words shape our perception of reality and determine the quality of our experience. Language programs the subconscious mind, which creates a filter through which reality is perceived and translated. This linguistic lens colors our every shred of experience with the codes and frequencies embedded in the words that comprise it. In other words, the language we use to program our subconscious minds has a direct correlation as to how we will choose to interpret our experience of reality.

To get an experiential understanding of what I am describing here, say the following sentences out loud, pausing to feel how each version lands in your body and to track the sensory responses they inspire:

> *I have to go to work.*
> *I am going to work.*
> *I get to go to work.*

In essence, all three sentences are communicating the same idea. But, notice how the edits shift the framing of the experience of going to work. Saying we "have to" makes work seem like drudgery, like something we are doing against our will. Saying we "get to" makes it seem like a treat. And simply stating, "I am going to work" is an objectively neutral framing. It is neither pro nor con; it just is.

All three versions communicate the same idea, and yet the perceptions they program have massive implications as to how we will experience this "work" and how the work experience will configure according to our beliefs and expectations.

These shifts aren't simply semantics. They are structural mindset frameworks that determine how we feel about our jobs, and how we engage our jobs, along with all the tasks they entail — whether we are going to feel weighed down and put upon and victimized, or whether we are going to feel inspired, and enlivened, and grateful for the opportunity to be of service. This framing orients our approach to every task we engage and every interaction that comprises our workday.

6. Frequency Magnet

Language's influence on our reality constructs isn't just about how we feel, perceive, connect and make meaning. It's also about physics, which tells us that like frequencies attract like frequencies. This means that the frequencies embedded in the words we use attract situations, circumstances and experiences that match those very same frequencies.

So when I use words that indicate excitement about going to work, then I attract exciting experiences at work. When I use words that indicate work is a joy, and work is fun, then I will attract joyful, fun clients, collaborations, projects and tasks. By the same token, when I language my work life as drudgery, those words will orient my subconscious mind to the frequencies of drudgery. Duly attuned, I will attract more burdens, more busy work and more roadblocks to my reality.

This is yet another way that words function — as frequency magnets. The words we use to describe ourselves and our experience of reality tune our internal vibrational frequencies. These frequencies attract people, circumstances and experiences that match our internally generated vibrations and the programming that influences them.

This is noteworthy and worth pausing to consider. The frequencies and perceptions that language program don't simply affect how we *translate* our experience of reality; they engage reality on a co-creative level, creating a feedback loop of interpretation, meaning-making and creation, influencing how reality fundamentally configures itself.

And so it is that the subconscious mind doesn't just determine how we are going to *interpret* our experience of reality; it *shapes* and even *creates* reality. The subconscious mind isn't some passive observer hanging out on the sidelines, waiting for reality to happen to figure out how to frame it. It is an active co-creator, directing reality to configure according to its programming (aka: the words we feed it).

7. The Linguistic Gunas: Expansion, Contraction, Neutrality

Another way we can describe the frequencies emitted through the three aforementioned versions of the "going to work" scenario is as *contractive*, *expansive* and *neutral*. The "I have to go to work" framing triggers contraction and restriction in the body, mind and emotions, while the "I get to" version invokes feelings of expansion and openness. The third option, "I am going to work," transmits the frequencies of neutrality.

I refer to these categories as the *linguistic gunas*. A Sanskrit word meaning "quality" or "tendency," "guna" is a concept that hails from ancient yogic philosophy and is usually employed to refer to the three qualities of being — *rajas*, *tamas* and *sattva* — which characterize all things in existence. While the gunas delineate a more extensive array of distinctions, for our intents and purposes here, we can think of rajasic qualities as *expansive*, tamasic qualities as *contractive* and sattvic qualities as *neutral*.

Just as the three gunas distinguish all things in existence, so too do the linguistic gunas categorize every word or phrase in the lexicon, which each vibrate at one of these three frequencies — expansion, contraction or neutrality.

Contractive Languaging

Contractive languaging shuts down both the speaker and the receiver alike, making it infinitely more difficult for our messages to land. Contractive languaging directs the body/mind to shut down, armor up and prepare for hurt, defeat, disappointment or death — hardly states aligned with optimal receiving or harmonious communication exchanges.

When we utilize words coded with contraction, we are unconsciously directing the people we are addressing to close themselves off to our ideas and to shield themselves from impending awfulness. When we, as communicators, utilize contractive languaging, we are sabotaging the conversation, as it makes it challenging for those we are addressing to receive and embrace our messages, given the deleterious frequencies with which we are couching our messages.

But it's not just those we are addressing that contractive languaging does a disservice. When we use contractive languaging to reference ourselves, tell our stories or frame our behavior, our projects, our aims or our life, to say nothing of the looping thoughts that comprise our self-talk, we are absolutely sabotaging ourselves, while reinforcing our worst fears and our most destructive habits and degrading our psycho-emotional wellbeing in the process.

Neurocientists have proven that contractive languaging takes a variety of tolls on our health and bodily integrity, having identified certain classes of these kinds of communication that direct the brain to release chemicals that strain the nervous system, shorten the telomeres and accelerate the aging process.[21]

---

21 "Some assessments of the amygdala's role in suprahypothalamic neuroendocrine regulation: A minireview." Talarovicova A., Krskova L., Kiss A. Endocrine Regulations. 2007 Nov; 41(4):155-62

Expansive Languaging

Expansive languaging opens both the speaker and the receiver alike, rendering our messages infinitely easier to absorb than when phrased with contractive languaging. Expansive words generate feel-good neurochemicals, which have myriad beneficial impacts on the body/mind, not to mention the fortuitous vibrational matches and experiences they magnetize.

As I mentioned above, neuroscience has recently turned its attention toward the effects that language has on the brain. While the surface has yet to be fully scratched, and the depths beckon deeper exploration, researchers have already discovered that expansive words and phrases are encoded with frequencies that stimulate the part of the brain that moves us from procrastination into action, and that the act of adopting expansive languaging patterns strengthens our ability to follow through and manifest.[22] In this way, expansive words function as fuel for growth and generation (aka: getting shit done).

Those clever neuroscientists have also proven that expansive languaging programs the brain to perceive people and circumstances as good and kind.[23] This coding allows the body/mind to more easily receive, engage and explore, as it programs our systems with the fundamental frequencies of trust and safety. Remember that trust is one of the hallmarks of the Feminine, which means that employing expansive languaging that engenders more of it is a great way to help rebalance the Masculine/Feminine polarities and harmonize the collective field.

Expansive languaging regulates our attitudes for the consistently positive,[24] while allowing us to maintain an open state, wherein flow, triumph, possibility, synchronicity and solutions color our lives. This means that one of the swiftest ways to up-level our experience of reality is to consistently employ expansive languaging.

---

22 "Grasping language – A short story on embodiment." Jirak D., Menz M. M., Buccino G., Borghi A. M., Binkofski F. Consciousness and Cognition. 2010 Sep; 19(3):711-20

23 Ibid.

24 "In search of the emotional self: An fMRI study using positive and negative emotional words." Fossati P., Hevenor S.J., Graham S.J., Grady C., Keightley M. L., Craik F., Mayberg H. American Journal of Psychiatry. 2003 Nov; 160(11):1938-45

Neutral Languaging

Neutral languaging has no qualitative effect on the speaker or receiver's state of being. Neutral languaging is a clean way of expressing our ideas, and a helpful communication strategy to employ when we're not feeling authentically aligned with expansive languaging, and still don't want to go perving the morphic field, or sullying any subconscious minds with contractive languaging. Because, while expansive languaging is an effective betterarchical badass reality-framing/creation tool, it isn't necessarily appropriate for every mood or situation.

Life is complicated, and full of contrast. No one's path is sparkles and sunshine all the time. Shit happens, shadows exist and loss is par for the course. So, when I'm heading to the vet to put down my anxiety-riddled, geriatric dog, "get to" isn't going to do squat to convince my subconscious mind that the task is anything but a big, heartbreaking bummer. Because I'm not a psychopath, and death sucks.[25]

That being said, I am still a conscious reality creator, and thus know that languaging the process of putting down my dog is a *choice* I am making of my own volition. And so it is that I eschew the urge to victimize myself with contractive languaging, in saying, "I *have to* take my dog to the vet," instead choosing a more neutral framing with, "I am taking my dog to the vet," which doesn't make the experience any less traumatic, but also doesn't exacerbate the suckiness inherent to the task or program my field with disempowering victim vibes.

Neutral languaging allows us to communicate what *is*, without mucking up our subconscious terrain or the quantum field at large with negativity, bummer frequencies or icky circumstances we'd really rather not attract, create or sustain.

---

25 Having not yet died myself (in this incarnation), I don't actually know for certain that death sucks. What I do know is that losing the ones we love to death is super painful.

Reality Is Plural

One of the most common misconceptions about reality is that it is singular — that there is one, and that it is the same for everyone. The truth is, there are many realities. Reality is multidimensional and subjective and plural. There is no singular reality. There are real*ities*.

Reality — as in our own personal version — is an immersive reflection of our own individual thoughts, beliefs, experiences, perspectives, karma and cosmic/energetic/genetic blueprints. This iteration of reality is subjective and unique to every person. It is also extremely malleable. Each and every one of us has the power to change our personal realities. Language is our go-to tool for this very task.

> *"All that we are is the result of what we have thought: it is founded on our thoughts, it is made up of our thoughts. If a man speaks or acts with an evil thought, pain follows him, as the wheel follows the foot of the ox that draws the carriage."*
> **— Dhammapada**

There is also a collective reality that we share with every Earthling on the planet. This reality is an amalgamation of the projected individual realities of all living beings, combined with the Laws of Nature and a handful of Universal Truths. Our every thought, word and deed contribute to the formation of this collective reality construct in which we all exist. Collective reality is also malleable, provided that enough members of said collective are consistently thinking, speaking and enacting the proposed shifts together.

The Morphic Field

According to evolutionary biology, the morphic field[26] is an invisible web of consciousness — a dynamic field of habit, behavior and experience — that links the entire human race, as well as every living species on the planet.

The frequencies we transmit through language program the morphic field, which directs our shared, collective reality to configure according to the synthesis of the individual frequencies programming it. Every word we think, ink, speak, write, type and read programs the morphic field and contributes to the shape, structure and continued unfolding of our shared reality construct.

This is a hugely impactful and extremely important concept to grok as we master the art of reality creation, and evolve our global culture for the betterarchical. Many people are operating under the misconception that we are mere inheritors of an otherwise static reality structure that is pre-destined, carved in stone, and thus, out of our control. Alas, this could not be further from the truth.

We are the ones creating our reality constructs. Reality conforms to the thoughts, words, beliefs and actions with which the majority is programming the morphic field every second of every day. The sooner a critical mass adopts the simple shifts compiled in this book, the sooner we quantum leap our collective reality construct into an infinitely more wonderful, sustainable, betterarchical world in which to live, love, create and thrive together.

---

26 Also referred to as the quantum field, collective field and morphogenetic field.

Frequency Bands

The morphic field is composed of frequency bands that hold the energetic signatures for all Earthly life forms, as well as for all the energies, emotions and qualities of experience that exist in the infinite weave of possibility.

We can imagine the frequency bands that make up our morphic field like grooves on a record — a giant, Earth-encompassing record. Our words, thoughts and beliefs are what attune us to these frequency bands, these grooves, in our metaphorical record. The frequency bands with which we choose to align ourselves most often are what determine our experience of reality.

For example, if I repeatedly utter the phrase, "I can't afford it," then I am consistently attuning myself to the frequency band of lack, and am thus commanding the universe to create more lack in my life.

If I consistently think the thought, *People suck, and nobody gets me*, then I will consistently attract people who suck and misunderstand me, while programming a reality construct in which I continue to feel isolated, by consistently empowering the frequency bands of loneliness and separation.

As I shake my booty while singing, "Money comes to me easily and often," I am attuning myself — my subconscious mind, my inner landscape and my default vibration that radiates out into the multiverse — to the coding of abundance. When I choose to make it a ritual, and I program my internal frequency this way first thing every morning, you can be damned sure that I am living an abundant life.

When I thank my body for being strong, limber, healthy and agile, I am choosing to program my subconscious mind with the frequencies of health and wellbeing. As I have taken it upon myself to make this a daily practice, is it really any surprise that my ballet game is stronger than ever, and that I can't remember the last time I was sick?

The frequencies we embody and transmit most often become the primary characteristics of our reality constructs. As more and more of us use language to activate positive frequency bands in in the morphic field, as well as in ourselves, the more quickly our shared reality configures to reflect an ever-expanding array of favorable energies and experiences.

8. Future Seeders/Shapers

Words shape our nows and seed our tomorrows. The world we are living in today is a result of the thoughts, words and deeds with which we programmed the morphic field in the past, just as tomorrow's world is forged of the words, thoughts and behaviors we engage today.

The future isn't something that just happens of its own accord, and that we are stuck with when we arrive there. The future is something we are co-creating in every moment and have full agency to craft according to the thoughts, words and actions we are employing *now*.

For example, let's say I'm leading a meeting, and I spend the bulk of it complaining about how inefficiently my team is producing our widgets. All I am doing is ensuring that my team will continue to produce those widgets inefficiently. I am perpetuating the existing situation by continuing to affirm and empower it with my words.

Now, when I choose to use the time brainstorming solutions as to how we can increase our efficiency, and envisioning how this increased productivity will affect our operations and our bottom line, I am creating the conditions to *change* the present moment reality. I am creating a future widget production scenario that is more efficient than the one I am currently experiencing, because I am speaking that up-leveled reality into existence *now*.

"*THE POWERS THAT ~~BE~~ WERE*"

When we complain about "the powers that be," we legitimize their hierarchical authority and seed more of it into our future. The phrase ratifies their power by languaging it in the present moment, thus perpetuating their so-called "authority," and all the shenanigans that come along with it.

When we edit the phrase to reflect the future into which we are choosing to live in by saying, "the powers that were," then we are seeding the way for a changing of the guard. When we refer to them as "the powers that were," we remove our consent from their imposed/alleged legitimacy, and we place their authority in the past, where it belongs.

The subconscious mind is extremely literal. These tiny languaging shifts undo lifetimes of programming and empower us to take the reins and to steer our Earth ship and our culture onto an infinitely more fun, free, peaceful, sustainable, abundant path. To say nothing (okay, a little) about the implications it has on our collective reality structure when this phrase becomes established in the lexicon, and enough people are uttering it on the regular such that the morphic field has no choice but to reorganize to reflect a reality devoid of false authorities.

- oh, please.
so, we're ditching
linguistic accuracy
+ replacing it with
straight-up lies, now?

Despite All Social Engineering to the Contrary, Time Isn't Actually Linear

From the train wreck that is the Gregorian Calendar, to the consistent and deafening narratives that seek to convince us that "old" is bad, "young" is supreme, time is perpetually scarce and we are ever and always "behind," our temporal indoctrination has the vast majority of us massively misinformed about this thing called "time."

Think about it. A calendar is a system that organizes time. Shouldn't a system that organizes *anything* be consistent, coherent and easy to follow? Our calendar is a veritable clusterfuck of irregularity, with some months clocking in at thirty days, some thirty-one, not to mention the spazzy, cross-eyed stepchild that is February, with its nonsensical twenty-eight days, and that whole leap year that shows up every fourth sun spin. I mean, how does that make any logical sense whatsoever? To top it off, December is the twelfth month, even though "dec-" means ten, and October is the tenth month, even though "oct-" means eight. How can we possibly be expected to come into a functional and harmonious relationship with "time" when the very system that organizes it is so janky and ass-backwards?

According to this longstanding cultural fiction, time operates much like a linear conveyor belt, moving us from past to future, birth to death, with a handful of noteworthy stops/life events along the way. This distorted (mis)understanding of our temporal organizing construct has folks waiting for things to materialize in 3D reality to feel like they have the right to language them in the here and now.

birth | 1st period | graduation | marriage | mid-life crisis | retirement | death

> *"The distinction between past, present and future*
> *is only a stubbornly persistent illusion."*
> — **Albert Einstein**

The truth is that time is omnidirectional, multidimensional and simultaneous. Past, future and present exist concurrently, now. This means that — in a world of infinite possibility — when we hone in on a desire, a goal, a wish or a dream, we are connecting to a reality that *already exists* on a parallel dimension.

I invite you to pause for a moment to really let this sink in. Everything you want, you already have — *now* — on a different level of reality. This means that to materialize these desires in *this* reality construct, we must collapse the illusion of time and of future and claim said desires in the present moment.

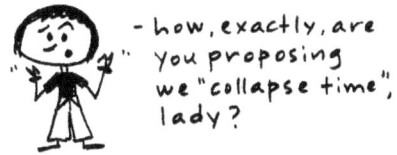

- how, exactly, are you proposing we "collapse time", lady?

We collapse the perceived distance between ourselves and the dreams and visions we are wanting to have and experience by languaging them in the here and now, with present tense positive language. We do not wait for them to appear to have then earned the privilege of languaging them as so. That's more inverted ass-backwardsness.

Reality configures according to vibration — primarily, the vibrations encoded in our words. Reality creators know this, and choose to live *into* their languaging, instead of simply assigning words to the default reality that has already happened, after the fact.

MANIFESTATION HACK: PRESENT TENSE POSITIVE

We utilize the present tense positive when we are in the process of manifesting by talking about the things we are calling in as though they are already here. I do not affirm the state of not-havingness by talking about how much I "want" a fat tire electric bike. I confirm my havingness by talking about how excited I am to be riding my fat tire electric bike through the desert, and how amazing it feels to use pedal assist up the ski mountain. This simple shift — from languaging my desires in the future to claiming them in the present moment — directs reality to deliver my dreams to me, now.

Similarly, when it comes to recreating culture, instead of complaining that there are no women leaders in the psychedelic space, I cultivate excitement, while envisioning more women taking the lead when it comes to teaching and speaking about entheogens. Instead of whining about how badly my hands hurt after a writing session, I say, "I look forward to my hands feeling better and better." I don't lament the frustration that comes from watching unconscious and misinformed people willingly avail themselves to tyranny; I simply hold the vision of our swift collective awakening and the restoration of a transparent democratic republic.

Let's Not with the Sucky Speak

Reality creation is a two-way street. Okay, it's an interlapping omnisection of every-which-way paths, portals, roads, alleys, thoroughfares and wormholes; *and* you get the gist, yes? Reality creation isn't just about claiming/languaging the goals, visions and experiences we are calling forth in the present moment, it's also about NOT summoning the things we reject, revile, regret and aren't digging, by empowering their *is*-ness in naming them.

When we focus on a substandard status quo, we perpetuate that substandard status quo. When we habitually tell our sad victim stories, we program our reality to create more icky experiences with which to craft more sad victim stories. When we give voice to worst-case scenarios and all the world's suckiness, we vote for the materialization of these worst-case scenarios, while sustaining suckiness the world over.

To be clear, this is not to deny anyone's trauma, transgressions, plight or suffering. It is simply to explain how language functions to perpetuate these experiences, energetics and feelings, and to invite us to examine how we are perpetuating suckiness in our own reality constructs, while encouraging us to switch it up.

Change comes when we shift our attention from problems to solutions, from worst-case scenarios to best possible outcomes, and we stay tenaciously focused on the solutions, and the best possible outcomes, and the up-leveled circumstances and reality constructs they portend, with our every word, thought and deed.

PART 3
THE LANGUAGE OF
BETTERARCHY

"If we speak a different language,
we would perceive a different world."
— Ludwig Wittgenstein

The language of betterarchy is the tool that will reprogram what Terence McKenna called "our fundamental, ontological conceptions of reality," and allow us to evolve our outdated hierarchical iteration with ease and grace. As I explained in Part 2, this evolution is a collective endeavor, which will happen all the more swiftly when we, the people, are speaking an up-leveled language of betterarchy.

Mastering the language of betterarchy is a two-step process: First, we train ourselves to recognize the outdated hierarchical languaging patterns infusing our lexicon, while educating ourselves as to how they are working against us. Then, we replace these words and phrases with betterarchical upgrades. Only when we are crystal clear as to what constitutes hierarchical languaging are we resourced to go about evolving our lexicon for the betterarchical.

In this section, I detail the ten categories of hierarchical languaging: *separation, conflict, identity, victimhood, wrong-use-of-will, lack, limitation, fear, fixity* and *status*. Each category serves as a helpful linguistic lens of perception as we familiarize ourselves with the nuances and subtleties informing these disempowering languaging patterns.

The more attention we place on examining the frequencies encoded in our words, the more patterns we start to see, and the quicker we recognize that language vibrating at any one of these ten frequencies is — *shocker!* — hierarchical. Duly attuned, we can then lean into the bettterarchical upgrades that are liberating our species from the shackles of hierarchy, and evolving our culture accordingly.

AUTHOR'S NOTE

I feel called to acknowledge that there is some categorical crossover amongst the hierarchical words and phrases we are examining in this section, and that some categories are like giant, overarching umbrellas, encompassing multiple categories at once. For example, all conflict languaging falls under the category of separation, as well. Judgment can be examined from the angle of three "different" categories, as it vibrates at the frequencies of separation, fixity and wrong-use-of-will, all at once.

I thought long and multidimensional about how to handle this, and toyed with the idea of limiting the scope of our examination to one category per word, as a way to streamline. Ultimately, this felt like a reductive and one-dimensional approach. As such, I have opted to ditch my historical allegiance to streamlining, while prioritizing your — the reader's — multidimensional understanding as to the various ways that hierarchical languaging functions to enslave and disempower us.

Thank you for resisting the urge to freak out when certain words appear in multiple sections, or when you realize that "can't" vibrates at the frequencies of both limitation and victimhood, which — when we tilt our heads at a certain angle — we can see are pretty much the same thing, anyway.

HIERARCHY: A VISUAL METAPHOR

Because hierarchy is an abstraction, I find it handy to have a visual reference for easy-peasy hierarchy recognition. It gives my brain something tangible with which to connect, thus grounding the concept into material metaphor, and making hierarchy's influence all the easier to spot, feel and familiarize ourselves with. To this end, I envision hierarchy as a tiered winners' podium upon which Olympic medalists — or really, any competitors — stand.

The winners' podium is the perfect metaphor for hierarchy: While the silver medalist is thrilled to have beaten the bronze medalist, above whom she is positioned, she is simultaneously resentful of the gold medalist, whose position she both envies and covets.

That medal should have been mine, Second Place thinks, replaying the race over and over in her mind, cataloging the gold medalist's perceived cheats, shortcomings and affronts to the integrity of the competition, as she scrapes the edges of her imagination for reasons why she should be standing on the top-most tier, wearing a gold medal and not this janky silver one, which clashes with both her skin tone and her wardrobe.

The bronze medalist resents both the silver and gold winners, while thanking every lord to which she prays that she placed at all. Still, she is acutely aware that she is the lowest person on the medalists' totem pole, and is already plotting ways to take down the other medalists in the next competition, while pitying the losers who didn't even place at all, and cultivating a nice, fat batch of superiority in the process.

The gold medalist is top dog and super proud of her accomplishments, while surprisingly anxious about defending her medal/title, lest the other two attempt to snag it away from her in the next competition. While our winner is infused with a flurry of happy chemicals dancing through her bloodstream, she still can't really relax, because she knows that there are plenty of others vying for her position, which she is now expected to "defend."

Granted, it's an imperfect metaphor given that the competitors in question are all Olympic medalists, succeeding in the uppermost echelons of their sports. Still, the visual remains a useful tool for us to employ moving forward. Shall we?

SEPARATION

"In ordinary life, we are not aware of the unity of all things, but divide the world into separate objects and events. This division is useful and necessary to cope with our everyday environment, but it is not a fundamental feature of reality. It is an abstraction devised by our discriminating and categorising intellect. To believe that our abstract concepts of separate 'things' and 'events' are realities of nature is an illusion."
— Fritjof Capra

One of the matrix's primary functions is to keep the populace jacked up on programming that persuades us into believing that we are not, in fact, a singular species of human Earth stewards, but that we are separate beings, who cannot be trusted, and with whom we must perpetually compete if we are to survive. Alas, this is false.

Now, this concept can be a little tricky to grasp, because one of the many things we humans have in common is an ego structure that aims to convince us that we are super special, precious snowflakes who are categorically and fundamentally *different* from everyone else. And in some ways, this is true. We are, each of us, amalgamations of a distinctive set of circumstances, characteristics, biology, belief, experience and perspectives that absolutely differentiate us as individuals.

Still, there exists no fundamental value judgment that we can objectively overlay upon our infinite sea of differences. One person might be a blonde-haired, blue-eyed carpenter who likes to cook, knit and yodel, while another person might be a dark-skinned, dreadlocked anthropologist who studies ballet, small batch fermentation and esoteric spirituality. There is no qualitative difference between either of them. One is not *better* than the other. They are simply different flavors of a singular consciousness expressing itself through a shared humanity — each animated by a unique cosmic blueprint, and each equally valuable, precious and super very special.

The ego loves to believe that we are separate, and goes the distance to convince us of such fictions in its incessant judging, comparing and criticizing. But we are not our egos, nor are we the frenetic machinations of our minds. We are a singular unified energy field, sharing a fleeting, individualized experience here on Earth.

And so it is that despite all divisive, hierarchical propaganda to the contrary, we humans really, truly are all One. And while the limitations of our 3D monkey minds can make this fundamental axiom challenging to fully grok, it remains a truism that has been confirmed across multiple scientific disciplines, as well as in countless spiritual and mystical traditions the world over.

To be clear, this is not New Age, kumbaya, love-and-light mumbo-jumbo. This is physics. This is Unified Field Theory. This is the scientific understanding that what appear to be multiple, individual people populating our planet — are actually temporary concentrations of energy existing in a vast, singular field of energy. Like drops of water in the ocean, we are but concentrated blips making a temporary appearance within a unified field of energy called *humanity*.

> *"We are one, after all, you and I, together we suffer,*
> *together exist, and forever will recreate each other."*
> **— Teilhard de Chardin**

But, unity doesn't sell malware, insurance or political ideologies. Nor does it serve hierarchy's agenda, which needs us divided and disgruntled so that we will continue to play into its shenanigans. And so it is that hierarchy uses language to brainwash us into conflating individuation with separation.

Otherizing

The act of otherizing takes individualism a step further in skewing our differences through the lens of hierarchy, and stapling them to an implied judgment, which purports that some people are better, kinder, smarter and more worthy than others, while said "others" are worse, broken, stupid, ignorant, inferior — take your pick.

Otherizing is one of hierarchy's more dangerous communication practices, because otherizing is fundamentally dehumanizing. When we place people in boxes labeled "other," we inadvertently extract their humanity from the equation, along with our underlying connection as brothers and sisters. This disconnect is what allows us to commit atrocities upon our fellow man, because the act of otherizing blinds us to our essential connection as human beings.

The Shame/Blame Game

One of the more unfortunate trends we have been witnessing in our recent cultural discourse is the knee-jerk habit of leaping away from the topic at hand — be it facts, figures, policy, ideology, conflicts of interest, etc. — to instead point fingers, project negative intentions and disparage large swaths of the population, as well as individuals we've never met, and even our nearest and dearest. Alas, leaping off topic to pinpoint a villain to blame and deride is an inefficient and extremely damaging communication strategy.

Some of us are operating at less developed levels of consciousness and come by this pattern honestly. Others are being manipulated by the social engineers, who use media[27] to prey upon our critical thinking skills, and manipulate our desires, beliefs and perspectives from there. It works well for the divide and conquer agenda, because instead of unifying and collaborating to evolve the system for the better, we align ourselves with our oppressors' programming, which pits us against one another. Duly manipulated/divided, we waste our time tearing each other down, instead of sharing and expanding perspectives, collaborating on solutions, and evolving our Selves and our culture for the better.

Shaming has become bloodsport these days, what with the ubiquity of cancel culture, wherein folks are publicly discredited and humiliated as they lose jobs, friends, social media accounts and payment processing services, alongside reputations and dignity for affronts as epically egregious as making an off-color joke, using the wrong pronoun or being a cisgendered, heterosexual, Western European biological man in 21st-century upside down world.

While I am inspired to posit that shaming is "never" constructive, there are indeed times when we are out of line and out of integrity and are well-served by a conscious, tough-love ass-handing that interrupts the pattern and shakes the ego out of unconscious autopilot, alerting us to the damage it is doing. This is but one example of the inefficacy of absolutes like "never" — exceptions abound. Still, the ubiquity and ferocity of shaming, as it is currently being employed in the cultural landscape, is far more sadistic than it is constructive.

Shaming entire races, genders, religions and cultures, along with individual humans who pray, think, vote, heal, ally and behave differently than we do does nothing to educate, illuminate or shift anyone's positions. All it does is engender feelings of ill will and resentment, thus rendering our communities less and less safe, given the undercurrent of negative emotions boiling beneath the surface of the individuals and groups comprising them.

There is not a person alive who bears one shred of personal responsibility for slavery, colonialism or systemic anything-ism. We are, all of us, born and reared in the same hierarchical control matrix, and we are, all of us,

---

27   And other nefarious technologies.

ill-served by it. To blame the incarnate beings we have been programmed to pinpoint as the perpetrators responsible for today's societal imbalances is to miss the mark, while succumbing to the *divide and rule* bait that empires have been using since empires were created. And to shame these alleged perpetrators on top of it? To instruct another being to feel bad about themselves because of something as insignificant as their race, gender or creed? Well, that's just straight-up cruel.

SEPARATION-SPEAK

Separation-speak is an umbrella term that describes the shadowy Masculine linguistic patterns we use to distinguish ourselves from groups or individuals with the implied intention of blaming, shaming, judging, deriding, slandering or ascribing higher/lower status. Most of the hierarchical words, phrases and habits we unpack in this book fall under the category of separation-speak.

Separation-speak does our human family a grave disservice, as it is the linguistic coding that programs separation consciousness. Separation consciousness is what allows us to disassociate from our fellow humans, to dehumanize and inflict any number of indignities and atrocities upon one another, because — well, hierarchy.

Polarities

Hierarchy is a very *black/white*, *good/bad*, *Left/Right*, *us/them* sort of system. Hierarchy relies upon reductive polarities to divide and control the populace, because hierarchy needs us to be at perpetual odds with one another to function. This endless pitting keeps us in a near constant state of fight or flight, wherein cortisol and other lizard brain hormones flood the bloodstream, freak-out the nervous systems, shroud our perceptions and put us on the defensive.

In attempting to whittle an omniscopic[28] world of every-which-way possibility and expression into reductive binaries, we shape a reality forged of dualistic division. Implications abound: If you're not *Right*, you must be *Left*; she's *better*, therefore he's *worse*; we're *good*, so they're *bad*.

Polarities are encoded with their opposites, verily forcing those communicating within the confines of the construct to choose a side. It is a subtle though powerful form of neurolinguistic bullying that lends itself to various psychological manipulations, including the infamous *false dichotomy* — a kind of reductive oversimplification in which two diametrically opposed points of view are presented as the only options, thus attempting to fragment the world into antithetical categories.

But polarities are divisive in and of themselves, without needing to leap to established propaganda tactics to fragment the people. Take the seemingly innocuous example of *better/worse*, as follows.

The Polarity Pickle: An Example

I was once listening to a podcast in the car with a girlfriend. The controversial psychology professor who was being interviewed posited that two-parent households were "better" than single-parent households. My friend — a single mother — was incensed.

---

28 **omniscopic**, *adj*; every moment access to every possibility that ever was, is or will be. A QL synonym for "limitless" or "unlimited" that doesn't tether us to the frequencies of limitation in its uttering.

"Who the hell is this bozo to say my child's household is any worse than anyone else's?" she barked at the speakers.

While the professor didn't actually *say* that my single mother friend's household was "worse," the implication was obvious. Because this is how polarities function. They attempt to shove people into reductive little boxes defined by implied diametric opposites that defy nuance, exceptions and in-betweens.

When we are being catalogued as "worse," or "wrong," or what have you — either by implication or straight-up accusation — our lizard brains go into defense mode, registering the words as a signal that we are not safe. Duly alerted by the linguistic coding, the amygdala releases a flurry of fight-or-flight hormones into the bloodstream, which armor us up, put us on the defensive and render us at immediate odds with whomever hurled the polarity in the first place.

So, while the professor may have had some solid points to offer, couched inside this reductive polarity, my friend was now thoroughly deaf to them, her nervous system having been hijacked by the neurochemical flood his contractive, polarized languaging signaled.

amygdala hijack

Had the professor eschewed the polarizing "better" descriptive, instead specifying "more balanced," "more effective" or "more resourced," he would have communicated his idea in a way that allowed it to be embraced by my friend and all the single-parent households to which he was making his comparison. These more meticulous descriptives vibrate at a neutral frequency, while painting a clearer picture of the point he was making, without triggering any defensiveness or pushback in the process.

Betterarchical Upgrades for Polarities

Eschew them, while being specific. Adjectives are our friend.

"Us/Them"

As long as we're on the topic of polarities, let's drop in with the separation-a-go-go motherload that is "us/them." It's one of hierarchy's crowning achievements,[29] having bamboozled the collective into believing that there is an "us" and that there is a "them," and that they are at perpetual, irreconcilable odds with one another.

The illusion of an "us" and a "them" seeks to cordon us off into evermore-fragmented tribes and camps based on blood, belief, allegiance and behavior. Everyone who believes and behaves as we do lands in the "us" category, while those who choose differently become a "them." Our allegiance, of course, is to the "us."

Don't get me wrong; humans are a tribal species. We gravitate towards those who share similarities and context. Still, as a culture currently and ostensibly obsessed with "diversity," wouldn't it be wiser to expand our definition of "us" to include the very differences that have previously landed folks in the "them" category?

Despite any illusions or propaganda to the contrary, "us" and "them" are not neutral polarities that hold peaceful, respectful space for dissimilarities and distinctions — not by a long shot. The issue with "us/them" lies in the "versus" that — whether stated or implied — separates the two. The implicit "versus" frequency pits the "us" and the "them" against one another by way of the adversarial conflict vibes encoded in the word. It's the deleterious downside of the inferred "versus" inextricably bound to all polarities — the frequencies encoded in that contentious little preposition infect the opposites bookending it, rendering the imposed chasm between them antagonistic and seemingly uncrossable.

"Us/them" seeds the morphic field with unnecessary conflict, while perving any kind of real-deal, lived experience of diversity, because "us/them" disassociates from differences. How can we expect to create a culture of authentic inclusivity when our differences land us in so many "them" categories?

---

29 In terms of effective control operations and sadistic enslavement constructs, that is.

The "us/them" polarity implies that the differences between us eradicate our shared humanity, and goes about mucking up the morphic field and our collective reality construct with the corresponding separation vibes.

As a means of course correcting, I am in the practice of utilizing language that affirms our shared humanity, while acknowledging the differences I am addressing from *inside* the construct of our underlying unity. This means ditching the "them" and the "they" and expanding our concept of "us" and "we" to include those who believe and behave differently than we do.

For example, instead of claiming that "they" are Republican, and that "we" are Green, I expand my ability to hold these differences in saying, "There are those of us who vote Republican, and there are those of us who vote Green," which allows me to hold these differing choices under the umbrella of our togetherness, instead of the illusion of separation.

Betterarchical Upgrade for "Us/Them"

"us/we"

THE DREADED OUTCAST

The "them" half of the "us/them" polarity construct is encoded with the frequencies of primal outcast terror, because being pinpointed as a "them" means we are necessarily excluded from the tribe.

Despite our evolutionary trajectory and all the logic and reasoning capacities it's gifted us, humans are still mammals beholden to chemistry and biology, just like all the other plants, animals, insects and Earthlings with whom we share the planet. Sure, we are blessed with evolutionary advantages, like opposable thumbs and self-reflective consciousness, but these useful tidbits don't discount the effects of those primal neural responses we inherited from our primitive hunter/gatherer ancestors and that still drive our triggers and reactions.

Outcast fear runs deep within every human's DNA — a longstanding carryover from tribal days of yore, when being cast out and sent to wander vast expanses of wilderness all by our lonesome translated to certain death by exposure, starvation, carnivorous predator or any number of threats to our safety and survival.

Threat, status, exclusion and authoritarian imposition are some of the frequencies embedded in hierarchical languaging that trigger outcast fear. This means that when we find ourselves on the wrong end of an "us/them" comparison, our lizard brains register the frequencies encoded in the communication as an exclusionary threat, and thus go about releasing chemicals that signal the physical and psycho-emotional bodies to armor, attack and/or freak-out, accordingly.

This is why a simple conversation about ideas or political figures we've never even met can get so heated and so volatile. Because even though there's not a saber-toothed tiger anywhere in sight/existence, the amygdala registers the casually dropped "them" category into which we are suddenly cordoned off as a survival threat that is just as deadly and immediate, and thus goes about readying the physiology to defend itself.

It's an outdated mechanism that's hampered by inaccuracy and exaggeration, but it's what we're dealing with, as hairy mammals trapped in third-dimensional meat suits. Given that it will likely take a minute/millennia for us to evolve out of fight or flight, our wisest move is to hone in on the languaging patterns that trigger this response in ourselves and others, and to adjust our communications accordingly (i.e., stop using them).

Prescriptive Languaging

Prescriptive languaging is a kind of second-person languaging–specifically, a bossy-pants, domineering kind of second-person languaging that alleges it knows best and is authorized to tell others what to do. We see this mostly wherein a person in a position of perceived authority (i.e., coach, parent, doctor, teacher, manager, principal, podcaster, celebrity) addresses others by telling them what to do using "you" statements.

"You" statements are sticky, as, by their very nature, they vibrate at the frequency of separation. The second I say, "You," I am differentiating this "you" from "me" and drawing an imaginary dividing line between us.

"You" statements are veritable landmines of projection. They have this niggling habit of putting folks on the defensive, as they are so often received (and sometimes intended) as accusatory.

"You're triggered," a man tells his partner, who immediately explodes in a *Don't you dare allege to tell me the quality of my own internal state* kind of freak-out, which could easily have been sidestepped with a slight edit, wherein the speaker takes responsibility for his own experience, in saying, "I'm getting the feeling that you're triggered."

Alas, we're not here to regurgitate Marshall Rosenberg's *Nonviolent Communication* teachings.[30] We are here to dive deeper, and to dance multidimensional and nuanced, which brings us back to prescriptive "you" statements, and why we are wise to eschew them.

The issue with prescriptive "you" statements is that they allege that she who is doing the prescribing knows better and has some sort of authority over those she is addressing. The prescriptive "you" statement is quintessential hierarchical languaging, in that it places the speaker on a pedestal above the person/people she is telling what to do — a pedestal that implies authority over those to whom she is delivering her prescriptions.

---

30 While I do highly recommend them.

Now, to be fair, hierarchies do exist. And there are plenty of instances wherein it is absolutely appropriate for a person who is holding a position of authority to give others instruction, direction or advice — be it a work task, a self-help technique or a collective call to action. Still, *appropriate* doesn't necessarily translate to *effective*.

Managers have every right to tell their team what action steps to take on a project. Still, it's *the way* the manager delivers the instructions that will determine the morale, coherence and efficacy of the team.

"Your numbers are way down," gripes the department head to his sales team. "You need to close, and you need to close big. I want a twenty percent sales spike from you by the end of month."

Compare how that communication lands to the following version, wherein the speaker switches from the second-person prescriptive to the first-person inclusive:

"Our numbers are way down," empathizes the department head. "We need to close, and we need to close big. Let's rock a twenty percent sales spike by end of month."

The empathetic department head isn't separating himself from his team. He is sharing responsibility for the sales dip (as well as the task of raising the team's numbers), while the griping version blames the team he is otherizing. The empathetic leader uses the first-person-inclusive call to action as an invitation for a group-win all parties can share, rather than a demand placed upon others to meet the expectations of the figurehead at the top of the status ladder.

Whereas the griping department head creates a clear dividing line between his team and himself, and goes about blaming, shaming and demanding accordingly, the empathetic department head includes himself as part of the team. He is choosing to share the disappointment and the responsibility for the sales dip, just as he is including himself in the task of raising the numbers.

Inclusive "we" statements are infinitely more effective than domineering "you" statements, as they don't transmit the separation codes that trigger the amygdala and the corresponding contraction/pushback. Ideas tethered to "we" statements are infinitely more likely to be received and integrated than those offered as prescriptive "you" statements, which inspire shut down, defensiveness and a host of negative emotions that aren't conducive to constructive action or collaboration.

Betterarchical Upgrades for Prescriptive Languaging (aka: "You"/"Your")

"we"/"us"/"our"

Notice how the betterarchical upgrades for separation-speak invite us to *include* those we had previously otherized. These languaging shifts program our consciousness to quantum leap into a paradigm of unity consciousness, wherein we hold loving and respectful space for the differences that had previously (and erroneously) inspired us to divide ourselves from one another. This is how language functions to program our consciousness. Whereas the matrix had indoctrinated us to perceive differences as separation by way of hierarchical languaging and separation-speak, we are now correcting this fallacy by evolving into betterarchical languaging. Nifty, right?

IDENTITY

> *"When you call yourself an Indian or a Muslim or a Christian or a European, or anything else, you are being violent. Do you see why it is violent? Because you are separating yourself from the rest of mankind. When you separate yourself by belief, by nationality, by tradition, it breeds violence. So a man who is seeking to understand violence does not belong to any country, to any religion, to any political party or partial system; he is concerned with the total understanding of mankind."*
> **— Jiddu Krishnamurti**

Separation consciousness arises out of identification and the seemingly benign act of attaching to labels, aspects, images, stories and stereotypes. Identification happens when we lock into fixed notions of who we or others "are," and conflate choices, preferences, characteristics, behaviors and beliefs with the Self (aka: "the condition of being a specified person or thing").

Identification is like the metaphorical difference between seeing a pretty object on the ground, acknowledging its loveliness and then continuing on my way, or picking up the object, declaring it "mine," crafting an elaborate pouch for it and carrying it with me wherever I go.

The more we identify, confusing aspects and allegiances with the Self, the more fragmented we become, and the more suffering we create. Why? Because attaching to an identity is the action that sets us up to suffer.

– the root of all suffering is attachment.

One of the Buddha's primary teachings was that attachment is the root of all suffering. In a reality construct ruled by impermanence, attaching to *anything* is a set up for pain, loss and frustration. Attaching an identity construct to any of the various, ever-shifting aspects that coalesce to create our concept of Self is to lock ourselves in a stagnant cage of our own forging, and to set ourselves up for a great, big bunch of suffering.

When we grasp onto any one morsel of our infinite *I*/*me*-ness (or *us*/*we*-ness or *them*/*they*-ness or *anything*/*everything*-ness) and then go about crafting an identity construct around it, we become attached. This attachment creates what physicists call a *quantum entanglement*.

Quantum Entanglements

Quantum entanglements refer to co-dependent relationship dynamics forged of invisible bonds between objects, wherein one cannot be described without simultaneously referencing, invoking or activating the other. Sometimes this happens because of certain chemical reactions or environmental occurrences. Other times, it happens through language.

It's one thing to be a person who healed himself from cancer. It's quite another to be a "cancer survivor." The "cancer survivor" is inextricably bound to the experience of having cancer and all the sucky bummer coding it portends. When one self-identifies as a "cancer survivor," he is choosing to handcuff himself to a past trauma and is thus binding himself to the energetic frequencies of that trauma — the pain, the fear, the suffering. Every time he calls himself a "cancer survivor," he is activating those frequencies in his being, and sending them out into his individual reality construct as well as the collective field at large.

There are infinite examples of languaging choices that create and sustain quantum entanglements, a handful of which we will dive into in the ensuing pages. As a generalized point of reference, consider this: Some quantum entanglements are benign, as in a father referencing his progeny as "my son".[31] Other quantum entanglements prove more damaging, wherein we bind ourselves to people, things, circumstances and experiences we don't actually like or wish to sustain, but to which we are inadvertently handcuffing ourselves with unconscious languaging, as in "I am a recovering alcoholic" (entangling ourselves with an historical vodka addiction) or "I'm a widow" (entangling us with a dead spouse).

Fragmentation

Hierarchy is fostered by fragmentation — a tool the social engineers use to divide and undermine the populace. Fragmentation fuels disaffection and incoherence, keeping us in a state of stuttering discordance, wherein flow, ease, harmony and momentum evade us.

We can think of fragmentation like a skipping record or a speed bump in the road. It's that moment when the flow is interrupted by an unexpected hiccup or impediment that disrupts the momentum and pulls us out of our experience. As any athlete or high performer knows, momentum is pretty much everything, especially when it comes to achieving flow states. Fragmentation pervs our momentum by throwing a sudden wrench into the action at hand.

As a social engineering strategy, fragmentation operates on multiple levels, dividing and dehumanizing, while activating internal dissonance as a response to hiccups in flow, logic and acculturation, as a deliberate means of subverting and degrading our efforts to thrive, unify, harmonize and evolve.

Identification creates fragmentation, cordoning off our human family into smaller and smaller sections and subgroups, separating us from each other,

---

31 Though, there is a school of thought that acknowledges that this kind of personal, possessive framing/quantum entangling will have deleterious effects on both father and son, given that the son is being framed as an object belonging to his father.

as well as our shared humanity in the process. Identification creates more "us/them" divides, confusing folks into forgetting that we are one human family, who all bleed, laugh, cry, die, suffer, orgasm, giggle and want the best for ourselves and our loved ones. The fragmentation identification foments is a massive impediment to unification.

> "...fragmentation is an attempt to extend the analysis of the world into separate parts beyond the domain in which to do this is appropriate. It is, in effect, an attempt to divide what is really indivisible. In the next step such an attempt will lead us also to try to unite what is not really unitable. This can be seen especially clearly in terms of groupings of people in society (political, economic, religious, etc.). The very act of forming such a group tends to create a sense of division and separation of the members from the rest of the world."
> — *David Bohm*

THE MOTHERLOAD OF FRAGMENTATION: THE SINGULAR "THEY"

I was once reading a memoir written by a woman who identifies as part of the LGBTQ community. One of the characters in the book was described as a woman named Sam. The ascribing of a masculine name to a female character didn't throw me, given that I'm rolling the same way. What did throw me, however, was the author's choice to refer to Sam with the pronoun "they" throughout the entire story. The first time Sam was referred to as "they," I was supremely confused, thinking I must have skipped a page. I flipped back several paragraphs to see where I had checked out, only to realize that I hadn't skipped any pages or fallen asleep on the read; rather, the author was using the plural "they" to refer to this singular character named Sam.

The author's choice to ascribe the plural pronoun to a singular character proved extremely fragmenting throughout the entire reading process. The usage never got less disruptive, and really put a damper on the reading enjoyment factor, as every time this "they" was employed to refer to the singular Sam, I was — yet, again — pulled out of the story, confused and certain I must have missed something, which sent me back another few paragraphs, looking for the part I thought I'd missed.

The plural "they" has been a foundational anchor in the English lexicon since well before I incarnated. The word is bandied about so often I can't begin to fathom how many times my brain has processed it to function as a plural pronoun. To be expected to now ascribe it an inverted meaning is the penultimate in fragmentation, as it necessarily disrupts any and all conversational flow, necessarily pulling the mind away from the topic at hand to instead undergo a series of complex acrobatics, as it reorients to a new, completely oppositional definition/usage.

To be clear, this is not to infer any issues whatsoever with those who identify as gender fluid. This is simply to explain how the hijacking of this particular pronoun, which already has an established meaning, is functioning to foster fragmentation.

Just as hierarchy is a structure that organizes people and societal systems, language is a structure that organizes communication tools. We can assess the success or failure of any organizational structure by its coherence — by how easy it is to utilize and understand, by how streamlined, accessible and functional it is. To impose a change upon any organizational structure that renders it more abstruse, more confusing and more fragmenting, while less easy to understand, implement and utilize is not an upgrade, is not progress and is not something to laud or encourage.

Our wisest move would be to introduce a new set of gender-neutral pronouns into the lexicon, instead of attempting to re-define an already established set, while confusing the fuck out of the populace, who knows it to denote a plural. "Ze/zey/zem" feel like our most obvious and compassionate lexicon additions, as they can be easily embraced and employed without causing any fragmentation or confusion in the process.

THE LANGUAGE OF IDENTIFICATION

The language of identification delineates a class of words and phrases that foster attachment to ideas, experiences, archetypes and avatars which can engender suffering, division, fragmentation and limitation. While I generally advise eschewing identification as much as possible, not every identity construct is necessarily deleterious.

If identifying as a wordsmith has me feeling expansive and delightful, then the act isn't necessarily doing me a disservice. If, however, I'm being invited to volunteer on a cob building project and I defer to my identity as a writer as a means of dodging those more laborious tasks, now I'm out of integrity with the identity construct that I'm wielding as an excuse to separate myself from the endeavor/mission.

Ultimately, it's on us to choose which identity constructs are serving us and which ones are not — a task which invites us to hone in on the language of identification, which resources us to discern if and when identification is helpful and appropriate.

Personal Pronouns

"Man has no individual 'i.' But there are, instead, hundreds and thousands of separate small 'i's, very often entirely unknown to one another, never coming into contact, or, on the contrary, hostile to each other, mutually exclusive and incompatible. Each minute, each moment, man is saying or thinking, 'i.' And each time his 'i' is different. Just now it was a thought, now it is a desire, now a sensation, now another thought, and so on, endlessly. Man is a plurality. Man's name is legion."
— G.I. Gurdjieff

"My" is a personal pronoun that functions as a tool of identification, as well as an instrument of quantum entanglement. This works in our favor when we are choosing to identify with inspirational wonderfulness, like "my open heart," "my thriving permaculture garden" and "my number one best-selling book."

Alas, personal pronouns do us a disservice when we pair them with traits, afflictions, pathologies, experiences and circumstances that don't serve us. When I blame my frazzled mood on "my anxiety," or my mid-date tantrum on "my abandonment issues," I am effectively tethering myself to traumas and pathologies that aren't serving me and from which I would be wiser to distance myself. When I describe the aching in my foot as "my arthritis," I am binding said aching to my identity and inviting it to take up permanent residence in my physical experience.

Personal pronouns indicate possession. "My" is a claim for ownership of that which we are describing. Think about the differences between "*a* car" and "*my* car," or "*a* diamond ring" and "*my* diamond ring," or between "*a* lost child" and "*my* lost child." Notice the visceral difference this tiny pronoun shift inspires.

These sensations are indications of attachment — a state which is fostered by the linguistic entanglements that personal pronouns actuate. Pairing the word "my" with anything creates a quantum entanglement between ourselves and said thing by way of linguistic merging. So "my acne," "my shopping addiction" and "my questionable choice in boyfriends" all become inextricably bound to my identity as I choose to language them with this pronoun.

Instead of utilizing personal pronouns to modify aspects, cycles, circumstances and experiences we're not digging, and don't wish to sustain, we are wise to modify them with impersonal language that holds them at a distance.

THE SELF-SABOTAGING HUMAN POTENTIAL PODCASTER: AN EXAMPLE

I used to subscribe to a top-rated podcast hosted by a famous tech investor turned human potential author/optimized lifestyle guru. The podcaster spoke openly and often about his struggles with psychic weather, which he would frequently refer to as "my depression."

I sent the podcaster multiple emails explaining the self-sabotage embedded in this phrasing, going on to explain how the very act of pairing the pronoun "my" with "depression" (let alone pathologizing said weather as "depression" in the first place) was exacerbating his suffering a thousandfold, while keeping him stuck in a victim cycle. I offered a handful of alternative ways he could describe his experience that wouldn't victimize him to said psychic weather patterns.

The podcaster didn't respond to my messages and — to this day — continues to language his mood cycles in this manner. While I still tune into his podcast on occasion, I ended up unsubscribing — not because he didn't respond to/take my unsolicited advice, but because I found it painful to listen to a world-renowned human potential leader consistently undermining himself and modeling this kind of self-sabotage for his millions of listeners.

So, it's not "my acne"; it's "the bumps that sometimes appear on my face." It's not "my anxiety"; it's "the anxiety I have historically experienced." It's not "my ex-wife"; it's "the woman to whom I used to be married."

By depersonalizing the experiences that aren't serving us, we stave off the urge to identify, and thus we can create more detached space between ourselves and that which we are describing, which frees us up to have new and different experiences.

Betterarchical Upgrades for Personal Pronouning

"a"

"the/that"

ADJACENT LANGUAGING

Did you notice how when offering the personal pronoun upgrades above, I sidestepped the words "acne" and "ex-wife," instead describing them with adjacent languaging that points to the same concepts, without quite naming them?

Adjacent languaging is a helpful tool for un-identifying, as it liberates us from the many layers of coding, story and metadata embedded in words that represent experiences, circumstances, people or things from which we are choosing to distance ourselves.

When words are loaded with negative programming or associations, I highly recommend replacing them with adjacent languaging that points in their general direction, without activating the negativity embedded in the actual words themselves.

Labels

Hierarchy loves to put people into boxes and categories, which function as cages that make us all the easier to divide, conquer and control. One of the hierarchy's primary methods of doing this is by labeling people.

Labels function as shorthand for behavior patterns, preferences and ideological allegiances we latch onto, and conflate with identity constructs. When we conflate behaviors with identity constructs, we put people in narrow, limiting, stagnant boxes, while removing their humanity from the equation. Labeling turns opinions and choices into homogenized cages forged of stereotypes, reductionism and disdain.

> *"Groups are grammatical fictions; only individuals exist, and each individual is different."*
> — **Robert Anton Wilson**

The act of labeling takes someone who once said something that someone else interpreted as unkind to Portugese people, and turns her into a "racist;" a person who fudged his age on a dating app becomes a "liar" (despite the fact that most everyone incarnate has lied at some point in their lives, and there is a world of difference between the act of *lying* and being "a liar"). The practice renders folks who wear glasses "nerds," girls who put out on the first date "sluts" and dudes who are into crystals, astrology and holistic healing "woo-woo science deniers." Labeling has made "Bernie Bros" and "Trumpers" out of people who once voted for these silly monikers' namesakes.

Labeling has become a favorite pastime of the MSM, which has taken a turn for the astonishingly low-vibe, unethical and editorialized, in labeling those whose choices, beliefs and behaviors that run counter to the agendas of the interests they serve (aka: those paying their salaries and pulling their strings). And so it is that the MSM have programmed the masses to label folks who think all lives matter as "white supremacists," those who question the legitimacy of energy sanctions "climate change deniers," and parents who don't support curriculum that teaches children to be ashamed of their skin color and/or genitals as "domestic terrorists."

Slapping labels onto people with whom we disagree is a great way of shutting down constructive discourse around ideas, experiences and circumstances, while shifting to character assassination instead. This labeling trend has us evading any intelligent or relevant discussion of the issue at hand, instead leaping to label, effectively demonizing those who think differently than we do. It's like a social engineering shell game. Whereas the street hustler distracts someone who is about to be ripped off with sleight of hand that functions as a *Look over here, so you don't notice I'm stealing from you* hustle, this version operates as a low-vibe psyop[32] that distracts us from the actual topic at hand by saying *Look at what a terrible, awful person this is,* instead of discussing the validity of said person's perspective and ideas.

The hurling of invectives in this manner is a swift and effective way of otherizing people who aren't falling in line with hierarchy's agendas. It's yet another brilliant social control mechanism that has — until now — had us controlling, enslaving and dividing ourselves with our words.

---

32 **psyop**: shorthand for "psychological operation" — a class of secret operations used by governments, military, social engineers and intelligence agencies to manipulate the masses' emotions, motives and objective reasoning, as well as the behavior of groups, individuals, governments and organizations. Psyops are the larger operations which propaganda campaigns are employed to serve.

The Label Cage

When we put people in boxes, we remove their humanity from the equation, thus making it easier to inflict violence upon them. A "person" who said something racist is far more challenging to shame, blame, humiliate and cancel than a "racist" is. A "person" is deserving of kindness and compassion, but a "racist?" No way.

Labels fragment our human family. They create an ever-increasing array of subdivisions that allows us to reduce ourselves and others to a handful of shallow descriptors that function to divide, stereotype and exclude.

You see, labels don't come free. They are weighed down with stories, assumptions and associations that we project onto those we are labeling. Labeling attempts to homogenize people based on shallow, reductive stereotypes, alleging that every single person who votes for a particular party or candidate necessarily embodies the same values, prejudices and allegiances. Or that being born without a certain amount of melanin in one's skin necessarily equates to being racist. Or that all spiritual people are polyamorous vegetarians with punctuality issues and B.O. It's a dehumanizing perspective, given that it denies our individuality, and the notion of free will and free expression, instead implying that those who make up certain perceived groups are all cookie-cutter versions of one another, bereft of their own unique experiences, opinions and beliefs.

"Cis," "white," "feminist," "terrorist," "Nazi," "liberal," "alt right," "woketard," "Karen," "Zionist," "illegal alien" and "conspiracy theorist" are all nifty, reductive shorthand monikers that chip away at individuality and homogenize our experience based on shallow identifiers. These labels communicate how we are supposed to think about people in broad, sweeping, stereotypical generalizations that rarely line up with the unique lived experience of the individuals they are attempting to describe/smear. Labels, in general — and these labels, specifically — are coded with projections, expectations and assumptions that fly in the face of individuality and free will, while multi-tasking as cancel culture character assassinations that seek to exclude folks from the public discourse.

The Hierarchy of Identity

These days, it's not enough to turn a dietary preference into an identity construct called "vegan." To stay on top of the social hierarchy, we must further differentiate that we are a "non-binary vegan of color," which inches us ever higher in the status game, and allegedly qualifies us to talk to other non-binary vegans of color about non-binary vegan of color issues. Because these are the rules of the current divide, and divide some more social hierarchy racket — only those who exist in the same categories of marginalization are "allowed" to speak about the issues relating to these categories of marginalization. And, if our own identity doesn't line up with the category's checklist, then we are to keep our mouths shut about all related issues, because — well, hierarchy. It's not a written proclamation, per se, rather an implied, socially imposed identitarian agreement into which we've been programmed to play.

The game requires us to fragment ourselves more, and more, and more, while resting upon an inverted status framework, wherein those who are considered the most oppressed, and who have supposedly cornered the market on suffering, hold the highest positions in the identitarian hierarchy. To this end, those who can check off the most identitarian boxes, representing the most inferred suffering, exist in the highest echelons of the identitarian status game, and thus win the most imaginary points.

Labels Inhibit Change, Growth, Pivots and Whim

Labeling programs us to conflate our identities with trifles as insignificant as voting inclinations. As someone who has historically voted Libertarian, when I am authentically inspired by the Green candidate's proposed policy shifts, it's going to be way easier for me to vote for the candidate with whom I feel genuinely aligned when I haven't declared my Self "a Libertarian" or "a Republican" or "a Democrat" or what have you.

Were I to self-identify as "a Democrat" and then cast my vote for a Republican candidate whose platform I dig, I would necessarily force myself to navigate a heaping buttload of inner turmoil, conflict and existential angst, if I were to allow myself to vote against "my" party at all. The truth of the matter is that political identities are effectively prisons of our own linguistic forging that rarely allow us to honor any organic inclinations to step outside these conceptual prisons. In conflating historical voting preferences with our existential *is*-ness, we are infinitely more likely to evade that whole research and due diligence part of the democratic process, while blindly checking the boxes next to the bills and candidates with "our" associated letters — be they *R, D, L, I, J, K, L, M, N* or *P*.

Labeling denies the evolutionary process in attempting to pin us to singular choices and moments in our ever-unfolding Earth walks, and staple them to reductive pigeonholes, attempting to rewrite transient behaviors as permanent identity constructs/cages. We'll unpack this more in the *Fixity* section, but for now it's enough to know that when we label ourselves, we project permanence onto preferences and predilections that may otherwise shift, were we to allow ourselves to grow and evolve authentically, outside of the confining cages that are these identity constructs.

THE "VEGAN" VISITS
AN ARGENTINE CATTLE FARM

As a former vegan who was heavily identified with my preference for plant-based everything, I navigated this lesson myself while visiting a friend on her cattle farm in Argentina. Every day for the first week of my stay, my host family offered me various cuts and kinds of meat during our every meal together.

"No, gracias," was my stock response. "Soy vegan."

Still, my hosts continued to offer me world-class meat at every meal. And every time, I would reassert my identity construct, as though it adequately explained my choice to abstain from the albeit fragrant and tempting delicacies that were made from animals that were raised, slaughtered and prepared on their multigenerational family farm.

At some point, it dawned on me that I was denying myself a very special, possibly once-in-a-lifetime opportunity, based upon a self-imposed label. I flashed to myself at 90 — wrinkled and creaky, reflecting upon my life while preparing to take my leave of it, lamenting the rare opportunity on which I had missed out because of my attachment to an identity construct.

The next night, I decided to slip out of said identity construct, and leave it in the guest house. As a heaping plate of fresh beef Asado was passed around the table, I reached for it, and — much to la familia's surprise — helped myself to a strip.

"Ah!" laughed my friend. "The vegan eats meat ahora!"

"Quando in Rome," I shrugged, laughing along with the table, delighting in the experience of sharing something so special and so delicious with my friends.

Betterarchical Upgrades for Labels

There is no such thing as a betterarchical label. Our wisest move when it comes to evolving into a betterarchical language/society is to eschew the urge to affix labels onto others, as well as ourselves. Instead of attempting to homogenize our vast and varied human experience by way of labels, we are wise to instead focus on the actions and behaviors that inform the labels and to stick with those.

So, instead of describing myself as a "yogi," I acknowledge that I have a regular yoga practice. I'm not a "free speech absolutist"; I am someone who wholeheartedly believes in every human's God-given right to free expression. My cousin isn't a "capitalist"; she is someone who loves making a lot of money. Jesse isn't a "pessimist"; rather, he tends to focus on the negative.

In all these instances, I am replacing the labels with descriptions of the actions to which they point, thus languaging these predilections with more accuracy, as well as the spaciousness in which we are all free to make a different choice at any time.

VERBS > NOUNS

Labels attempt to contort otherwise fleeting choices, habits, behaviors, allegiances, preferences and likelihoods into fixed things (aka: nouns). It's the easiest way to clue into the identification trap: notice where nouns are being used to reduce choices, habits, behaviors, allegiances, preferences and likelihoods into personality constructs or classifications of humans.

The mainstream media machine has taken to labeling anyone who is making choices that don't align with the agenda(s) they are pushing by twisting said choices, beliefs and behaviors into clunky nouns, marked by the inelegant "-er" tacked onto the backside of said predilections, actions and tendencies. The short list includes: "Trumper," "anti-vaxxer," "science-denier," "anti-masker," "election-denier" and "flat-Earther" — each one conflating choices, preferences and intellectual allegiances (or non-allegiances, as the case may be) with a dehumanizing identity construct.

The spazzy, overused "-er" isn't the only suffix the matrix minions use to inappropriately noun choices, ideas and off-color jokes. There is "-ist" ("racist," "sexist," "white supremacist"); there is "-phobe" ("transphobe," "homophobe"); and there are plenty of other iterations of shorthand tag-ons, messily stapled to fleeting moments of expression that are then conflated with unflattering forms of personhood, duly imprisoned by way of clunky and inelegant nouns.

Nouns — organic and refined, or clumsy and contrived — imply fixity and permanence. Verbs, on the other hand, allow us to language temporary phases, states, choices and whatnot in motion, thus giving us the option and the spaciousness to make different choices as we evolve, grow and change.

Think about it. When I identified myself as "a vegan" (aka: a thing, a noun) it was nearly impossible for me to allow myself to eat meat. Had I simply (and more accurately) described my eating habits with verbs, by saying, "I have historically adhered to a plant-based diet" or "I normally eat a plant-based diet" or "I usually eat vegetarian" or even, "I don't eat meat," without conflating historical behaviors with an identity construct, then I wouldn't have painted myself into such a confining corner that required me to undergo a full-fledged existential unraveling so that I could simply share a meal with my friends.

Nouns take temporary choices and ideas and turn them into identity cages forged of projected permanence. Verbs, on the other hand, allow us to language actions as actions, choices as choices and beliefs as beliefs, without projecting permanence, rigidity or fixity upon them.

"Types," "Kinds" and "Sorts"

Let us consider the following statements:

"I'm not the kind of woman who wears miniskirts."
"Martinis for lunch? Please! I'm not that guy."
"I'm not the type of person who sends handwritten letters and remembers people's birthdays."

The implications are thick, loaded and limiting. Aren't they?

According to all three statements, choices and actions are prohibitive–not because of the actions or preferences themselves, but because of the character and values the speakers are choosing to project upon the "kinds" of people who would indulge in the behaviors they are referencing.

Reframed in the positive, wherein instead of *not* identifying as these sorts of people, the speakers claim to be exactly these sorts of people, the limitations of the cages into which they are placing themselves remain just as confining. Because they are limiting their experiences to an artificially narrowed set that align with the implied stories and behavior patterns that said "kinds" of people would enact.

Again, we see language being used to homogenize and stereotype. Whether we are aligning ourselves with a type or a group or we are separating ourselves from a type or a group, we are still enslaving ourselves to a conceptual cage (aka: identity) and limiting our behaviors accordingly. Someone can choose to wear a miniskirt and not ascribe to any of the values or character traits Speaker #1 is projecting upon them. A person can abstain from drinking 99.999% of the time and still choose to imbibe during a lunch meeting with out-of-town guests who are operating under different cultural standards, as long as that someone isn't conflating temporary choices with an identity construct. But given that he already has, when our teetotaler *does* decide to share a drink with his lunchtime cohorts, he must now endure an existential overhaul, as he has taken it upon himself to confuse a momentary choice/ pattern interruption with an indication of character, value and whatever other traits he is choosing to project upon "the kind of people" who imbibe at lunch.

Behaviors and choices are objectively neutral. The meaning we choose to project upon said behaviors and choices is entirely up to us. We get to decide which choices and behaviors align with our values and priorities in any given moment and to engage or not, accordingly. But to eschew or align with choices and behaviors based on projected character assessments and existential constructs is to tangle ourselves in the icky, sticky web of identity, and to proliferate separation consciousness.

Betterarchical Upgrades for "Types," "Kinds" and "Sorts"

Given that "types," "kinds" and "sorts" function as homogenized identity cages forged of stories, stereotypes and projections, our wisest move, as relates to liberating ourselves from the confines of hierarchical languaging, is to simply resist the urge to use them.

When it comes to projecting them onto others, I recommend a hard and fast *don't*. As far as self-identifying as any "kind" or "type," I encourage us to dig deeper and to unravel the stories we are projecting onto the actions and behaviors for which these "kinds" or "types" are serving as shorthand. Duly liberated, we are free to make choices based on authentic, present-moment alignment, instead of projected identity constructs. Freedom rocks.

Pathologizing

Slapping labels onto symptoms, tendencies, traumas, traits, phases, weather and whim is a hierarchical hustle that allows people and things to be easily categorized into reductive little boxes that come along with prefab "fixes," in the guise of medical procedures and pharmaceutical prescriptions, topped off with excuses, pity, perpetuation, degeneration and disempowerment.

Pathologies are umbrella assessments that healthcare professionals (or paranoia-prone people self-diagnosing by way of late-night, internet keyword searches) ascribe to patterns of symptoms. Pathologies can be useful, when it comes to determining treatments and healing protocols. But when held too tightly, they become prisons that impede the healing process, because pathologies are heavily coded, loaded with very specific stories — linear, progressive, regressive, worst-case-scenario roadmaps vibrating with fear, doom and gloom.

The coding embedded in pathologies is standardized and singular. A medical "authority" assesses our symptoms and then tells us we have *this thing* called _____ (insert terrifying pathology here). Because we have now been christened with *this thing*, we are to expect these *other things* to happen to us as time ticks on, and *this thing* progresses (insert a laundry list of evermore painful, debilitating symptoms and impairments that pathologies program us to expect and thus manifest).

Pathologies essentially function as curses, as they program the subconscious mind to organize symptoms into a very specific, predetermined progression, programming them to unfold in ways that may not have organically manifested as such had the body/mind not been instructed to follow this preordained pathway of illness.

They're also sticky. Pathologies are like magnets for personal pronouns and have this sneaky way of morphing into quantum entanglements. Once our symptoms have been christened with an official, medically sanctioned diagnosis, we carry these pathologies around with us like cardigan-wrapped purse Chihuahuas, making frequent reference to "*my* arthritis," "*my* diabetes," "*my* bipolar" and "*my* allergy." Hello, identification!

From there, it takes but the tiniest linguistic leap to move from *possessing* these pathologies to *becoming* them, as in, "*I am* arthritic," "*I am* diabetic," "*I am* bipolar" and "*I am* allergic." When languaged as existential identifiers by the "I am" preceding it, we allow ourselves to merge with these pathologies, thus opening the floodgates to all the deleterious coding embedded within them. This merging has the exact opposite effect of healing, given that pathologizing symptoms empowers and exacerbates said symptoms, while programming our bodies with more of them, thus ensuring that they stick around, indefinitely, or for as long as the story associated with the pathology tells us to expect them to stick around.

Betterarchical Upgrades for Pathologizing

The notion of *not* attaching pathologies to our symptoms is extremely radical for some folks. There lingers an unexamined, old paradigm attachment to the perceived authority of medical professionals, to whom we willingly give away our power. This is not to deny the value of a trained medical professional, who has education and experience that can be helpful in assessing symptoms and prescribing effective healing protocols. But there is no need to attach names, labels and pathologies to these symptoms to heal them, especially given that names, labels and pathologies have this insidious way of inspiring us to identify and to cling.

We'll tackle the pathology problem from the angle of projected permanence in the *Fixity* section, wherein we will also explore an alternate angle of upgrades to replace the outdated habit of pathologizing. In the meantime, let us resist the urge to pathologize symptoms and to instead distance ourselves with adjacent languaging.

So, instead of saying, "I have arthritis," I say, "I've been experiencing some inflammation," or — for extra expansive mojo — I say, "I am swiftly healing some inflammation." Instead of saying, "I am diabetic," I would say, "I have been expressing some symptoms similar to diabetes," or — even better — "I am transmuting some symptoms similar to diabetes." Instead of "I am bipolar," I would go with, "I sometimes experience mood swings," or "I am navigating some psychic weather."

We don't *have* pathologies, and we sure as hell *aren't* these pathologies. We "express" symptoms, we "heal" symptoms, we "transmute" symptoms, we "learn from" symptoms, we "navigate" symptoms and we "move through" symptoms. See the pattern? We distance ourselves from said symptoms with verbs that hold them at bay and acknowledge their impermanence. Deal?

"COSMIC UPGRADING"

"What's wrong with your wrist?" asked a colleague, referencing the web of copper compression tape criss-crossed around it, despite the fact that we were at a café, and not a boxing ring.

Whilst a handful of healers had tried to spew half-baked pathologies all over my aching, inflamed wrist, I cut them off at the pass, refusing to let a single one infect my mind with their curses. Sure, my wrist might have been expressing symptoms related to Pathology X or Syndrome Y, but I wasn't interested in hearing any of 'em. I was only interested in healing as quickly as possible, which meant not labeling/identifying with said symptoms.

"I'm integrating a cosmic upgrade," I smiled.
"Cool," she enthused. "Love that."

This was a distinctly different experience than I'd had sharing various half-baked diagnoses thrust upon me by healthcare practitioners in the past, wherein the moment these parroted pathologies left my lips, I was met with furrowed brows, downturned mouths and all the associated signals of pity and concern. These responses, while loving and empathetic, had the unfortunate consequence of creating a feedback loop wherein I absorbed their worry and their sympathy, allowing these low-vibe frequencies to glom onto my own, thus exacerbating the fear, pain and victimization I was already experiencing, and — let's be honest — milking.

The beauty of the "I'm integrating a cosmic upgrade" framing is that I am not shooting myself in the proverbial (or literal) foot. There is no deleterious or degenerative coding in this languaging. I am not giving voice to any frequencies that would program my body to configure or devolve according to any pre-fab fairy tales. This communication is efficient, next-level linguistic multi-tasking, allowing me to sidestep both contraction and neutrality by describing my experience with expansive languaging that commands an upgrade, while attuning the person with whom I am speaking to a higher vibrational resonance that then sets the tone for our exchange, thereby creating a positive, uplifting, expansive feedback loop between us.

Yay for quantum leaps, cosmic upgrades and divine magic flowing through my happy, healthy hands.

CONFLICT

"Fighting for peace is like screwing for virginity."
— **George Carlin**

Despite any and all propaganda, catchphrases or campaign promises to the contrary, hierarchy loves conflict. War makes for booming business, soaring profits and "justified" civil rights grabs. Widespread violence — whether real, or staged — is a stellar excuse to expand the powers of "authority" and government overreach. Engineered conflict amongst the populace is a fantastic distraction from the fuckery being imposed by the matrix and the structures serving the hierarchical agenda. The more conflict with which the public is programmed, the more conflict the public embodies and acts out, paving the way for Big Daddy hierarchy to step in and protect us from our savage selves.

In a sense, we are a culture addicted to conflict. We see this playing itself out in our media — our movies, video games, music videos and television shows, and especially our social media engaging — where the discourse has devolved to a level on par with dog fighting or Mongol sport murder.

Our addiction to conflict is clearly evidenced in our languaging patterns, wherein instead of proposing an "idea" or purporting a "theory," we label them "arguments" and then go about "defending" them. We see this in our ritual of political debate, wherein the masses tune in to watch the two-party system's candidates single-mindedly cling to their (corporate donors') ideas and then fight about why their perspectives are better than their opponents' — as though the ability to defend our egoic blind spots translates to effective leadership.

Conflict = Separation

Conflict languaging is an extension of separation-speak, sprinkled with animosity, aggression and ill will (*hello, Masculine shadows!*). Our lexicon is lousy and loaded with the stuff, inspiring us to inadvertently program our world and our Selves with violence and strife, on the regular.

As an eternal student of Quantum Languaging and the multi-layered intricacies of communication, I have become fascinated with pin-pointing the origin points of conflict. This study has me mining the languaging patterns expressing in heated dialogues, scouring the exchanges in question for cues and triggers that shift the energy/trajectory of our conversations. I've studied hundreds of conversations that have spun out into arguments, honing in on that singular moment wherein an imaginary switch is flipped, and peaceful discourse/respectful disagreement devolves into a fight. That moment is consistently defined by otherizing — be it a judgment, a projection or an *us/them* declaration. Conflict is activated by a line drawn in the sand that says, *Because you think, feel, look or do differently, you are **other***. That declaration of separation is where the conversation consistently goes sideways.

While arguments are obvious, conflict colors our lexicon in ways we may not realize. It's not just about conversations that escalate into squabbles or straight-up fights. It's also about the languaging patterns we are unwittingly utilizing to program our reality constructs with more strife, more violence and more aggression.

THE LANGUAGE OF CONFLICT

The energies of war and violence have been woven into the very fabric of our language such that plenty of peaceful folks are inadvertently speaking conflict into the collective field, all day, every day. Neither ignorance nor unconsciousness combat the coding embedded in our words. So, while it may not be my intention to be aggressive, oppositional or murderous, any and all associated languaging patterns are functioning to do exactly this and to program my and our realities accordingly, whether consciously or unconsciously.

What follows are some of the more common examples of conflict languaging infusing our lexicon.

"anti-"

There are plenty of toxic languaging patterns embedded in the collective lexicon. "Anti-" may be one of the most damaging, given its widespread weaponization and proliferation in this Junk Metal Age of outrage through which we, as a collective, are wading.

"Anti-" is a combative little prefix that alleges to oppose whatever it modifies — be it war, trust, poverty, aging, sexism, racism or any of the myriad ideological *-isms* pervading the cultural landscape. Modifying a word or a concept with "anti-" and thinking we are *not* invoking its energies in our reality construct is like painting a mural of a pink elephant and then putting a big red-X over it, meanwhile pretending that we aren't implanting the image of a pink elephant into the minds of everyone who sees it.

Stapling "anti-" onto whatever it is we claim to oppose is a Masculine shadow strategy that seeks to squash/barrel over the offending idea, instead of stretching itself to describe the solution or the pivot it would prefer to support.

"Anti-" is the epitome of the kind of force that Dr. David Hawkins wrote about in his seminal book, *Power vs. Force*, wherein he explained, "Force always creates counterforce; its effect is to polarize rather than unify." What this means is that — despite any and all intentions to the contrary — "anti-" functions to generate friction, opposition and pushback, while strengthening and empowering that which it attempts to counter in the process.

When we tether the prefx "anti-" to *anything*, we create a quantum entanglement between ourselves and the thing we are claiming to oppose. "Anti-sexists" needs sexism to have a mission, and to fulfill their purpose. Duly self-identified, without sexism, the anti-sexist's existence would be nullified. If there were no sexism, then there would be nothing to reject, detest or fight against. "Anti-sexists" are inextricably bound to sexism to succeed at their mission, which — essentially — is to ineffectively rail against the thing they claim to abhor, while fueling and empowering it in the process.

When my mission is to oppose sexism (as the "anti-" prefix denotes), then my task is to be consistently on the lookout for instances of sexism against which to rail. So, while I might *claim* to oppose sexism, I actually *need* sexism and — to a certain extent — even love sexism, because when I find it, I get to be on purpose. I can accomplish my mission. Without sexism, I am aimless. I have no identity. I don't exist.

As we identify as "anti-sexist," our perception of the world is skewed by the intent to combat sexism. Because we need sexism to accomplish our mission, we need to amass instances of sexism to be on purpose. Sexism becomes the dominant filter through which we see the world. Claiming to be "anti-sexist" is to experience the world from the perspective of sexism.

It's like slipping on a pair of sexism goggles, which filter our reality through the lens of sexism. From this vantage point, we are not objectively assessing situations as they are. We are looking for instances into which we can plug sexism. This filter renders our reality "sexist," because the universe gives us back that with which we program it.

SANDWICH-EATERS

I once dated a man who was heavily identified with his raw, vegan diet. He ate only fruit, greens, seeds, nuts, avocados and a handful of non-hybridized vegetables, and only with his hands, because — according to him — utensils were for disconnected, brain-dead American zombies. Not only did he eat this way, but he identified himself this way, loudly and often — announcing to every waiter, cashier and vendor we encountered that he was "raw vegan" and thus, by implication, superior.

This man, we'll call him RV, was perpetually on the lookout for those he branded "sandwich-eaters" — nutritionally inferior morons who, according to RV, clearly hated themselves, given how little they cared for intestinal integrity or proper food combining precepts. RV was nowhere near neutral about those who ascribed to different nutritional paradigms; rather, he was actively triggered by them, and thus went out of his way to survey his every immediate environment for these so-called "sandwich-eaters," upon whom he projected his derision, his eating disorder and his self-esteem issues with a contemptuous tone and wildly gesticulating, avocado-crusted fingers. For all intents and purposes, RV was "anti-sandwich-eaters."

Let the record show that I, myself, had no charge on humans who ate sandwiches and rarely noticed them. Conversely, RV's reality construct was verily drenched with sandwich-eaters, who seemed to follow him wherever he went — not because the world is overrun by folks eating sandwiches, but because RV was attracting them into his field by way of his obsession and the charge (aka: unintegrated trauma) he projected upon them.

"Anti-Sexism" = More Sexism!

Not only does the choice to self-identify as "anti-sexist" tether our personal identities to the very thing we claim to oppose, it strengthens sexism, in general. It doesn't matter what injustice we staple to the backside of the prefix, whatever it is we are claiming to be "anti-" will only be empowered and expanded by the declaration. Because every time I say I am "anti-whatever," I am activating the frequencies of *whatever*, and ratifying the existential validity of *whatever*, and giving my sacred attention to *whatever*, and calling *whatever* into my present moment and thus seeding my reality with more *whatever*.

Remember, the words we speak *now* function to program the quantum field as to how to organize our future realities. When we rail on about what we hate and what isn't working, all we are doing is seeding our realities with more of what we hate and more of what isn't working. To take it a giant, sabotage-y step further, to then *define* ourselves by the very things we detest is the utmost in absurdity, given that it means we are incessantly programming ourselves and our reality constructs with the precise thing that repels us enough to make it our mission to eradicate.

All this is to say, who cares what you're "anti-"? What are you *for*? It's fine and dandy if you're thoroughly *over* sexism. But what would you rather see in its place? What would you prefer? What's the solution? What does a world marked by gender equality look and feel like?

Think about it. Do we go to a restaurant and tell the waiter all the things on the menu we *don't* want? Of course not. Not only would we be activating the frequencies of our least favorite foods and icking ourselves out, the waiter would have no idea what to bring us.

The smart way to go about it is to tell the waiter what we want, so he knows what to deliver. The same goes for the multiverse. Instead of giving voice, energy and telomere-length[33] to that which we oppose, we are wiser

---

33 Cortisol shortens the length of our telomeres, which regulate the body's aging process. The more cortisol we run, the shorter our telomeres become and the quicker our bodies age. When we rail on about "-isms" and concepts and inequities and situations we don't like, cortisol is released into the bloodstream, where it goes about shortening our telomeres and taking a real-deal toll on our physiological health and wellbeing.

to speak to the visions and the solutions into which we are choosing to live. This is how a tiny shift in languaging creates a seismic shift in our experience of reality.

Personally, I want nothing to do with "anti-sexism." I am a humanist. I stand for equality amongst all human beings, regardless of race, color, gender, religion or belief structure.

When I identify as a humanist and choose to devote my efforts to fostering unity and equality (instead of fighting the opposite), then I am necessarily going to attract more and more experiences of unity and equality. This is how language programs our reality. This is how we use words to change our world for the better.

Betterarchical Upgrades for "Anti-"

"pro-"

The "anti-" fix is more frameshift than simple linguistic replacement (though it's that, too; thank you, "pro-"!). Instead of utilizing a different word to language what we're *not* digging, the betterarchical upgrade invites us to shift our attention onto the solutions and up-leveled reality constructs for which we are vying.

So, rather than declaring whatever it is we are "anti-," we stretch into the "pro-" we would prefer to replace it. Instead of languaging the scourges we would otherwise combat, we speak to the up-leveled solutions we are choosing to live into.

Some examples:

From:	*To:*
"anti-racism"	"pro-humanism"; "pro-equality"
"anti-sexism"	"pro-gender equality"
"anti-aging"	"eternal"; "eternity-activating"; "optimizing"
"anti-poverty"	"abundance-proliferating"; "resource-rich"

Murderous Inversions

Murderous inversions refer to a certain class of violent exclamations, utilized to connote something positive, despite their real-deal established meanings. Examples include, though are in no way limited to "killed," "slayed," "crushed," "dominated" and "bomb."

We've all heard variations of these sentiments and perhaps even articulated them ourselves:

Someone asks us how our presentation went, and we respond with, "I crushed it."

How'd our daughter's soccer team do in the tournament? "They slayed."

A comedian is in the zone and getting oodles of laughs. "He's killing it," the booking agent enthuses.

These kicky little phrases have come to reference peak performance, triumphant experience, a job well done and a point well made. The conflation of violent/murderous language with excellence seeds our culture with violence and murder. It blurs the boundaries in the subconscious mind, thus desensitizing us to the real-deal actions and consequences these terms connote.

It's interesting to observe people calling for peace and unity, while unconsciously programming the quantum field with these sentiments. Though I'm not one to place limits upon an individual, group or species, I really don't see how widespread peace is possible while we are normalizing violent acts like *smashing the patriarchy*, along with *killing, crushing, slaying* and *dominating*, and conflating these terms with otherwise laudable behavior. As these expressions have infiltrated the mainstream lexicon, we have become increasingly desensitized to their actual connotation, while drenching our collective field in their frequencies. The effects on the populace at large cannot be underscored. They are massive, and they are multiple, and they are deeply, deeply destructive to our society, our planet and our human family.

INVERSIONS

The malappropriation of otherwise violent, destructive terms to connote positive action is a type of inversion. Inversions are used as a method of weaponizing symbols and language by transposing their meaning. It's a trick the matrix's social engineers use to hoodwink us into doing their dirty work for them and perving our own lives/world by seeding the morphic field with deleterious programming.

It's why "gangster" has come to mean someone who is successful or leading well. It's why "bomb" is used to describe something attractive, good or tasty, as though shifting the collective connotation actually changes the actual meaning of the word or the coding it transmits. Because it doesn't. Not even a little bit.

When I describe my coconut custard flan as "bomb," I might think I'm transmitting the energetics of something positive, but even if the people to whom I'm speaking share this modern-day, butt-backwards understanding of the adjectivized version of "bomb" to indicate "yummy," the coding and the frequencies embedded in the word remain the same. And so, every time we use the word "bomb" to communicate something good, we are programming the morphic field with the proliferation of explosives, while desensitizing ourselves to their ubiquity and danger.

> *"War is Peace. Freedom is slavery. Ignorance is strength."*
> **— George Orwell, 1984**

This infamous slogan from Orwell's dystopian novel turned eerily prophetic 21st century reality is an example of an inversion. Others include our Western medical "health care" system and the mislabeling of violent, destructive uprisings as "peaceful protests."

Moving away from the realm of language, we see symbolic examples of inversions in the upside-down cross that has come to represent Satanism, along with the backwards ancient swastika employed by the Third Reich. In both instances, these sacred symbols were hijacked and flipped with the intention of perverting their meaning and sullying them in the eyes and minds of the public and those who worship accordingly.

Start to pay attention to inversions in culture: to symbols of division and homogeny being employed to signify unity, to poisons being propped up as miracle cures, to slavery being sold as freedom, to the many, many upside-down flippy-flops the matrix uses to control and disempower us. Duly attuned, we are now resourced to remove our consent from the inversion game, and to instead utilize language that really, truly uplifts, empowers, unifies and invokes the energies of peace, harmony and wonderfulness, thus transforming our world accordingly.

Betterarchical Upgrades for Murderous Inversions

While it may be fun to utilize expressions like "slayed," "killed" and "crushed" to effuse about triumphs and jobs well done, we are wise to take pause, feel into their actual definitions and coding and consider whether we want to experience more violence, murder and oppression in our lives and in our world.

Free will rocks, and it's certainly not my place to forbid anyone from using these words to connote the inverted wins with which they have been conflated. Still, I encourage us to get super clear as to what our every word and phrase truly means, while deciphering for ourselves whether it is in highest and best alignment to continue to seed our lives and our world with these frequencies and these directives.

The "Fights" We Don't Even Realize We're Waging

The language of war and conflict has seeped its way into our everyday lexicon to such an extent that the vast majority of us are wholly unaware of the violence and division we are weaving into our conversations, our relationship dynamics and our reality constructs.

"argue"

These days, those of us living in modern, institutionalized hierarchy don't "posit" theories, "propose" scenarios or "purport" ideas. Instead, we "argue" them:

argue, v.
to disagree; to speak angrily to someone
from Old French arguer, 1300s: reproach, accuse, blame

"I would argue that breakfast is the most important meal of the day," notes self-identified Intellectual X.

"That's ridiculous," counters Academic Y, leaping to defend his own perspective. "I would argue that lunch is actually the most important meal of the day."

Here's the thing: no one is actually arguing in this scenario. No one is triggered; no one is raising his voice, and no one is emotionally flustered. But in mislabeling our ideas as "arguments," we activate codes and signals that put us on the defensive and inspire us to armor our psycho-emotional bodies accordingly. In fact, one could argue — *clear, cancel, delete*[34] — one could *purport* that Academic Y might not have even pushed back against Academic X's assertion if it hadn't been framed as an "argument" in the first place. Had Academic X languaged her idea as either: "I think breakfast is the most important meal of the day" or "Breakfast is the most important meal of the day," Academic Y wouldn't have been on the receiving end of the vibrational signals that trigger conflict and resistance.

Framing our perspectives as "arguments" seeds the quantum field with unnecessary conflict vibes, programming the morphic field with contention. It's an unfortunate languaging habit we see coming out of the über-hierarchical academic paradigm, wherein doctoral candidates must "argue" the validity of their theses, and are taught to (mis)identify their ideas as "arguments."

While there can be a modicum of linguistic validity in countering another's proposition with an opposing "argument," to *initiate* a perspective as an "argument" is to invite unnecessary pushback from the get-go. When we couch our ideas as "arguments," we are — by default — seeding them with doubt, defense and skepticism. It's contractive, counter-productive and energetically inefficient. When I "argue" something I simply *believe*, I am instantly putting the person to whom I am speaking on the defensive, because I am transmitting communication codes that indicate we are in a fight.

---

34 A fantastic phrase to utter (aloud or internally) after speaking, thinking or bearing witness to a disempowering statement onto which we are not aligned with signing. It basically clears the field and directs the creative forces to disregard what they just heard.

ENERGETIC EFFICIENCY

Practically speaking, we all have a certain allotment of energy units to utilize each day. When we waste units of said energy allotments with leaks and distractions, we have less energy available to devote to our priorities, passions and — most importantly — our dharma.

Contractive languaging is energetically inefficient for the communicator, as well as those being addressed. When we are on the receiving end of contractive languaging, we must work that much harder to receive the information, given all the unconscious sidestepping we now must undertake to sift for the actual message.

By the same token, when we couch our messages inside contractive languaging, we are only making it more difficult for ourselves to be heard, because we are transmitting signals that shut down our audience. Duly defended, we must now work even harder to state, and re-state our ideas, while meandering around all the armor, personality distortions and egoic strategies we have inadvertently aroused and which are now functioning to keep our notions at bay.

When it comes to energetically efficient communication, expansive languaging is a game-changing tool, because it does the heavy lifting for us in opening up our audiences to receive. Like a just-right linguistic foreplay/penetration combo, expansive languaging is the ultimate in interpersonal multi-tasking.

Betterarchical Upgrades for "Argue"

"posit"	"offer"
"purport"	"think"
"suggest"	"feel"
"believe"	"see it as"

Let us note that "argue" isn't always erroneous. Sometimes our ideas really *are* arguments, and sometimes we aren't *purporting* or *suggesting*, but rather we are really, truly *arguing*, and sometimes it is even aligned and appropriate. Still, a lot of those times wherein "argue" is linguistically sound, it belies a lopsided communication paradigm, a closed mind and an unconscious need to be right, which is its own massive hierarchical distortion plaguing the larger collective discourse.

Proving We Are Right vs. Seeking to Understand

The proliferation of conflict languaging has turned discourse into a battlefield, wherein we are programmed to blindly defend our ideas and our indoctrination, instead of pausing to consider that we might not know every single thing there is to know about every single thing, and that perhaps — just, perhaps — the "other" perspective might be valid, relevant or — *gasp!* — true.

When we defend our ideas and go the distance to "win" our exchanges, we close ourselves off to other points of view. Proving we are right instead of seeking to understand is like erecting electric fencing around our worldviews, while (unconsciously) alleging that we are done learning, done expanding our points of view and done considering other possibilities. Alternate perspectives? No way, man. We have it all figured out, and have already assessed anything and everything that could possibly be relevant, and thus have no room, no space, no inclination and no interest in gleaning any additional information or perspectives, or in educating ourselves beyond our current storehouse of knowledge. Because we're omniscient, dammit.

Endeavoring to prove we are right instead of seeking to understand the other person's point of view is ego is in purest, most base form. It goes a little something like this: We align ourselves with a perspective that resonates as true with us. Someone proposes an alternative perspective that rubs up against said belief, and this — *THIS* — is the crossroads that will determine whether we are asleep or we are awake. How we respond in this moment will show us whether we are unconsciously acting out our hierarchical indoctrination, or are engaging from a balanced, betterarchical anchor point that holds space for diversity of thought and belief, and that doesn't perceive differences as threats. Those under the spell of hierarchy will leap to defend their beliefs without taking the time to receive or entertain the others' perspectives.

Defending our ideas is a deeply distorted, shadowy Masculine means of communicating that leans way light on the listening and the empathizing, while digging its heels into separation consciousness. In fact, calling the practice of blindly defending our ideas a "communication strategy" is a leap in and of itself, given that communication is defined as "the exchange of thoughts, messages or information, as by speech, signals, writing or behavior," and that the hallmark of blindly proving ourselves right indicates a disregard for the "exchange" portion of the communication process that renders us open to receiving and considering other points of view.

Instead of leaning in to learn about the others' perspectives, this strategy pushes them away — both the ideas as well as the humans articulating them. The orientation flies in the face of healthy relatedness, as it denies our fundamental unity and indicates all of zero interest in exploring said unity, or honoring the people we are attempting to prove wrong as fellow humans who have come to embrace their ideas honestly, and might not be the inferior, brain-dead morons we're judging them to be, just because they believe differently than we do.

The False Sense of Self

We defend our ideas without pausing to consider the perspectives we are opposing when we aren't comfortable or secure enough to accept real-deal diversity. It's too threatening to our worldview and our sense of Self. The unconscious egoic strategy goes a little something like this: *If someone doesn't believe what I believe, then how do I know that my belief is valid? How do I know that I'm a good person for holding this belief? Wait…Am I NOT a good person? What IS a good person, anyway? Shit, these questions are making me really uncomfortable, and I hate being uncomfortable. Fuck it. I'd rather just bully this jackass into believing what I[35] believe, instead of looking at/dealing*

---

35   have been indoctrinated to

with my own internal confusion and the self-esteem deficiency to which it is pointing. Heil, hierarchy!

This is what happens when our sense of Self is false, distorted or inauthentic: we can't handle expressions of Self that are different than ours (beyond the shallow optics we've been programmed to embrace as "diversity"). The pervasiveness of the false sense of Self has reached pandemic proportions, given hierarchy's penchant for programming us to seek outside ourselves for self-worth, success, security and happiness. When we don't source our self-worth, success, security and happiness internally, we become dependent upon external approval to glean a (false) sense of Self.

This outward-grasping makes us all the easier to manipulate and control, which is the point. The global self-esteem deficiency is squelching the human spirit, while preventing us from knowing ourselves whole, actualizing our potential and expanding our consciousness, our emotional capacity, our creativity and our genius.

When we leap to defend our positions, while attempting to "slay" those professing alternate versions, we are prioritizing ideological abstractions over our relationships with those we are engaging, instead of leaning in and attempting to forge a genuine understanding as to where they are coming from and what is informing their point of view. In terms of our hierarchical framing, we are elevating our own ideas, allegiances and worldviews above these differing ideas, as well as the humans professing them.

We can't claim to be inclusive if we are not willing to consider other people's ideas. Even if we can't authentically entertain them as our own, we can, at the very least, dig a little deeper to forge an understanding as to how other folks are coming to believe what they believe, such that we can authentically honor their beliefs as valid, even if those beliefs rub up against our own.

ET TU, TWYLA?

I once sent a video link to a group of girlfriends, one of whom was also a journalist. The journalist, we'll call her Twyla, replied to the group with a link to an article alleging to counter the information in the video.

That was fast, I thought, when her text arrived four minutes after I'd sent the link to a 90-minute video.

I dialed Twyla's number so that we could share a real-time conversation about the conflicting narratives, and — as journalists and friends — could find our way to the truth.

Honestly, I haven't even had a chance to watch the video you sent, Twyla texted, having let my phone call go to voicemail.

Let the record show that Twyla writes for some of the largest, most widely circulated mainstream media outlets in the country. And while Twyla raced to send the other folks on my email thread information that would indicate that I had been mistaken and that the video I shared was false, she hadn't, herself, taken the time to watch it or to educate herself on the perspective I was sharing. Instead, Twyla immediately assumed that I was wrong, because — from the title and the description — she ascertained that the information I was sharing rubbed up against her own beliefs and intellectual allegiances, and then went the distance in sharing alternate information with the intention of proving me wrong, even though she hadn't even explored any of it for herself.

Twyla's actions weren't just hurtful and dismissive, they were supremely arrogant. She was operating under the unconscious illusion of her own omniscience, assuming that she already knew everything there was to know about the topic at hand and indicating all of zero interest in considering additional information or entertaining another point of view.

It hit me like a sucker punch to the gut, not because I cared whether or not Twyla agreed with me, but because Twyla makes her living vetting and researching information, and "educating" the public accordingly. To this day, I am still struggling to wrap my mind around the implications of this integrity lapse, and the obvious disregard for journalistic ethics has on a people and a culture.

Proving we are right instead of seeking to understand is its own category of conflict languaging. What follows are a couple methods by which we see this practice being played out in the larger cultural exchange space as well as in our own interpersonal discourse.

Diplomacy > Debate

Debate is the globally sanctioned, competitive practice of proving we are right. It's an archaic and hyper-Masculine form of public discourse, a relic from dark days of yore, when the elite classes gathered to watch lions tear unlucky plebes to shreds in arenas packed with bloodthirsty barbarians.

Debate categorically dismisses the possibility that other points may be valid or true. Debate has nothing to do with learning, cooperating or bridging perceived gaps in knowledge or understanding. Debate is about clinging to a position at all costs. It's about combating one idea with another idea, to prove that our idea is better, stronger, righter and more valid than anyone else's idea. The aim has nothing to do with growth, evolution, cooperation, collaboration or mutual understanding; the aim is to win.

Debate is fine for sport, Tibetan monastic studies or the cultivation of mental dexterity, but as a means of vetting global leaders, facilitating genuine understanding or moving society forward in a positive, progressive way, it's the ultimate in ass-backwardsness. The process functions to sustain the imbalance between the Masculine and the Feminine, while empowering a ruthless, hierarchical system.

Take the Presidential elections we have here in the United States, wherein the populace gathers around their screens to watch a handful of carefully groomed candidates, representing the two dominant political parties (*Hello, polarization!*) defend the superiority of their ideas and their visions. There is no active listening. There is no compassionate, collaborative discussion. There is only combative ideological clinging.

As we shift our culture from the hierarchical to the betterarchical, from the Masculine-dominant to the Masculine/Feminine-balanced, we move away from debate, while embracing *diplomacy*. Diplomacy is what has our candidates demonstrating how well they can dialogue and listen, and then effectively collaborate with one another on creative solutions that serve all parties and perspectives involved. Diplomacy incorporates the Feminine practices of receiving and cooperating, deftly woven with Masculine vision, strategy and action. Granted, it's not nearly as exciting or theatrical as it is to watch our "leaders" catfight, name-call and sell each other down so many ad hominem-laced rivers, while defending the superiority of their ideas, platforms and positions and "slaying" their opponents. But is the purpose of politics entertainment or public service?

False Dichotomy

We've all heard versions of this idea before, whether implicitly stated in the geopolitical sphere (e.g., "If you're not with us, you're with the terrorists") or the social justice activism space (e.g., "Silence is violence") or implied in the digital realms of social media (e.g., *If you don't post this flag or this colored square as your profile picture, then you are an enemy of the cause*). It is a form of ideological bullying that is rarely true, while always, always serving to strengthen the grip of hierarchy in its reductive and wholly irrational, conflict-laden divisiveness.

The problem — well, one of them — is that the statement attempts to override the infinite array of potential reasons why one might not be "with"

another's cause, and to whittle our otherwise complex, multilayered reality into a narrow and contrived *either/or* scenario. It alleges that because I don't feel aligned with a specific cause or idea, or because said cause or idea is not something I am choosing to prioritize, then I am, by default, an enemy of said cause or idea and — when we get really bananas with it — of the people who stand with said cause or idea. It takes what could very well be ignorance, indifference or neutrality and flips it into a projected "anti-" stance that may never have been claimed or considered.

The allegation is a standard-issue logical fallacy that professional thinkers call a *false dichotomy*. The false dichotomy is a pitch-perfect example of how hierarchy operates — in vast, sweeping generalizations and black-and-white extremes that polarize the populace, while keeping neutrality at bay. This shadowy Masculine means of thinking rejects nuance, subtleties, grey areas and diversity, while attempting to project division where it doesn't necessarily exist or belong.

> **false dichotomy**, *n.*
> *A situation in which two alternative points of view are presented as the only options, when, in fact, infinite others are available*

The false dichotomy purports that my choice to *not* support a pro-toddler rights march (because toddler rights aren't really on my radar; and because I don't, personally, see the efficacy of marches; and because my attention is focused on other realms of service) becomes twisted into a fictional narrative that alleges that I hate toddlers, I am an enemy of toddlers, and I should be canceled for my assumed/projected/imaginary hatred of toddlers and my (totally made-up/nonexistent) disdain for the toddler cause.

The *If you're not with us, you're against us* line of (erroneous) reasoning requires the self-esteem deficient advocate to make continual leaps of self-aggrandizing illogic, because it infers that I care enough about the person or cause in question to align myself "with" or "against" it. The false dichotomy rebrands neutrality as conflict, placing itself front and center in everyone else's narrative, instead of resting in the albeit uncomfortable possibility that no one is thinking of us, acting *for* or *against* us or considering us, at all.

Like the *victim languaging* we will be exploring in the pages ahead, the false dichotomy is supremely narcissistic. It's the height of self-involvement to assume that just because my cause doesn't resonate with another, that this "other" must then be positioning herself *against* me. Do you see how this framing renders *me* the subject in this false equivalence? Either the other *supports* me, or the other is *against* me. In both instances, it's all about **me**. *I* am the reference point. There is no space for neutrality or indifference. There is no room for the notion that I am simply not on said other's radar, because said other is focused elsewhere, or because said other has extracted a different meaning or interpretation of the thing against which I am railing against or for which I am lobbying. When dealing in false dichotomies, the world revolves around us and our causes, and anyone who alleges to orbit differently is branded the enemy.

Betterarchical Upgrades for Moving from Proving Ourselves Right to Seeking to Understand

As you can imagine, the shift from *proving ourselves right* to *seeking to understand* is more of an evolutionary leap than it is simple languaging upgrade. There is no one lexicon replacement that is going to instantly transmute the urge to prove ourselves right into a genuine openness to/ curiosity about other people's perspectives.

That being said, *witness mode* is our friend. When we are operating in witness mode, we observe the urge to defend ideas and perspectives, instead of taking action on any such urges. We rest in the Feminine and simply witness how we show up in our exchanges. Are we genuinely interested in others' ideas? Are we allowing ourselves to receive their words without racing to combat them with our own? What happens ~~if~~ when we resist the urge to counter another's ideas and simply rest in the spaciousness of listening and allowing?

Let us challenge ourselves to cultivate our Feminine listening skills, to receive others' ideas and perspectives without leaping to offer our own versions. And, when we are faced with ideas and perspectives that do rub up against our own, before we leap to defend and counter, let us consider the following questions:

- *What if this perspective is valid?*
- *What if this idea could co-exist with my own, without anyone needing to be wrong?*
- *What kind of internal self-reorganization is necessary for me to hold this idea as valid and a-okay?*
- *What kind of inner work am I being called to do — within myself — to be able to honor this perspective?*

"Fight"

The social sphere is cluttered with humans occupied with the task of "fighting"– be they fighting age, time, violence, poverty, cavities or an ever-expanding assortment of evermore egregious cultural scourges marketed to us as *-isms* and atrocities on a 24/7 information cycle.

One of the most ineffective "fights" I've observed is the one I see self-identified feminists waging by "fighting the patriarchy," and "smashing the patriarchy," and "fighting for gender equality." It's the ultimate in tail-chasing hypocrisy, as "fighting" is a shadowy patriarchal strategy that empowers the Masculine polarity, and further exacerbates the imbalance of energies between the Masculine and the Feminine. The truth of the matter is that the act of "fighting" the patriarchy is actually delaying that whole "return of the divine feminine" so many New Age feminists claim to serve, while inadvertently sabotaging.

"Fighting" functions much the same way that "anti-" does, in that it transmits the frequencies of force, thereby creating counterforce. As well, "fighting" places our attention on the thing we oppose, creating yet another quantum entanglement and fueling the object of opposition. It's violent, contentious and energetically inefficient, as it's sooooo much easier to simply "stand *for*" that with which we are aligning ourselves, rather than to "fight *against*" whatever it is we're not digging.

When we declare our allegiances and our alliances along with the word "fight," we are activating the frequencies of conflict, opposition and pushback. "Fighting" delegitimizes our stance in signaling contention to our audience. When I say, "I'm fighting for freedom," it weakens freedom's *no-duh* legitimacy, as it immediately invokes its opposition, while validating and empowering it.

To "fight" for ANYTHING is to empower the energies, systems and folks who oppose the things for which we are claiming to fight. I don't "fight" for freedom, because my freedom is not in question. I "stand" for freedom. I "rest" in freedom. I "foster" freedom. I "empower" freedom. I "claim" my freedom. I "am" freedom. I do not legitimize any potential opposition to my freedom because my freedom is not up for grabs. Period.

Betterarchical Upgrades for "Fight"

"stand"
"claim"
"rest"
"foster"
"empower"
"am"

VICTIMHOOD[36]

"If you could kick the person in the pants responsible for most of your trouble, you wouldn't sit for a month."
— Theodore Roosevelt

Hierarchy's social engineers have gone the distance in convincing the collective that there is value in victimhood. This fallacious and ridiculous notion has people clawing, fighting and scrambling for most marginalized status, because we've been suckered into believing that disempowerment is the new black and that "most oppressedest" is a title worth lobbying for.

The rub is that, while the "most oppressedest" might win sympathy and a certain kind of low-vibe social status, the claim doesn't come along with any actual, real lived value. Sure, victims are rewarded with pity, sympathy, hand-outs, *tsk-tsks*, furrowed brows, concerned coos and all the emotional junk food upon which we binge when we're not resourced enough to know ourselves whole and empowered. But none of these external reactions translate to a robust, abundant, creative, fulfilling incarnation.

Victimhood is a tiny, contracted, go-nowhere corner into which we paint ourselves, cheered on (read: enabled) by friends, follows, likes and social credit. Victimhood is the crutch that allows us to rationalize shrunken, lackluster lives, while blaming *Excuse X* or *Perpetrator Y* for our crummy lot and our unrealized potential.

---

36 Author's note: The Victimhood section is quite a bit longer than the other hierarchical languaging chapters, because the victim virus is one of the most virulent pandemics plaguing our culture, and thus warrants a more in-depth unpacking. I trust it's all evening out on some dimension.

uh, yay
victimhood?

Victimhood = The Feminine Shadow

While we've unpacked quite a few ways in which the Masculine shadow is perving our language and our society, it would be disingenuous to pretend that the Feminine shadow isn't also informing our current cultural clusterfuck. Victimhood is verily drenched in the Feminine shadow, which surrenders its center, its dignity, its compassion and its critical thinking capacities to the emotional hysteria and drama queen antics that so often color victim consciousness.

One of the ways the Feminine shadow expresses is through unchecked emotional leaks or outbursts that indicate little to no consideration for truth, propriety, professionalism or anyone else involved. The emotional hysteria attached to victimhood cares not for time, place or context; rather it will throw its hissy fits wherever it damn well pleases — other humans be damned. Victim consciousness is reactive, blinded by its trauma and its stories, and beholden only to its hurt, to which the world is expected to kowtow.

Victim consciousness defers to the Feminine emotions and the sad, sorry stories manipulating them, while abandoning reason and logic in the process. Were we to think of victim consciousness in terms of the scales of justice representing the Masculine and Feminine polarities, the Feminine side would be pressing into the Earth's core, weighed down with self-righteousness and *woe is me* vibes, while the Masculine side would be floating up in the outermost edges of the atmosphere, weighed down by all of nothing, having surrendered its will, power and critical thinking skills to the Feminine histrionics that typify victimhood.

Cancel Culture = The Masculine Shadow

While victim consciousness is inherently Feminine in its tendency to languish in the negative emotions for which it compulsively denies responsibility, its current cancel culture-wielding is a telltale sign of the Masculine shadow, which shoves, forces and bullies in its attempts to get its own way, and prove itself right.

Whereas victim consciousness used to be satisfied languishing on the sidelines, pouting and feeling sorry for itself, while accepting — nay, embracing — its sad, sucky lot, nowadays, victimhood takes it light years farther by insisting that others bend to their hurt, and bow to their hurt, and contort their expression, their behavior and their everything so as not to trigger their hurt.[37]

Cancel culture is an expression of victimhood's violent, aggressive insistence that everyone else contort themselves around its pain. It is the quintessential Masculine shadow in full effect, barreling over any and all contrary ideas, beliefs or perspectives by assuming and projecting the worst possible intentions, while seeking to destroy careers, reputations and relationships in its wake.

And so it is that victimhood is an expression of both the Masculine and Feminine shadows, dancing together in destructive, unconscious tandem.

---

37 Which — when we're dealing in objective reality and not victim-wonky fantasy land — is only ever the self-identified "victim's" responsibility to manage, heal and integrate.

Blame < Taking Responsibility

Victimhood is a fundamentally disempowering identity to which to lay claim, because it places responsibility for our lives outside of us, giving way to blame, bullying and cancel culture, as we deny our own agency and accountability for our lives. When we deny our agency and accountability, we martyr ourselves to the issue at hand, effectively abandoning our ability, as reality creators, to change the situation.

When we are operating in the frequency band of victimhood, and something unpleasant or uncomfortable happens, we leap to blame, immediately seeking an external agent upon whom we can pin the responsibility for our misfortune, hurt feelings or inconvenience. Victim consciousness is perpetually focused outside of itself, ever and always looking for a(nother) scapegoat upon which it can project responsibility for its triggers, discomfort and contractions.

Empowered, betterarchical badass consciousness, on the other hand, seeks inward when experiencing something unpleasant. Empowered, betterarchical badass consciousness (the polar opposite of the victim variety) takes responsibility, and scours the situation for clues as to where we, ourselves, are accountable, and where we can shift, pivot or adjust to avoid similar outcomes in the future. The beauty of taking responsibility is that when we acknowledge that we are 100% accountable for our experience of reality, then we are resourced to change reality for the better.

The Oppression Olympics

Hierarchy loves it some victim consciousness, because a society full of disempowered people is easy to control. And a society full of disempowered people fragmented into tiny identitarian subgroups, fighting over who "wins" most marginalized status, while blaming and shaming *each other* for their plight? Well, that's the divide-and-rule jackpot.

Twenty-first century hierarchy has gifted us an imaginary, though strictly socially-enforced marginalization rating scale that alleges we can quantify adversity based upon a handful of superficial character traits — race, religion, gender, skin color, sexual preference, et al. This surface-level scale of implied suffering seeks to convince us that people with lighter skin necessarily suffer less than people with darker skin do, period and always; and that people with darker skin and gender dysmorphia necessarily suffer more than people with darker skin without gender dysmorphia, who still suffer more than people with lighter skin and gender dysmorphia, because — well, melanin. This same victimization rating scale alleges that women suffer more than men, homosexuals suffer more than heterosexuals, and on, and on, and on. Skewed by this shallow, reductive means of assessing something as multilayered and immeasurable as *suffering* disregards other contributing factors and considerations, such as trauma, tragedy, illness, injury, family, geography, neurology, environment, circumstance, et al. When competing in the Oppression Olympics, these are all but inconsequential irrelevancies that count for nothing because melanin, and pronouns, and vaginas, and...and...*ugh*.

I'm going to let you in on a little secret the social engineers don't want us to know. I suggest pulling on your big girl/boy panties for this one, because if you've swallowed the latest batch of ideological indoctrination, you may very well be triggered. Here goes:

Everybody suffers.

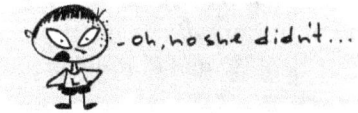

Now, this is not to deny anyone's trauma, tragedy, pain or plight on any level whatsoever. People endure some really fucked up shit on this planet, which is, essentially, a swiftly spinning rock, hurtling through unexplored realms of deeper and deeper space at a breakneck pace. As if this wasn't unsettling enough, this spinning rock we call home happens to be populated by deadly plants, predators, microbes and pathogens, along with ass-kicking terrain and deep-sea *God knows what*, while also being predisposed to epic environmental upheavals, and buttloads of hard knocks and unfair licks for those of us making our homes upon it. Nothing about this set-up is safe, nor was it ever meant to be.

Granted, it can appear as though some people suffer more than others do. Look at countries like Haiti and India. Look at the entire African continent. Look at Flint, Michigan. Why are some people born into poverty, upon parched pieces of Earth marked by famine, violence and corruption, while some are born in peaceful, resource-rich paradises?

I can't answer this with any certainty. What I do know is that no one has exclusive rights to suffering. Everybody suffers, regardless of race, gender, skin color or belief structure. Everyone is blessed with gifts and talents, and boosts and boons, while also given their share of shadows, burdens and short sticks. I don't know how it's all doled out, or what factors determine who gets what, but I do know that we all get a mix of all of it—the good, the bad, the ugly and the wonderful.

Victimizing ourselves to the challenges we are dealt amplifies the weight and power of said challenges. The more we talk about our challenges and lament our challenges and define our lives and our lot by our challenges, the heavier and more cumbersome these challenges become.

> "...we all must struggle with the downside of human nature. Everyone is crippled in some area, and everyone is somewhere on the path of evolution, some ahead of us, and some behind."
> — *Dr. David R. Hawkins*

The language of victimhood seeps into our vocabulary in a hefty handful of subtle and insidious ways. The implications are many and varied, but—at its most basic level — the more we talk about our sad stories and all the terrible things that happen to us, the more life and legitimacy we give to these frequencies, simultaneously empowering them and seeding our collective field with them, thereby creating more experiences that match these very same frequencies.

This is not to advocate rug-shoving, repression or denial. It is important that we acknowledge our suffering, and that we take the time and care necessary to process and integrate our suffering such that we are not inclined to attach or identify, and thus give these experiences any more power over us than they have already leached. There is a time and a place for telling our stories — like, with trusted healers, guides, friends and family who can hold space and support us in milking these experiences for the lessons and upgrades they hold for us, and in integrating them, such that they do not run or define our lives.

FOR THE TRIGGERED...

Some folks seem get their panties in a great, big bunch at the suggestion that we not identify certain groups as "victims," because — according to the panty-bunchers — said groups have had it sooooo bad that to deny their victimhood is tantamount to a hate crime.

And while it may be true that there are particular groups that really did or do have it waaaaaaayyyyy worse than any other historically marginalized groups, the laws of reality creation still apply to everyone. The subconscious mind and the forces of nature don't suspend their operating instructions to accommodate inequality or unfairness, genocide or slavery. They simply respond to the frequencies embedded in our words and go about organizing reality accordingly.

There are no exceptions to the reality creation game. It doesn't matter how justified we think our victim stories are. Identifying with victimhood keeps us disempowered, while ensuring that we continue to manifest unfair licks in our lives. And so, while no one is denying the sucky lot that various groups and individuals endure, the only way for all of us to transmute inequality, unfairness and suckiness is to stop identifying with it.

Suffering + Identification = Victimization

Everyone undergoes experiences and indignities to which we can, if we so choose, victimize ourselves. How tightly we cling to these experiences and indignities is what determines whether we victimize ourselves to them, or not. Victimhood has nothing to do with *what* we experience, rather *how* we choose to frame and language our experiences.

When we identify with our traumas or our shadows or our challenges, we victimize ourselves to them. Victimization isn't determined by being discriminated against or having a terrible thing perpetrated upon us. Victimization is determined by how we author our stories, interpret our experiences and choose to perceive the world.

> *"In the final analysis, the questions of why bad things happen to good people transmutes itself into some very different questions, no longer asking why something happened, but asking how we will respond, what we intend to do now that it happened."*
> — **Pierre Teilhard de Chardin**

By and large, those of us who claim to be victims and who are stuck in victim consciousness are not victims because life has given us an unfair shake or because others are doing terrible things to us,[38] but because we are habitually identifying ourselves as victims, and utilizing the language of victimhood to describe our experiences. When we identify as victims, we don't just program our internal frequencies to configure themselves to victimhood, we align ourselves with victimhood frequency bands in the morphic field, thereby setting up a feedback loop that attracts perpetrators and experiences that will continue to affirm our self-proclaimed victimhood.

> *"The structure of language determines not only thought, but reality itself."*
> — **Dr. Noam Chomsky**

---

38 Though, when we consistently align ourselves with the frequencies of victimhood, we are absolutely programming our realities to organize in this fashion.

The Victim/Perpetrator Polarity

Remember, a few chapters back, when we discussed how hierarchy is propped up by reductive polarity constructs like *good/bad*, *Left/Right*, *better/worse*? Well, the *victim/perpetrator* variety might just be the most insidious and disempowering polarity construct of them all.

Victim/perpetrator is a program. When we plug ourselves into this program, the frequencies we emit through our words and our thoughts code the morphic field to configure to affirm our victimhood.[39] It does this by sending us perpetrators.

As you recall, polarities are magnets for that which they oppose. Each component is both repelled by and attracted to the opposite to which they are inextricably bound. It's how quantum entanglements work.

So, when I am in the habit of telling my sad, sorry stories and proclaiming that terrible things "always" happen to me and languaging my lot as unfair and less-than, I am emitting victim vibes. Those frequencies are going to magnetically attract agents that will abuse, disrespect and take advantage of me. The more perpetrators I attract, the bigger and stronger my victim identity grows, thus creating a closed-circuit loop that attracts more abusers and more situations in which I experience short shrift.

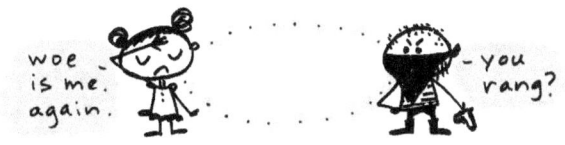

---

39 Reality creation is consistent like this. It really doesn't matter what program we choose — victim, visionary, loser, lover — whatever we give it, that's what it's going to give us back.

THAT TIME I PLAYED SMALL, MEEK AND VICTIMY WITH A PREDATORY PIT VIPER

Not long ago, I found myself in sudden and unexpected need of new digs. My landlords had decided to the sell their house, and gave me 30-days notice to find shelter in the middle of winter/global lockdown in an extremely over-stretched, over-priced rental market.

Instead of framing the circumstance as an opportunity — to move some energy, to up-level my living situation, to finally have a bathtub that didn't require an inflatable pump — I victimized myself to it. I complained that my landlords were cruel and heartless to give me the boot before their house had actually sold, while whining about the horrific injustice that had me trudging through the snowy streets of Northern New Mexico to find shelter for my sad, sorry self.

Cut to me sitting down with a potential landlady to discuss the specifics of a pitch-perfect, free-standing casita with raised garden beds and a fresh water well, in my very favorite neighborhood, less than a week before I was slated to vacate.

Why am I acting so small and disempowered? I wondered, watching a bunch of frantic, desperate words slip forth from my lips, as I kissed the landlady's ass and behaved like a trained seal, eager to demonstrate how obedient I was and how well I'd perfected the tricks that earned me praise, anchovies and — with any luck — a twelve-month lease.

While I landed the casita, the landlady booted me six days after I moved in. Appearing with a burly handyman at her side, she presented me with an aggressive letter from her high-powered attorney, threatening to sue me for a lengthy list of imaginary transgressions if I wasn't out in only ten days, demanding that I sign over the last month's rent I paid in cash as a security deposit, which — you guessed it — she pocketed.

It was an incredibly jarring experience that made little sense — that is, until I reflected back upon my whining and pity partying and remembered that first meeting with the aforementioned pit viper* — I mean, landlady — and got really honest with myself. I flashed upon a vision of a shrunken, wool-wrapped version of me, vibing small, meek, disempowered and desperate, and realized that I had manifested the experience, and I had magnetized a scamtastic pit viper of a landlady by victimizing myself to the situation, and vibrating at a frequency that was a match for such sketchy bamboozling.

Lesson learned.

* While, as we've already learned, name-calling is a divisive and dehumanizing practice I really don't recommend, this is one of those rare instances wherein I am rationalizing it as appropriate, because I: a) am, myself, a work in progress; and b) still cannot fathom how another human could possibly treat someone this way and be able to sleep at night; and I'm pretty sure pit vipers are nocturnal, so it's kinda the only way it makes sense.

Victim Goggles

At any given moment, there are infinite morsels of input, and objects, and nuance, and circumstance that are amalgamating to create our experience of reality. There are buildings, and weather, and soundscapes. There are flashes of color and texture, along with snippets of conversation. There are insects, and clouds, and chemtrails. There are birds and honking horns. There are walls, and window frames, and billboards, and telephone wires. There is a horizon.

The human sensory apparatus can only take in but a tiny fraction of the myriad elements competing for our awareness in any given moment. Language determines how our brains filter this endless onslaught of input, as well as the meaning we will project upon it. This meaning will consistently confirm the stories and egoic projections that are coded into our identity constructs, as well as the languaging habits informing them.

Reality, and all the elements and experiences that comprise it, is fundamentally neutral. It is our own personal programming that will determine whether we judge our experiences as "good," "bad," "right," "wrong," "fair," "unfair," etc. The words we habitually use and the stories we consistently tell determine our outlook on the world and whether we will surmise that world to be kind, loving, fair, fucked-up or out to get us.

As the language of identification consistently distorts our lens of perception to affirm the stories that beget our identity constructs, identifying as a victim is tantamount to gluing a pair of victim goggles to one's face and then perpetually seeing the world through victim-tinted lenses.

When observing the world through victim goggles, otherwise neutral experiences and exchanges become tinged with ill will, nefarious intentions and implied omniscience. When I am operating in victim consciousness, and the waiter forgets to bring me a side of lemon, it's not because he's slammed, stoned or incompetent; it's because he's an anti-Semite. It doesn't matter that I don't actually know the waiter, or that I have zero evidence that the waiter holds any ill will towards Jews, or even knows that I'm Jewish. Because I am seeing the world through victim goggles, I am operating with a duly distorted lens of perception, which has me interpreting otherwise neutral interactions to fit my victim narrative.

Let's take a less charged example: I volunteer at a local farm. The farmer — a sweetheart of a man, as well as a Capricorn[40] — is rather identified with his organizational system. While working in the greenhouse one morning, the farmer was incensed to find his rag bucket was missing. Instead of chalking it up to unconsciousness, forgetfulness or stupidity, the farmer insisted that his helpers were pitted against him and were dead-set on sabotaging his organizational structure. Interpreted through these victim lenses, the farmer's helpers don't just suck at their jobs, they are shady perpetrators with sinister intentions.

For our final example, let's touch in with the woman who identifies as a feminist, believes the world is awash with gender discrimination and has thus taken it upon herself to "fight sexism." When she gets passed over for a raise, her mind will leap to conclude that it is because she is a woman. When the car salesman won't budge on the price, it's because she's a woman. When she is seated at a wobbly table instead of a cushy booth, it's because she's a woman. The pasta that gave her food poisoning? Obviously, it was prepared by a man. If a woman were in charge of that kitchen, she would never have gotten sick in a million years.

There are multiple through lines here. It's not just that folks who are choosing to victimize themselves to circumstance are operating through distorted lenses which bend reality to fit their programming, it's that they are also — allegedly — all-knowing psychics. In all of our examples, the victims were able to clairvoyantly read their perpetrators' internal motivations and to know that they were operating out of nefarious intent.

---

40 The practical, grounded, get-shit-done sign.

The (Imaginary) Omniscience of Victimhood

Victim consciousness has this uncanny knack for knowing what others are thinking and intending. I'm not sure whether those running victim consciousness are clairvoyant, clairaudient, clairsentient or simply omniscient, but their perception that others are targeting them specifically because of whatever elements define their victimhood is wholly dependent upon the victims' ability to read other people's minds. It would be equal parts eerie and cool, were it true. But the reality is, this "knowledge" is but the delusion of a victim-goggle-blind mind.

Not only do those seeing the world through victim goggles claim to know other people's thoughts, preferences and intentions, but said thoughts, preferences and intentions are conveniently and consistently malevolent. It's extraordinary how every mind victim consciousness reads just happens to be pitted against it, in precisely the same way(s) that their identity constructs dictate.

In case my sarcasm is too subtle, I'm being facetious. Of course people who are running victim consciousness are not omniscient or clairvoyant; they are just letting their language-warped minds mess with them. It's this great leap that victim consciousness demands we take, wherein we project negative intent upon our so-called perpetrators.

Why Not Assume the Best?

The assumption of ill intent is responsible for quite a bit of our cultural strife, wherein the social engineers minding the matrix encourage people to believe the worst of one another and to project nefarious intentions and hateful stories onto their fellow humans as a means of dividing and controlling the populace.

The problem with projecting negative intent upon folks whose minds we are not actually reading is multi-faceted. For starters, it's unfair and disrespectful to whomever it is upon whom we are projecting ill will, because it sets them up to be the bad guy when they may not be. When we project negative intent, we demonize a person/people who may not deserve our demonization, while degrading our inherent unity as a human family, because we can't demonize someone without otherizing them first.

When we project negative intent, we're not just otherizing and therefore shitting on our morphic field, we are sabotaging *ourselves*, because we are activating the frequencies that we are projecting upon our so-called perpetrators in our own bodies, minds, spirits and realities. We are taking it upon ourselves to stress out our systems, and shorten our telomeres based on unfounded assumptions that may very well be false, and that are incompatible with a healthy, happy, optimized human vessel/experience.

In the space of lack of information, it makes little sense to fill in the blanks with negativity or stories that paint the players in the worst possible light. When we don't have all the information — and even when we do — we are wise to assume the best, as a means of programming ourselves and the morphic field with *those* frequencies and *those* associations, if for no other reason than they feel better. As long as we are going to take leaps of knowingness by guessing and presuming and filling in missing blanks, why not assume the best, given that the best is going to optimize us, and program our reality construct in fortuitous ways? If we glean new information that runs counter to our best-case scenario assumptions, we can adjust our assessments then. But, in the meantime, why not cultivate as many best-case scenario frequencies as we can and allow those vibrations to program our bodies and our world accordingly?

THE FALLACY OF EXTERNAL AUTHORITY

Hierarchy is sustained by the myth of external authority — by the narrative that paints authority as a force outside of ourselves, which has legitimate agency over us as individuals as well as the collective.

This is false.

Hierarchy has us convinced that "authority" means someone or some institution that has power *over* us. According to this misconception, authority is an entity that can tell us what we can or cannot do, and how to go about doing the things it deigns to allow us to do. Hierarchy has us asking permission to drive a motorcycle, rub someone else's shoulders and take two weeks off work to be with our wife and newborn baby. Silly hierarchy.

The fallacy of external authority is what has free-thinking grown-ups telling us that they "can't" sell us a side of guacamole (even though the restaurant serves it in their breakfast burrito *and* their taco salad, which means they definitely have it in the kitchen), because it's "not on the menu" and they're "not allowed." The fallacy of external authority effectively shuts down our critical thinking capabilities, along with our humanity, allowing us to sleepwalk through half-lived lives on autopilot, worshipping at the altar of external validation/permission and all that we've been told we are and are not "allowed" to do.

Authority Is an Inside Job

Alas, despite any indoctrination to the contrary, authority is not actually an externally sourced situation, nor is it bestowed upon us by someone with a badge, a gun, a tie, a certificate or a bunch of initials trailing their name.

Modern day dictionary definitions of *authority* are many and varied, and tend to lead with multiple entries attempting to convince us that authority is a variety of external overlord imbued with the power to act over others. And sure, this is a secondary kind of authority that is indeed rampant in our hierarchical culture. Alas, when we look to the etymology, which gives us the origins of the word before the matrix had its way with it, we get quite a different picture.

au·thor·i·ty

"Authority" comes from the Latin *auctor*, which — in verb form — means: "to do, to originate." As a noun, "auctor" means: "originator, creator, founder; one who causes to grow." When combined with "-ity" (meaning "condition or quality of being"), we understand "authority" to (really, truly) mean: "the quality of being a doer, creator, originator," or — my favorite — "one who fosters growth and evolution."

As much as I love etymology, there's really no need to overthink it. You can't spell "authority" without the word "author." What does an author do? Writes stories. "Authority" speaks to our power to write our stories for ourselves — to our own agency/divine right to *author* our own lives however we damn well please.[41]

---

41 As long as we are not imposing our will upon anyone else. Duh.

How Are We Choosing to Author Our Stories?

Let's say I show up to lead a workshop overcaffeinated and underprepared. Afterwards, when describing how it went, I can self-flagellate for being an irresponsible fuck-up who forgot her notes and spoke too fast, or I can choose to frame it as a learning experience that is teaching me the value of preparation and the benefits of adaptogenic tea. Both versions are equally accurate, while vastly different in terms of tone and tenor. Which version of this story do you think will serve me best?

The cool thing about *authority* is that — now that we know what it really, truly means — we can reclaim it in its true essence. Duly educated on the real-deal connotation, we are resourced to reclaim our own sovereign authority and to use it to *author* our lives for the bigger, better and more empowered. Now that we grok that authority is an inside job, let us adjust our lenses of perception accordingly and write better stories — stories wherein we are casting ourselves as heroes instead of victims.

Lalla, the "Single Mother": An Example in Victim-Framing

"But, it's true," my client Lalla insisted when I invited her to drop the word "single" from the "mother" part of her identity. "I *am* a single mother."

It is *a* truth, yes, but it's certainly not the whole truth. Lalla is also a creative mother, a funny mother, a caring mother, a competent mother, a witchy mother, a tall mother, a crafty mother, a hands-on mother, an omnivorous mother and a Libra mother. Lalla could have chosen any number of descriptives to modify her "mother" identity, but she consistently chose "single," and articulated it loud and often, garnished with a heavy tinge of self-pity and resentment.

Lalla went on to explain that she wanted people to know she was a single mother because single mothers have it harder than mothers with partners do, and she wanted to be acknowledged for the burden she was carrying.

External Validation-a-~~Go-Go~~ No-No

It's yet another hallmark of hierarchy — the incessant seeking of external validation. Instead of fostering our authenticity, empowerment and self-esteem, the matrix programs us with frequencies of *not-enough-ness* as a means of selling us their infinite array of bigger, better, faster, slavey-er fixes for our lackluster lives and our eternally broken selves. This incessant *lack* programming has us perpetually chasing external fixes, be they bling, babes, boners, booze, pills, rides, likes, follows, fame, Fendi or eternal youth, instead of resourcing our answers and our succor from within.

As we utilize the language of betterarchy to re-program ourselves and our world, we transmute unconscious external acknowledgment-scavenging patterns into internally-sourced, empowerment-embodying ones. The shift resources us to prioritize our own lived, felt experience over the external validation we have been programmed to unconsciously collect for experiences we'd prefer not be living or feeling.

Victim Consciousness = Masochism

When we language our experience as a burden, we amplify the weight of said burden. Every time Lalla identified herself as a "single mother," she was invoking the energetic frequencies of challenge, unfairness, exhaustion and victimization. For Lalla, and many single mothers, the simple act of aspirating the phrase "single mother" is akin to watching two people struggling to carry a heavy oak desk up a steep staircase, and then sitting on it.

Lalla's languaging was programming her to perpetually prioritize the act of pity collecting, instead of choosing to up-level her relationship to parenting by re-languaging it, thereby making it less challenging.

Let's be clear: I'm not disputing Lalla's perspective, or suggesting that single moms don't carry a heavier load than multi-parent families do. If the phrase "single mother" held no charge for Lalla, and she carried her motherhood lightly, then I wouldn't have pressed the issue. But because I had witnessed Lalla consistently victimizing herself to her solo mama journey, I nudged her to drop the qualifier from her identity construct, as a way to lighten her own load.

= victim languaging

"What are the tangible benefits of having others recognize that you have it harder?" I asked Lalla. "Does their understanding of your burden make your burden lighter? Does it make the task of child-rearing easier? And when it comes down to it, would you rather have people pity you because parenting is hard, or would you rather have parenting be easier?"[42]

It finally clicked. Lalla realized that her choice to consistently self-identify as a "single mother" was exacerbating her burden. As she willingly rewrote her identity construct as simply "mother," she was liberated from all that extra heaviness and hardness encoded in the modifier "single." She was free to create a future wherein the load was lighter, and the task was easier. The edit allowed Lalla to dial up her enjoyment factor, while relinquishing the bummer vibes, because she claimed her *authority* to author her story for the kinder and more supportive.

No One is Coming to Rescue You

Hierarchy goes the distance to encourage us to keep telling our sob stories, and identifying with our sob stories, and competing over whose sob story is the saddest and the sorriest of them all, because while we're busy dithering over who wins the Oppression Olympics, the control system grows bigger and stronger, fortifying itself upon our distraction, division and dependency.

The inverted program that alleges to have authority *over* us has some folks believing that we need hierarchy to survive. Using language, images and symbols in media, entertainment, advertising, education and pretty much everything else, the matrix force-feeds us a singular lifestyle formula that

---

42 Except, I didn't pummel Lalla with a barrage of confronting questions all in one batch like a sadistic bully. This is a truncated paraphrasing of a slower, gentler coaching process, restructured for reading ease.

comes along with various safety nets: credit lines, mortgages, insurance, installment plans, 401ks, fluoride, Viagra, Botox, etc. Duly programmed, we allow ourselves to become dependent upon the very mechanism that is enslaving us.

When we buy into the fiction that authority resides outside of ourselves, we get lazy. We sit around, apathetic and complacent, assuming that someone else is going to handle the various issues plaguing our world and our species for us. We assume that "they" have it handled — blindly trusting the minions minding the matrix to drive our Earth ship for us, without stopping to consider where exactly "they" are taking us, and if we're really, truly aligned with their intentions/destination. And so it is that we dilly-dally in passive acquiescence, dropping the ball on our responsibility as custodians of this beautiful spinning rock that is ALL of ours to mind, manage and serve, and which we would be wise to steer onto a more functional, peaceful, sustainable trajectory on the sooner side of later (aka: now).

Our current cultural iteration has the blue team blaming the red team, and then sitting around waiting for the blue leaders to fix everything for them, while the red team blames the blue team, and twiddles their thumbs while waiting for the red leaders to do the same. Except it's not about blue, or red, or black, or white, or *x,* or *y,* it's about *us* — a singular humanity of Earthlings, who are all equally responsible for the wellbeing of our species and our planet — stepping into our power and up-leveling our world for ourselves.

No one is coming to save us. It is on us to save ourselves, by taking responsibility, claiming our authority and crafting a better Earth story. The task demands that we root victimhood out of our personal and collective lexicon — and thus, out of our personal and collective consciousness — while affirming our sovereign agency and our unfuckwithable empowerment with our every word. Only then are we resourced and ready to design a better game.

VICTIM LANGUAGING

Every time we language ourselves as victims to our reality, our circumstances or to other people or entities, we disempower ourselves. And every time we language ourselves as masters of our realities, and we acknowledge our own co-creative agency in our experience of them, we empower ourselves. The determining factor is neither the circumstance, nor the experience itself; rather, it is how we choose to frame the circumstance or the experience with the words we use to describe them.

The VLF

Victim languaging programs us to perceive the world as though outside agencies are acting against us. The victim narrative is dependent upon being a person whom (unfair) things happen *TO*. While victim languaging is copious and varied in our culture, there is a distinct pattern that clues us into one of its more common iterations. It is a version of: *Someone did something to me* — a pattern wherein the person claiming victimhood languages himself as the object or aim of another's actions, thus garnishing his victim identity with a telltale sprinkling of narcissism.

> ***Victim Languaging Formula:***
>
> *entity A + verb + something terrible + "TO" + victim X*
>
> *ex: "Someone did something really bad to me."*

The Victim Languaging Formula (VLF) allows us to evade responsibility for our actions by alleging that we are but passive objects to whom terrible, unfair things are happening. The structure enables us in denying our onus, while hiding behind the actions of the perpetrator(s) we are blaming.

We can use this pattern as a means of cluing into victim languaging, and to how those claiming victimhood language themselves as passive agents upon whom terrible things are being perpetrated. We can also use the VLF to examine our own languaging patterns and root victim consciousness out of our personal lexicons. When we notice ourselves languaging our experience with the VLF, our wisest move is to switch it up by re-languaging the statement with ourselves as the subject, which necessarily places us in a position to take responsibility for our actions and our experience.

Betterarchical Upgrade for The VLF:

entity A + verb (neutral action)

ex: "Someone did something."

WHAT IF LIFE IS HAPPENING FOR YOU?

"Why is this happening to me?" whines Victim X, assuming — to his detriment — that the universe is conspiring against him.

Whilst curiosity rocks, and I'm all for open-ended inquiry, it's still a loaded, self-sabotagey question. Framing ourselves as victims of circumstance and a malevolent multiverse only blinds us to the truth of the matter, while inviting reality to configure to affirm that those larger cosmic forces are stacked against us.

Ask and ye shall receive, a rebel mystic once said, cluing humanity in on our role as co-creators here. And so it is that when we ask for proof of our victimhood, we will absolutely receive it.

But what if the cosmic forces are actually working in our favor? What if we were to switch up our mindset to consider that everything, everything we are experiencing is happening for us — for our growth, our healing, our illumination and our evolution? When we re-frame the question, and open our minds to the possibility that the universe is kind and loving, and that our experiences are actually serving us instead of working against us, then we choose empowerment over victimhood.

The Narcissism of Victimhood

Victim consciousness tricks us into believing that outside agencies are acting against us. *He made me cry. She fucked me over. He misgendered me. She abandoned me.* All these statements cast us as lead actors in other people's stories, implying that we, ourselves, were front and center of our alleged perpetrators' consciousnesses as they were deliberately trying to hurt us. The statements aren't just inaccurate, they allow us to avoid taking responsibility for our trauma, our triggers and our shoddy discernment.

The narcissism of victimhood has us casting ourselves as lead actors in other people's stories. So, were I to mistakenly address someone by the wrong pronoun, to the person running victim consciousness, it isn't a matter of me being careless or distracted or simply not habituated to using a plural part of speech to represent a singular human, it becomes a "microaggression," a deliberate attempt to hurt another person — another person who is not taking responsibility for the unintegrated trauma they are using to victimize and disempower themselves.

The Indiscretion: A Lesson in Framing

Let's say I'm in a committed, monogamous relationship, and my partner chooses to share intimacy with someone else. *Ouch.* Now, how I choose to frame the situation, position myself within it and author the story will determine how I heal, how I grow (or shrink), how the relationship continues to unfold (or doesn't), how I construct my present moment identity and how I seed my reality moving forward. ALL of these factors will be determined by the words I ascribe to the situation.

"He cheated on me," I sob to my best friend over cocktails, followed by a heaping plate of deep-fried comfort food before I engage in some reckless canoodling with the chiseled stranger slurping mezcal at the end of the bar.

I think it's fair to say we've all either languaged our own experience this way, or — at the very least — heard a friend do so. And while it's not necessarily inaccurate, it is disempowering, as well as masochistic, as this framing will only exacerbate the pain and the agony of what is already an ouchie enough situation as it is.

Let's break it down:

When I claim, "My partner cheated on me," I am victimizing myself to his actions. We don't need to have any additional information to know that, in this story, I am the victim and he is the perpetrator. So, right away, we are inferring a good/bad, black/white, reductive, polarized framework. We are empowering the hierarchical structure/prison by conforming our own multilayered, multidimensional life, with all its unique components, characteristics and circumstances, to fit into a pre-fab box: *Him: bad. Me: good. Insert drama here.* No nuance. No distinction. Just standard-issue victim framing.

Here's the thing: "cheating" is an interpretation, not an action. It's not an objective assessment of the circumstances in question. It is a judgment. As well, "cheating" implies nefarious intent, suggesting that my partner's primary action was to betray/hurt me. This is trauma-based conjecture that only muddies the truth of what happened, which — more than likely — is that my partner chose to explore an attraction with someone else, *despite* our agreement, rather than *to spite* our agreement.

Don't get me wrong; I'm not in favor of deception or broken agreements, nor am I advocating for covert extra-relational explorations. But the problem with this particular framing — which is one of the primary issues with victim languaging, in general — is that it places the person who is claiming victimhood front and center as the protagonist in the alleged perpetrator's story.

For the person running narcissistic programming/tendencies, it's far more excruciating to imagine that we were totally absent from our partner's mind than it is to believe that our partner was trying to hurt us. Being ignored, forgotten or unconsidered is infinitely more painful than being abused. Framing ourselves as the object of another's mistreatment gives us a certain level of importance in the other person's mind and indicates that we matter, and that we exist. But to be forgotten — to be off someone's radar altogether — well, that's a painful place to be.

Relationships Are a Two-Way Deal

From the vantage point of "He cheated on me," the "he" in question is the bad guy who is to blame for breaking my heart. Alas, the allegation denies the fact that I am 50% of our relationship, allowing me to sidestep the most relevant and empowering inquiry, which is: *Where can I take responsibility for my partner's choice to seek outside of our relationship for affection or attention or whatever energetic experience he was seeking? Where did I drop the ball on my discernment? Which red flags did I sweep under the rug, and why? Where did my apathy, my distraction, my career devotion or my codependence contribute to his decision to seek outside our relationship for connection?*

Granted, the answers might very well put me in the clear, but without taking the time to examine our own responsibility, and without the willingness to see how we might have co-created the situation, we will forever be stuck in victimhood. We will continue to be passive victims upon whom terrible things are perpetrated, instead of empowered co-creators who choose to consciously craft lives and relationships we love.

Quantum Entanglement Alert

This story, *He cheated on me*, is sticky, as it creates and sustains quantum entanglements. In languaging myself as the object of this sentence, and linking myself to my partner's actions through language, I am codependently handcuffing myself to him on multiple dimensional levels.

This framing allows me to insinuate myself into my partner's story (even though I wasn't even there) and to frame his actions in relationship to me, verily stapling myself to my unfaithful partner and to this painful moment in our relationship. These words allow me to attach myself to his actions and to this hurt, thus exacerbating the pain with which I am choosing to identify.

Now, feel into the energies that are transmitted when I rewrite the story this way:

"My partner had sex with another person."

This statement is both accurate and objective. There is no judgment. There is no entanglement. It simply communicates what happened. There is infinitely more spaciousness in this assessment, because I haven't inserted myself into the story.

When we language the scenario with neutral facts — hold the victim languaging — there is infinitely more space for healing and reconciliation. Now we are dealing with what is real and with what actually happened, instead of giving our power away to a hierarchical program that attempts to shove my relationship into a generic, one-size-fits-all box and cast me as the victim in my own life.

Betterarchical Upgrades for the VLF

- *Language ourselves as the subject, rather than the object of the statement.*
- *Resist the urge to place ourselves or the alleged "victim" front and center in the alleged "perpetrator's" narrative.*
- *Present neutral facts, and hold the judgment.*
- *Take responsibility.*

"Can't"/"Have To"

"Can't" and "have to" are essentially two sides of the same disempowering coin. They both vibrate at similar frequencies of victimhood, and they both function to deny our own agency, which is why we are examining them in tandem, here.

Let's start with "can't."

"can't"

As with most words, there are multiple uses of/applications for "can't." Mostly, we use it to deny our competence and our agency, while bowing to codependent relationship dynamics.

From a connotation standpoint, "can't" refers to an actual *inability* to do something, whether that inability is steeped in physical, ideological or psycho-emotional impediment, or in authoritarian constraint — evident, imminent or implied.

Regardless of its actual meaning, we often employ the word "can't" to get out of things we don't want to do, without taking responsibility for the fact that we don't want to do them. This well-intended though thoroughly disempowering languaging habit enables our collective emotional retardation by assuming the folks we are turning down "can't" handle the rejection this erroneously misused word seeks to quell.

Take, for example, the following statement:

"I can't go hiking with you today, Hannah. I have to work."

"Have to" operates much the same way as "can't" does, except while "can't" implies inability, "have to" alleges to have zero agency in the situations it modifies. We'll delve deeper into the domineering frequencies encoded in "have to" in a bit. For now, though, let's stick with "can't."

When I say "I can't go hiking," I am taking all of zero responsibility for my *choice* to go to work over hitting the trails with Hannah. It would be accurate were I a leg-less slave handcuffed to my desk. Alas, in the vast majority of instances, this isn't actually the case.

When I say "I can't go hiking. I have to work," I am victimizing myself to my job and denying my own agency in how I choose to allot my time and attention. The truth of the matter is that I am not a leg-less slave handcuffed to my desk, and I *can* go hiking with Hannah, though I am *choosing* to work instead. I choose to work because I like having a steady income, and I like being able to pay for the goods and services that enhance my life — be it regular bodywork and a pantry filled with superfoods, or simply shelter, running water and the electricity necessary to run my laptop. Working is a *choice* I make in service to the lifestyle I have created for myself.

Granted, there are aspects of me that would rather hike with Hannah than work, but when I language my choice to work instead of hike with "can't" and then go the distance by pairing it with "have to," I am disempowering myself to my job. The aspirated "can't" + "have to" combination harmonizes my internal vibration with the frequency bands of victimhood, disempowering me to whatever it is I am claiming I "can't" or "have to" do.

Remember, the frequency bands to which we attune ourselves most frequently determine the energies and experiences that characterize our lives. And so it is that "can't" and "have to" direct the universe to configure in service to our victimization and our disempowerment, ensuring that external agencies squelch our fun and our freedom on the regular.

The same applies for the various "can'ts" and "have tos" the matrix attempts to impose upon us. Examples include: "I have to renew my passport," or "I can't see you for a session at my house, because I don't have insurance."

Except, I *can* see anyone I want for a session in my house, though I may *choose* not to if I'm feeling uncomfortable about the insurance thing. Similarly, I don't "have to" renew my passport, though I might *choose* to if I have my sights set on international travel.

Even when we are choosing to adhere to the matrix's rules and protocols, we are wise to continue to affirm our sovereign authority by languaging our choices to comply as *choices*, instead of as "can'ts" and "have tos." Sovereignty and empowerment are frequency bands in the morphic field. When we use language to align with these frequencies, we are programming ourselves, as well as collective reality, with the qualities of empowerment and sovereignty.

"can't" + "have to" are Co-Dependent Bullshit

Oftentimes, we employ "can't" when we don't want to do the thing we are attempting to forgo. Maybe I don't "have to" work, and I really "can" go hiking with Hannah, but I just *don't want to*. Maybe Hannah is needy and prone to gossiping and complains a lot and often feels sorry for herself. Maybe I notice that when Hannah and I hang out, I leave feeling drained and depleted. But because I don't want to hurt Hannah's feelings, and I don't really feel like getting into a whole big thing, I dodge what might be an uncomfortable conversation by saying "I can't," because I "have to" do something else, instead of sharing my truth and being honest with my friend.

This is one of the more ubiquitous uses of "can't"/"have to" in our culture. I guess we figure it's easier to disempower ourselves and deny our own agency than it is to show up honestly and integrously in our relationships. "Can't" and "have to" are like the motherload of toxic multitasking, allowing us to dodge responsibility for our choices and enable codependent relationship dynamics, while disempowering us to victim consciousness.

The intention informing this codependent linguistic evasion is — by and large — compassionate and speaks (mostly) to the kindness of the human spirit. I say *mostly*, because there is still the matter of our emotional immaturity and the corresponding reticence to share tough truths in our unconscious efforts to avoid discomfort. What it really boils down to is fear — fear of conflict, fear of drama, fear of being disliked and misunderstood

— and fear of losing our proverbial shit. Alas, the strategy is short-sighted, serving to corrode and distort our relationship dynamics, while enabling everyone involved to stay stunted and small.

The truly compassionate response is to be honest. It is to take responsibility for our own experiences, while languaging our choices as choices, instead of pawning them off on imaginary tyrants and constraints. It is to acknowledge that we are utterly and completely, 100% in charge of our time, our attention and our calendars, and that everything we do or do not do is a choice.

— what if i'm already booked, though?

Still, there are indeed instances wherein we really do have prior commitments. What if I am scheduled to work, if that's a commitment that I've already made to my team, my clients and my supervisor? How would I go about languaging this in such a way that I'm not disempowering myself to my calendar and my responsibilities?

Great question, superstar. Replacements abound, while honesty and precision rock. I am a fan of telling people "I'm already committed" or that "I have other plans." If it's authentic, I add that "I'd love to arrange for a raincheck" and suggest a couple alternate day/times to connect. In other instances, I let folks know that while "I appreciate the invitation, I'm not feeling aligned with _____" (whatever it is they have invited me to). Sometimes, I simply say, "No, thank you," and leave it at that.

Betterarchical Upgrades for "Can't"

"not going to"
"not aligned with"
"not available"
"No, thank you"
"already scheduled/committed"

The Hierarchical Henchman that Is "Have To"

Whereas "can't" isn't *always* a victim-vibey cop-out, because there are, indeed, some things that we really, truly *can't* do (e.g., walk to Iceland, outrun a cheetah), "have to" is never, ever true, while always functioning to align our vibration/seed our realities with the frequencies of victimhood and disempowerment.

"Have to" implies that we have no say in our own lives. The phrase invokes the idea of a real or imaginary overlord pulling our strings, driving our ships and bossing us around. Employed as an excuse, it makes for a handy *Get out of anything-free* card, as when we allege that we "have to" do something, we are signaling that the case is closed, and that it's out of our hands. It's the ultimate in responsibility-dodging, as the inference is that — while we may really, truly *want* to be doing the thing we're using "have to" as an excuse to not do — it's not up to us. Instead of speaking our truths, we blame the invisible "have to" gestapo; they're in charge here.

When we deny our agency with "have to," we place ourselves in an inferior status position to whatever it is we are claiming we "have to" do. This very act empowers the overarching hierarchy construct by way of the fallacy that we, ourselves, are not in charge of our lives. In this way, hierarchy has become a veritable crutch upon which we lean to avoid uncomfortable conversations. Instead of being honest, we blame hierarchy and are thus let off the hook, because — well, "the Man."

And then there are those teetering stacks of "have tos" that fill our days, serving to signal lack of agency and implied enslavement to whatever it is we are claiming we "have to" do — be it eat, work, clean, bathe, parent or exercise. The coding has us affirming our victimhood with every "have to" we utter. And so it is that we willingly place ourselves on the bottom rung of the hierarchy ladder, playing subordinate to our laundry list of "have tos."

And while none of this is to deny our responsibilities or the chores, projects and to-dos peppering our days, it is to acknowledge that every time we modify these tasks with "have to," we are empowering hierarchy, denying our own sovereign agency, disempowering ourselves to an imaginary external authority and aligning ourselves with the frequency bands of disempowerment and victimization in the morphic field and in our lives.

Every "have to" we employ notifies our subconscious mind that we are not in charge of our Selves, instructing it to go about configuring/sustaining a reality construct reflective of disempowering victimhood. When we language our tasks as "have tos," we inevitably attract more "have tos" as well as more external authority figures attempting to tell us what to do.

The same goes for the "have tos" we employ to get out of doing things we don't want to do, or to gather pity for the weight of our loads, when we are lacking the courage, consciousness and tools to support us in being honest. When we abdicate responsibility for our choices to an invisible overlord who is allegedly pulling our every string, we attune our internal vibrations to the frequencies of disempowerment and victimhood, thus inviting our reality construct to configure and perpetuate accordingly.

Here's the thing: no one "has to" do anything. I *choose* to do laundry because I like clean clothes. I *choose* to work, because I like having money to purchase goods and services. I *choose* to drive my eight-year old to art classes, because she's passionate about color and aesthetics, and the whole reason I decided to procreate in the first place was to raise an empowered, expressed human to contribute to the betterment of the world.

"Have to" is — essentially — a one-way track to Victimland and a surefire way to build a disempowered life devoid of agency or empowerment. The upgrade is super simple: stop saying it. Instead of victimizing ourselves to our responsibilities and commitments, let us own our choices as choices and simply language our actions as actions, without tossing in the extraneous noose that is "have to."

And so it is that "I have to do the laundry" becomes "I choose to do the laundry" or simply, "I am doing the laundry" along with, "I am going to work" and "I am taking Trixie to watercolor class."

Choice allows us to flip the positional script on hierarchy and claim our status at the tippy-top of our own lives. Choice is a magical frequency that amplifies our empowerment and signals to the multiverse, as well as to any and everyone who enters our vibratory fields, that we are empowered reality creators standing in our sovereign agency, and crafting our lives as we choose.

Betterarchical Upgrades for "Have To"

"am doing"
"choose to"
"get to"

BETTERARCHICAL BADASS
EXTRA CREDIT EXERCISE

As you, superstar, are inspired to step into your full power and claim complete, sovereign agency over your life, I recommend making a list of every "have to" on your to-do list — big, little, immediate, future, easy-peasy and excruciating. Once you've jotted down every task weighing upon you, re-write each one as a choice as "I choose to..."

While languaging our tasks as choices isn't necessary in our daily communications (i.e., "I am paying the gas bill" vs. "I am choosing to pay the gas bill"), for this exercise, it's crucial. The act of re-framing our every "have to" as a choice has a palpable effect on the subconscious mind, instructing it to re-organize these tasks into a different set of neural networks–the ones associated with empowered agency, instead of victim — drenched enslavement.

Take your time with the second part of the exercise, reverse engineering the "have tos" to find your way to the desired result that is informing it, just as I did with the schlepping my imaginary progeny to art class example. When we pull back and examine our "have tos" from a wide-angle perspective, honing in on the Why? that ultimately informs them, we see that what we had been languaging as a "have to" is simply another choice that is supporting us in achieving our goals, realizing our dreams and enjoying our lives.

"Make"

"Make" (and its various derivations) is yet another hallmark of victim languaging. When slipped into a sentence and attributed to an alleged perpetrator, "make" is a fantastic way for those operating in victim consciousness to deny responsibility for their choices, lives, traumas and triggers, while pinning the blame on an external entity.

Some examples to ponder:

"My boss made me stay late."
"Jamie made me do shots with her at the club."
"Frank is making me go to his parents' place for Christmas."
"My girlfriend makes me feel like shit."

Unless we are dealing with the egregious imposition of one's will upon another, none of these statements are true. And by "egregious imposition of will," I mean physical force, as in my boss duct taping me to my chair, or Jamie pinning me to the ground, pinching my nostrils shut and literally pouring shots down my throat. But this isn't what happened.

What actually happened is that my boss asked me to stay late or told me to stay late, and — as an autonomous adult with free will — I *chose* to comply. As for Jamie, she might have asked, encouraged or even pleaded with me to do shots. She may have even stooped to emotional manipulation, but — when it came right down to it — *I* was the one who chose to toss 'em back. Same goes for Frank and our holiday plans with his parentals. Again, unless we are dealing with a rufi + duct tape + trunk combo travel plan, Frank isn't actually "making" me do anything. While I may not like the choice I am making, when it comes right down to it, *I* am still the one making it, while attempting to dodge my responsibility by way of the *m*-word in question.

What about that whole "My girlfriend made me feel like shit" schpiel? The statement purports that someone else has control over my emotional state and is imbued with the power to "make" me feel certain emotions. Except that no one has the power to "make" us feel anything. All anyone can do is trigger the feelings attached to our own hurt, our own beliefs and our own unresolved trauma, which are only and always our responsibility to heal and integrate for ourselves.

Betterarchical Upgrades for "Make"

The betterarchical upgrade for "make" and its various derivations is much the same as it is for other VLF: take responsibility. The upgrade invites us to re-frame the statement such that we are self-responsible subjects in the sentence, rather than passive objects being victimized to other entities' demands and behaviors.

As well, it is yet another opportunity to exercise the practice of owning our choices as choices, regardless of preference, and to reverse engineer the larger *Why* to help us reframe the situation at hand as the choice it really, truly is.

Here are some rewrites of our initial "make" statements, duly upgraded to place us in the driver's seat of our own lives, instead of in the back of that proverbial victim bus where they had initially put us:

"I chose to stay late at the office because I had a couple proposals to finish off, and these kinds of things go a long way with my boss, who is eyeing me for a promotion."

"I did shots with Jamie because the music was bumping, and I was feeling nostalgic, and she looked so cute and excited when I said, 'Fuck it, let's get smashed.'"

"I'm going to Frank's parents' place for Christmas because he came with me to Bermuda in February, and I know how much it means to him."

"I notice that I consistently feel sad and hurt and less-than when I spend time with my girlfriend."

Can you feel the difference in the coding these upgrades transmit, as compared to their original framing?

While the implications are vast and varied, I am inspired to point our attention towards the agency embedded in these upgrades, and how all these frameshifts put us in the drivers' seat of our own lives, acknowledging our agency, free will and choice in every situation we find ourselves. Duly harmonized with the frequencies of agency, free will and choice, we are now resourced to pivot, shift and change reality to our liking.

MICROAGRESSIONS, LANGUAGE POLICING AND THE TWENTY-FIRST CENTURY TRIGGER BAN

Triggering each other's trauma (kindly and compassionately) is a truly valuable service, as the process shines a light on the cracks in our consciousness and the gaps in our psycho-emotional integrity which are inviting healing and integration. While this is not to suggest that we mistreat one another or deliberately activate people's unhealed hurts, it is to invite us to take responsibility for our own triggers and emotional reactions and to push back on the current culturally implied/imposed ban on triggering folks.

One of the hallmarks of the Victimhood is the New Black trend the language of betterarchy is uprooting and evolving is the tendency for folks to get (off on getting) supremely offended by things that are said and by things that aren't said, but that the offended think should be said, and to twist everything (or as much as humanly possible) into an affront and a reason to be offended.

This fad not only has people strapped into victim goggles, ever and always on the hunt for oppression affirmations, but now it has big tech, big government and the minions representing their interests lobbying for censorship and rigorous limitations (implied and overt, as well as regulated and socially-imposed) on what we can and cannot say, lest folks we've never met and with whom we have no beefs claim to be triggered. No longer does the onus lie on us to take responsibility for our own emotional states; rather, the responsibility lies on everyone else to pre-emptively mind and hold their tongues, just in case our feelings get hurt and we decide to cancel/tattle on them.

The issue is manyfold and multi-layered, perched atop a massive distortion of will and an alarming inversion of responsibility. Alas, the tendril that feels most pertinent to presence here is that the trend seeks to prohibit triggering and being triggered, which is akin to outlawing growth and evolution.

When we treat each other like emotionally stunted squirrels who can't handle truth, jokes, irony, rejection, shadows or negative emotions, we are doing hierarchy's bidding for it, ensuring that we all remain small, stunted and stuck by denying one another the opportunity to strengthen our emotional intelligence muscles and rise to the occasion(s).

It is precisely the triggering of unhealed wounds that allows us to heal said wounds, because it is their triggering that draws our attention towards them and illuminates what is calling for love, acknowledgment, compassion and integration. Duly alerted, we can embark upon the necessary inner work to reclaim these fragmented aspects of ourselves, while cultivating tools and techniques which will support us in remaining calm, poised and centered in the face of them.

Hierarchy is dependent upon our emotional infancy to function, relying on a populace that is easily triggered, quick to shame, blame and freak-out, such that we are too distracted with our division and our drama to notice how depraved and dysfunctional the system really is. Duly distracted, disempowered and unhinged, we are all the easier to control.

Grit, character and inner resolve must be cultivated. This is not to advocate for insults, bullying or any kind of deliberate mistreatment; rather, it is to remind us that emotional intelligence is a muscle that must be flexed to grow bigger and stronger. When we deny one another the opportunity to exercise these muscles, and go the distance by outlawing the kinds of weights and practices that would allow us to strengthen them, we are doing ourselves and each other a grave disservice.

Those Sad, Sorry Stories

Part of hierarchy's *Victimhood is awesome!* scam entails fostering and encouraging the social sport of sharing our sad, sorry stories — casually and often — in otherwise inappropriate situations. This trauma-chronicling trend has nothing to do with healing, integrating or mining the lessons on our ever-unfolding path to wholeness. Rather, it is an unconscious pity collection strategy — a means of vampirically feeding ourselves off other people's sympathy, while clocking imaginary social credit points for our suffering.

Again, this is not to minimize anyone's hurt or the overarching effects of tragedy or trauma on the multidimensional human condition. Rather, it is to say that we have been tricked into milking our tragedies and indulging our sad, sorry stories as a means of keeping ourselves small and stunted, which has allowed hierarchy and its various minions to control us, while steering our Earth ship onto some really questionable trajectories.

Telling and retelling our sad stories only serves to strengthen and perpetuate the shadow frequencies informing them, while keeping us trapped in victim consciousness. Think about the worst experience of your life. Every time you tell the story of that experience, you are activating those frequencies in your own body, mind, heart and field. You are choosing to revive those energies, while connecting to their corresponding frequency bands in the morphic field, thus programming your reality construct with more of them. You are tethering yourself to that experience and allowing it to control your now, while seeding your future with its residue.

But sucky stuff happens, I can hear some folks protest.

Indeed, it does. And there is great value in talking about our sucky stuff as a means of healing, integrating and learning from it, in a supportive and appropriate context, with loving, compassionate ears and hearts who can hold space for our process. Sharing our sucky stuff with people we barely know during otherwise casual exchanges to stockpile their pity is only to empower the victim stories we are attaching to our experiences, to identify with our self-proclaimed victimhood and to program the morphic field with more of it.

Podcast or Sucky Storytime?

I was once invited on a podcast, ostensibly to talk about Quantum Languaging. Alas, instead of discussing the power of language to create and transform reality, I spent 90 minutes nodding and holding wide-eyed space for the emotionally wobbly host, who was fixated on her ancestral trauma, and spent the bulk of the show steering the conversation into off-topic stories about her mother's death, and her father's drinking problem, and her sister's borderline personality disorder, while lamenting how sad, sorry and tragic her life had been.

Now, had we agreed to do a proper coaching session, the host's tales of trauma and woe would have been welcomed and appropriate. We could have dropped into a deeper, more internal space, and I could have guided her into some real-deal healing. Alas, her choice to insert them into a podcast interview was highly inappropriate and made for a stilted, one-way exchange, wherein her unintegrated traumas claimed the space, and steered the dynamic, and sucked all the oxygen out of the conversation.

Because this is what victim consciousness does: it takes. It takes, and it takes, and it takes some more, ever and always attempting to fill an empty hole, a hungry ghost,[43] a wound that needs constant tending and reassuring, incessant nodding and *tsk-tsk*-ing. Feeding victim consciousness is akin to pouring water into a bucket with a hole in it. That bucket will never, ever, ever be full until the hole itself is mended. And no amount of water in the world is going to fix that hole. The only way to fix that hole is to heal and integrate the trauma. And the only way to heal and integrate trauma is to stop identifying with it, which is antithetical to talking, talking, talking, talking about it, any chance we get.

---

43 In the Buddhist tradition, a hungry ghost is a spirit afflicted with constant cravings and sensual longings, which it desperately tries to quell through endless consumption.

Earth: An Evolutionary Realm

Keep in mind that Earth is a planet of evolution. We came here to learn and grow, expand and evolve. And, oftentimes, our growth and our mettle, our grit and our character develop as a result of having our asses kicked over, and over, and over again. This is not to advocate for trauma, tragedy or sucky stuff; rather, it is to help us reframe these oftentimes excruciating experiences such that they don't steal our power and control us.

Yes, horrible things happen that make no sense,[44] and that shatter our hearts, and our souls, and our trust, and our innocence. Ours is a brutal planet that is in no way, shape or form fair. Is it fair when a bobcat snatches up a mama bunny, rips it into pieces and eats it for breakfast, leaving her litter of tiny, fluffy baby bunnies alone and afraid, only to die of exposure and starvation in a cold, detached landscape that offers no bunny rabbit orphan services to care for them? Is the bobcat a cruel, selfish, racist bunnyphobe who should be canceled, punished and forever outcast for being a bobcat? No. She's just being a bobcat. Brutality and unfairness are baked into this planetary romp from the get-go, and no rules, laws, legislation or social safety nets are going to change that. Ever.

So, when sucky stuff happens, we have a choice; we can feel sorry for ourselves, languish in the pain and victimize ourselves to it, or we can mine the experiences for whatever buried treasures they have to gift us, while trusting in a larger organizational perfection that makes sense on some dimension, and move on with our lives — better, stronger and wiser for our every initiation.

---

44   From our limited, third-dimensional, linear time-bound perspective.

Every Trial an Initiation

When framed as *initiations*, our challenges are transmuted into fuel that encourages growth and forward motion, portending quantum leaps and evolutionary upgrades that are always serving our expansion and our betterment.

As 21st-century Western culture has — until now — been devoid of rituals and initiations that mark the crossing of so many important thresholds, it is on us to recognize these moments and to claim them for ourselves. Sure, there are the usuals that get all the attention and the play — graduation, marriage, birth, death and retirement — but there are also infinite other initiatory experiences peppering the spaces in between. The more we acknowledge and language these infinite others as such, the more sacred, elevated, connected and transformational our paths become.

To this end, I have taken to languaging epic challenges and painful experiences as "initiations." The labeling fortifies my spirit and allows me to endure the journeys with courage and strength, while programming my spirit with the frequencies of upgrades and evolution.

The language of healing has become a pillar of my coaching practice, wherein I guide folks who have been diagnosed with cancer, and other chronic/ degenerative diseases, in reprogramming their bodies for accelerated healing, total remission and optimized wellbeing. One of the first steps in the process is to re-language what doctors refer to as "cancer," or "diabetes," or "disease" as "an initiation" — as a transformational healing journey that necessarily portends evolutionary upgrades and quantum leaps in consciousness.

I encourage us to utilize this word when life throws us lemon-flavored journeys we'd really rather not tread. Notice how the languaging shifts what may otherwise be a *Why me?* scenario we are resisting into a hero's journey that changes us for the better.

CHARLIE'S SPIDER MEDICINE INITIATION

When my friend Charlie, age three, experienced his first spider bite, his eye swelled up like a baseball, and his nervous system took a major hit. Charlie was sad, and scared, and suddenly, supremely afraid of spiders.

"What an auspicious initiation," I told him, going on to explain the magic of spider medicine, reframing the bite as an otherworldly induction into the sacred realms of arachnid magic.

Charlie's entire countenance changed. He went from being bummed and blue to honored and emboldened. It wasn't just spider magic that shifted him, it was the reframe itself — the choice to author the story of the experience as an empowering honor, instead of a victimizing cruelty.

Every Experience a Teacher

When I choose to language the foibles, face plants, misfires and challenges I experience as teachers, I frame them in such a way as to unlock the lessons they have to gift me. Instead of victimizing myself to them, I am inviting them into a co-creative dance wherein I am acknowledging that they — like every single circumstance the universe throws my way — are serving my growth, my evolution and my wholeness.

Remember, we all have the *authority* to author our lives however we want to. We have every right to author ourselves as victims to external reality, but know that — in doing so — we are, by default, choosing to live lives of limitation and disempowerment.

When we choose to author our circumstances as teachers, while taking responsibility for our experiences of reality, we are resourced to milk the lessons out of all of them. This framing is what allows us to expedite our growth, realize our potential, actualize the lives of our dreams and transform our world for the infinitely more wonderful, sustainable, empowered, peaceful and unified.

Remember the landlord who gave me the boot and then pocketed my last month's rent? She was a teacher. She taught me what happens when I play small and subordinate, and don't ask for a receipt after paying rent in cash. The TSA agent who relieved me of my organic hair gel and favorite tweezers? A teacher who gave me the opportunity to learn what happens when I don't read the airline's carryon rules. The tyrant — I mean *politician* — in the elected leadership position who's trampling on my civil liberties? She's teaching me what happens when I drop the ball on my responsibility to mind, manage and participate in the democratic process.

....

Purifying our personal lexicon of victim speak is the single most empowering act we can take. It is a bold statement, I know, and I stand by it. I encourage you and me and all of us to really sit with all these angles of victim languaging, and to allow them to sink in, while summoning the will and the courage to examine our own languaging habits, and to transmute the remnants of victim languaging that have historically rolled off our own tongues, duly programming our minds and our field(s) with the disempowering pathogen that is victimhood. When we make the leap from victim speak to empowerment speak, a whole new paradigm opens itself to us — a reality marked by creative agency, wherein perceived limits are obliterated and every possible world is our oyster. Yummm...

WRONG-USE-OF-WILL[45]

"Stop acting so small.
You are the universe in ecstatic motion."
— Rumi

This category of hierarchical languaging was inspired by one of my very favorite books, *Right Use of Will*, by Ceanne DeRohan. Among other things, the book examines the various ways we humans misuse our will by attempting to impose it upon others. The work invites us to take responsibility for our own responses, reactions and emotions, while honoring others' freedom, agency and authority.

Hierarchy loves to impose its will upon the populace and to (attempt to) deny our free will, sovereignty and God-given agency over our own lives. Hierarchy is rife with wrong-use-of-will. It tells us we can't drive a car without a license, cut another person's hair without a certificate, build a home without a permit, breed without registering our children as chattel or expand our consciousness as authentically inspired by ingesting certain plants that grow naturally from the Earth. Hierarchy loves to tell us what we can and cannot do.

---

45 Polarity caveat: I feel inspired to note that because I do not advocate for reductive judgmental polarities like right/wrong, I feel a bit ambivalent about using them to delineate this specific category of words and languaging patterns. And because *Right Use of Will* has had such a powerfully positive/transformative impact on my life and the lives of so many folks in my high-vibe tribe, and because it's one of a handful of books I am excited to be embraced as mandatory reading/high school curriculum the world over, I am paying homage to its wonderfulness by playing off the polarity embedded in its name, trusting that you, dear reader, won't confuse tribute for advocacy.

This is one of the more glaring ways in which the Masculine shadow has seeped its way into the culture, where it continues to over-exert itself — *clear, cancel, delete* — where it *has historically been* over-exerting itself[46] by controlling and dominating through wrong-use-of-will.

The truth of the matter is that no one — I repeat, **no one** — has the right to impose his or her will upon anyone else. This applies to laying hands on others and to telling folks what to do, what to believe and what they are or are not "allowed" to say, read, write and think. This also applies to coercion and manipulation tactics that would sway folks into making choices that run counter to their best interests and their authentic desires.

Wrong-use-of-will is inherently hierarchical, as it implies that an external entity has authority *over* us — whether that entity be an agency, organization or embodied person, or a nebulous, unspecified abstraction (e.g., *hope*). We'll dive deeper into the specifics in a moment. Just know that this class of languaging is characterized by a misuse of will, which — when wielded — disempowers our audience as well as ourselves, while inspiring contraction and pushback in the process.

---

46 While we will unpack the practice of "past-tensing the shadows" in the ensuing pages, I encourage you to take a moment to feel into the difference between framing this over-exertion in the present moment, where I am validating it, and thus seeding the future with more of it, versus being more exacting with our languaging, and framing it in the past, thus signaling to the forces of reality creation that we are available for a different experience.

WRONG-USE-OF-WILL LANGUAGING

Wrong-use-of-will languaging describes hierarchical words and languaging strategies that insinuate the imposition of our will upon others, whether overtly or inadvertently. In addition to being fundamentally out of integrity, wrong-use-of-will languaging inspires amygdala freak-outs and contractions galore, while fostering imbalanced power dynamics in our relationships and our culture as well as all the inequality, resentment and low-vibe ickiness that come along with 'em.

Wrong-use-of-will seeps into our languaging habits in the most nuanced and insidious of ways. And while the majority of these communication patterns are unconscious and unintended, the consequences of their bandying are in no way tempered by the ignorance informing them.

One of the primary issues with wrong-use-of-will languaging is that it inspires contraction in whomever we are addressing. The coding transmitted to those on the receiving end of wrong-use-of-will frequencies indicates that they are in a lesser status position, and that the person who is addressing them is trying to control or dominate them. Whether conscious or not, this coding directs our neurochemistry to armor up and defend, which renders us deaf to the real-deal meat of the message(s) being delivered. As such, our wisest move as conscious communicators and empowered, betterarchical reality creators, is to transmute any and all wrong-use-of-will languaging patterns into their "right use" variety, wherein we are honoring the sovereign agency of our audience and whomever we are addressing.

"Should"

When looking up the word "should" in the dictionary, we find that the very first definition is "to express obligation," which ~~should~~ *will likely* clue us in on its coded frequencies. "Should" implies that we have authority over those to whom we are speaking, suggesting that they don't actually have a choice in the matter, but rather are *obliged* to follow our commands.

This kind of communication strategy might be appropriate for the CCP, Third Reich or Random Dictatorship X, but it's hardly effective or appropriate for free-thinking, autonomous adults living in a(n allegedly) democratic society. When directed towards another human, as in, "You should try the new sushi joint around the corner" or "You should really invest in precious metals," all our well-meaning intentions are obliterated in the face of the wrong-use-of-will vibes encoded in the *s*-word.

Because "should" is programmed with wrong-use-of-will frequencies, when wielded, it communicates that the person we are "should"-ing is in a subordinate position and is expected to follow our commands. The receiver's amygdala then responds with its own *You're-not-the-boss-of-me* reaction, by flooding the body with chemicals and coding that put us on the defensive and inspire contraction, as we prepare to fight back against being controlled or overpowered.

I can personally attest to the inefficacy of "should," as — when I find myself on the receiving end of this tyrannical little verb — my brain literally blocks out every word that trails it. It doesn't matter how brilliant or insightful the recommendation may be, when preceded by a "should," my brain puts up a wall of temporary deafness, insistent as it is upon sovereignty and free will.

Granted, I am highly attuned to the frequencies encoded in language and likely navigate more extreme reactions than some folks do. Still, even for those completely unaware of the wrong-use-of-will coding embedded in "should," the subconscious programming and the neurochemical reactions *are* happening, even on the most subtle of levels.

To be clear, most "shoulds" are well-intended and aren't necessarily conscious attempts to control, dominate or trample on anyone's freedom or authority. Regardless, the effects of the word's careless bandying are undeniable as well as inefficient, because what is the point of offering recommendations if we are inadvertently shutting folks down and rendering them deaf to our wisdom in the process?

Betterarchical Upgrades for "Should"

Instead of mucking up the morphic field with the self-defeating "should," I recommend inviting folks to "consider" our perspectives, while owning them as *our own* perspectives, instead of projecting them as empirical truths and prescriptions for those we are addressing. The upgrade invites us to stay in our lanes, while honoring the free will and sovereign authority of those we are addressing.

"I recommend"
"Are you open to considering"
"A wiser/more effective way may be"
"Have you considered"/"I invite you to consider"/
"You may want to consider"

"Hope" (v.)

"Hope" is a tricky one. As a noun, it vibes supremely positive, encouraging us to live into our optimism and our knowingness that the universe is kind and always coalescing on our behalf. As a verb, however, it's pretty flimsy — thoroughly devoid of agency, confidence or willpower. In this section, we will be examining "hope" as a verb.

The problem with "hope" is that it pins its dreams, goals and visions on a nebulous, external *something* to make them all materialize. "Hope" has no agency, authority or conviction of its own. It's too busy waiting for a mythic superhero to come swooping down from the heavens to render its visions so. "Hope" is reliant upon an implied externality to realize whatever it's referencing, while dodging any and all responsibility for following through on the actions it modifies.

Some examples:

Q: "When are you going to finish writing your book?"
A: "Hopefully, by summer."

The writer doesn't seem all that convinced, does he?

Q: "Is our team gonna win this scrimmage, coach?"
A: "I sure hope so."

If the coach isn't committed to the win, then how can we expect the team to have confidence in this outcome?

"I'm hoping to get the garage cleaned out this weekend," says Janice, who isn't likely to finish the task, what with this attitude.

"Hope" has big dreams. "Hope" paints giant visions of future wonderfulness that it (claims it) really wants to happen. Yet "hope" lacks the trust, commitment, execution and follow-through to actualize its stated aims, too busy as it is dilly-dallying in passive acquiescence, waiting for some outside agency to magically appear and take care of it on "hope's" behalf.

"Hope" is chock-full of potential. Alas, potential is useless without the confidence and follow-through "hope" lacks. "Hope" is wishy-washy evasiveness gussied up in the razzle-dazzle optics that suckers folks into believing in it, despite the non-committal *maybe-ness* encoded in its frequencies. If "hope" doesn't believe in itself (and let's be very clear: it doesn't), then why would the multiverse waste any energy supporting its actualization?

When I "hope" for change or "hope" my book becomes a number-one bestseller, I am connecting to the frequency bands of wrong-use-of-will, thus letting the multiverse know that I am claiming no agency here, but that it would be swell if it would send me some magic beans or a fairy godmother to make it happen for me. Or not. *Whatevs.*

Alas, the multiverse doesn't work this way.

As an empowered reality creator, instead of "hoping" for change, or "hoping" I get a raise, or "hoping" my book becomes a number-one bestseller, I collapse the perceived distance between my dreams and my present-moment reality, and I claim them in the here and now in stating:

"I am ready to receive a 20% raise before the end of the second quarter, along with a five-figure bonus."

"I am writing a number-one bestseller."

How do I know my book will be a number-one bestseller? Because I am *committed* to writing a number-one bestseller. I don't "hope" for it. I claim it. I decide, and I language my decision with definitive conviction and then watch (and take inspired action) as the multiverse responds accordingly.

As for change? Change is not a future concept for which I hope and dream and pray. Change is here now, which gives me the confidence to claim, "My landslide victory and my leadership mark a new era of change for every citizen in our great nation, now." Change is not some wishy-washy fantasy that might maybe happen, just as soon as my magic wish-granting genie arrives. Change is something that materializes when we lay claim to it with confidence, conviction and definitive languaging, now.

But how do you know? I hear a small doubting voice wonder aloud. *How can you be so sure? How can you lay claim to something that hasn't happened yet?*

Again, I remind you that time is not linear, and that the whole reason we are connecting to the energies and timelines of change and pay hikes and number-one bestselling awesomeness in the first place is because — on some parallel dimension — they already *are*. We don't collapse the perceived distance between these dimensions and our here-and-now by "hoping," but rather by "claiming"–with conviction, confidence and definitive languaging.

Transmuting "hope's" wishy-washy, wrong-use-of-will vibes demands our confidence. This means ditching any and all *kinda, sorta, maybe* futurizing languaging and laying claim to our visions with assurance and conviction *now*, instead of pushing them off into an idealized future that may or may not come.

Betterarchical Upgrades for "Hope" (v.)

"will"[47]
"trust"
"forsee"
"am/is"
"am devoted/committed to"
"envision"
"choose"
"am living into"

---

47 While still future-based, "will" vibrates at the frequencies of commitment and certitude, rendering it stronger and more confident than "hope." "Will" is an effective transitional upgrade to employ while we are in the process of up-leveling our present-moment claiming competency.

"If"

"If" shares the same downfalls as our flaky friend "hope," refusing to commit to the realization of whatever it's supposedly modifying, while waiting for some imaginary *something* to come along and render the realization so. "If" vibrates at the frequencies of doubt, failure and commitment-phobic, while allowing us to play small and uncertain, dilly-dallying in perpetual procrastination mode.

Let's look at a few examples, shall we?

Example #1:

"If I ever finish writing this dissertation, I'm going to treat myself to a trip to the Maldives."

A trip to the Maldives sure sounds like a swell reward for finishing a dissertation, but the speaker doesn't sound all that convinced that he's going to pull it off. "If," in this instance, makes it seem like he's not completely in charge of the dissertation-finishing task. It's more like a question mark — a *possibly, maybe* type of endeavor over which he has no control.

My take-away from this statement is that the speaker is not going to the Maldives, because the speaker is not going to finish his dissertation — that is, unless a magic typewriter falls into his lap from the heavens and polishes it off for him. Writing a dissertation is hard enough when we are operating with agency, self-responsible authority, discipline and a daily word count. But with this kind of wishy-washy commitment-deficient framing? Not so much.

The speaker's languaging choice infers that the dissertation-finishing task isn't up to him, but rather it is the responsibility of some external agent or occurrence. The "if" allows him to defer to a nebulous something-or-other to determine whether his dissertation will magically finish itself. Or not. *Whatevs.*

still - not a word. please stop disrespecting the language.

The obvious upgrade for the writer's statement is, "**When** I finish my dissertation, I am treating myself to a trip to the Maldives."

Alternatively, as he is inspired to step into superstar reality creator mode, he will collapse the distance between this perceived future moment and his present version, in saying:

"**As** I am finishing my dissertation even faster than I'd imagined, I'm looking into flights to the Maldives."

Example #2:

"I think we are going to be ready to launch in the spring, if we can raise enough investment capital, that is."

I don't know about you, but if I had been considering investing in this venture, this statement alone would inspire me change my mind. If the company's founder doesn't have enough faith in her project to commit to raising the capital, why would I invest my own resources in it? Entrepreneurial endeavors require commitment and follow-through. This sentence tells me that all the speaker is committed to is a half-assed approach to business-launching, and that she is passively waiting to see if some external X-factor sweeps in to allow her to raise enough funds, so that she can possibly, maybe launch in the spring. Are you inspired to invest your resources in such a flimsy future vision? Yeah, me neither.

Notice that I tossed a couple "ifs" into the sentences trailing the statement in question, to help demonstrate that "if" does indeed have its time and place and doesn't always portend failure. Still, when it comes to describing our goals, visions, achievements and manifestations, "if" is straight-up sabotage.

Our entrepreneur would be wiser to lean into a betterarchical languaging upgrade, such as:

"We are going to be ready to launch in the spring, **when** we raise all the necessary investment capital."

While the most pressing upgrade was shifting the topical "if" to the committed "when," notice that I removed the doubting "I think" piece and tightened the investment capital chunk to make the whole statement stronger. "Once" would also work well for an "if" replacement here, as in:

"We are going to be ready to launch in the spring, **once** we've raised all the necessary investment capital."

As our entrepreneur is inspired to step into superstar, betterarchical reality creator mode, she can accelerate the process in saying:

"We are launching this spring, **after** we have surpassed all of our investment capital goals by at least 44%."

Betterarchical Upgrades for "If"

"when"
"as"
"once"
"after"

Judgment

When we judge, we separate. We don't just separate; we (attempt to) diminish the other's status. They're not just *not* us; they are *beneath* us. The act of judgment kicks that which or whom we are judging down a notch or two or twelve. Their status plummets through the lens of our judgment. It's hierarchy-a-go-go.

Judgment alleges that we are objective arbiters of capital-*T Truth* and are divinely authorized to project our opinions as facts. Judgment implies that we hold superior knowledge that something is bad, that someone is immoral, that an object is overpriced, that a garment is ugly or that yesterday's workshop sucked. When we judge, we project our unintegrated traumas, distortions, wounds, shadows and programs onto that which we are judging, while unconsciously claiming omniscience and impartial, almighty-decider status that gives us license to smear our opinions all over the world at large.

Aside from the psychological distortions to which judgment points, as a communication strategy, it's ineffective. Judgment shuts down the audience in its reductive generalizing, inspiring contraction in the process. Shorthand assessments like "good/bad," "right/wrong" and "pretty/ugly" marginalize the ideas, entities and circumstances they are modifying, while doing a half-assed job of describing the scenario in question.

Let's revisit that podcast I mentioned a few chapters back, when we were unpacking polarities as an aspect of separation-speak. As you likely recall, the show featured a controversial psychology professor, who claimed it was obvious that two-parent households were "better" than single-parent households. "Better" is a judgment — a hierarchical, qualitative assessment that necessarily places itself *above* that to which it is comparing itself — in this instance, the single parent household. "Better" is a sweeping, inexact generalization that — as I witnessed firsthand — will absolutely shut down the single parents listening to the talk, as they are effectively being told that they are qualitatively *worse* than the partnered parents to whom they are being compared.

In this instance, the "better/worse" framing isn't just acting as a divisive, reductive polarity distinction; it's also functioning as a judgment. The professor was judging two-parent households as "better" and — by the implication embedded in the polarity framing — single-parent households as "worse."

Again, this is not to say that two-parent households don't have advantages over single-parent households, but to default to a sweeping judgment that one situation is "better" and that the other is "worse" is to generalize, as well as to insult the single parent. It's also a sloppy, inexacting means of (not really) assessing the situation.

"Better" is a vague, and relatively useless judgment that tells us very little — qualitatively speaking — about the difference between the two household structures in question. What does "better" actually mean? Does it mean *safer*? *More efficient*? *More effective*? *More diverse*? Does he mean that two-parent households offer a more balanced energetic framework for the family unit itself? "Better" is a vague, judgy, sub-par assessment that does little to explain the upsides or downsides informing the professor's opinion or to inspire his audience to embrace his stance on the matter.

If I tell you my method of onion-cutting is "better" than yours, I'm posturing and playing the hierarchy game. If I tell you that my method of chopping onions is "faster and more efficient, because it allows me to chop onions into finer slivers in a tenth of the time," now we're dealing with meaningful facts that paint a clearer picture of the scenario, while sidestepping the hierarchical dig that will cause pushback and inspire negative feelings in she who chops more slowly and methodically, but perhaps prefers the meditative state in which her rhythm anchors her as well as the sacred geometric shapes she takes her time carving. Perhaps she isn't interested in speed or width, but in her own lived experience of the chopping, which means she's operating with different priorities that attune her to different aims and that render assessments like "better" or "worse" wholly irrelevant.

So often, we defer to "good/bad," "better/worse" polarity-based judgments out of laziness, as we race to make our points, wholly unconscious of the contractive, separation-steeped, wrong-use-of-will frequencies we are transmitting. Alas, this kind of shorthand only serves to shut down the listener, while empowering hierarchy, as we claim a superior knowingness which grants us the authority to deem certain ideas, experiences, people and things more or less worthy, based upon our implied omniscience.

In addition to being supremely arrogant, reductive judgments like "good/bad" and "better/worse" are — for the most part — vagueries that do little in the way of transmitting constructive feedback. If we're in a brainstorming session, and I dismiss your idea as "bad" or as "worse" than my own, there's not really any meaningful feedback for you or anyone to take away from my assessment, which serves more as a sweeping dismissal than an illuminating critique.

In this and most instances, it is far more helpful to frame feedback in terms of efficacy and efficiency, as in whether something "serves" the participants, the mission or the greater good, or whether I, myself, am experiencing it as "aligned," or "resonant," or "coherent," or "supportive" or "harmonious." This is a helpful strategy when it comes to transmuting judgment. Instead of projecting our own opinion onto something or someone as though it is an objective assessment, we are wiser to own our own experience of the thing or being in question and to align our communications accordingly.

THE "BETTERARCHY" CAVEAT

But, your book is called *The Language of Betterarchy*, lady!! What kind of steaming hot hypocrisy are you shoveling here, anyways?

I know. I know. It's why I wrestled with the whole "___-archy" question for so long, dilly-dallying with linguistic organizational overhaul, when this languaging paradigm and this book were frothing at their imaginary faces to come through.

Let us keep in mind that these communication tools that comprise the language of betterarchy are not rigid or definitive. For every precept, there is an exception, or two, or twelve. Remember, while hierarchy is itself a Masculine construct, the language of betterarchy alchemizes both the Masculine and the Feminine as a means of restoring balance to our species and our world.

Notice I said "alchemize." Alchemy is not a static, singular formula into which we plug our every component. Alchemy is a dynamic process of transmutation that cannot be whittled down to anything hard, fast or dogmatic. That would bring us back to the cult of scientism and the domineering shadow of the Masculine. When we are dealing with alchemy, there are guidelines and there are principles, and still, it is up to us, as self-responsible, betterarchical reality creators, to synthesize the elements involved as we are authentically inspired by wisdom, intuition, circumstance and experience.

The Feminine principle (which the language of betterarchy is helping to restore and integrate into our field, our world and our consciousness) is fluid and flexible. The Feminine honors nuance and holds space for exceptions. The Feminine acknowledges that everyone and everything is unique and cannot be whittled down to a singular, all-encompassing rule (minus that whole free will one).

"Betterarchy" is a placeholder for the up-leveled organizational solution into which this communication paradigm is guiding us. It is a great, grand unknown into which we are together leaping. Yes, a better unknown. And if that framing triggers or shuts down those who are engineering the old, hierarchical version, so be it.

For example, instead of saying, "Musical theater is corny and cheesy," I would say, "Musical theater doesn't resonate with me."

It's not that, "Lasagna is disgusting"; rather, it's that, "My belly doesn't do well with lasagna."

I don't purport that "Anne is a fake, petty snob"; I say, "I don't resonate with Anne's vibes or communication strategies." Or if I'm being really candid, I would say, "I prefer not to hang out with Anne because I find it challenging to connect with her, and I find myself craving more depth in our conversations." Notice how none of the upgrade options have me alleging to offer an objective assessment of Anne, while they all have me taking responsibility for my experience of Anne, without slandering her character or throwing her under any proverbial buses.

The judgment upgrade invites us to hone in on descriptive adjectives that more accurately depict any preferences we may be communicating, while taking responsibility for our own experience of people, things, activities, circumstances and behaviors, such that we are not projecting our opinions as objective assessments; rather, we are taking responsibility for our feelings as precisely that: our own subjective responses and reactions that have nothing to do with the empirical status of whatever it is we are describing.

Betterarchical Upgrades for Judgments

"is/is not aligned"
"is/is not resonant"
"is/is not harmonious"
"is/is not coherent"
"does/does not land"
"has/doesn't have traction"
"is/is not inspiring"
"is/is not efficient"
"is/is not effective"
"is/is not serving"
"does/does not resonate"
"am/am not attracted/drawn to"

"Toxic Masculinity"

It's hard for me to type this phrase — let alone attempt to utter it aloud — without choking on my own vomit. But because I love you so much, dear reader, I'm braving barf mouth and death by gag reflex in service to the swift eradication of this divisive, damaging phrase from our collective lexicon.

"Toxic masculinity" is a low-vibe euphemism for the Masculine shadow. Let us remember that we ALL have shadows — both Feminine and Masculine — to our own unique and varying degrees. "Toxic masculinity" is a phrase that aims to deride and demonize the Masculine shadow, while it is, in and of itself, an expression of the Masculine shadow in its aggressive, judgy-pants divisiveness. The hypocrisy of the phrase being hurled with the violent, polarizing invective that defines the Masculine shadow those doing the hurling seek to shame is worth noting and relinquishing.

"Toxic masculinity" goes the distance in marginalizing the Masculine shadow and shaming men for expressing it. The phrase references the unconscious, shadow aspects of the Masculine polarity, while taking the umbrella descriptive a caustic step further in judging said shadows as noxious and repugnant and then multitasking as a kicky catchphrase/ hashtag, to boot.

When we judge or disparage something, we hold aligned relationship with it at bay. Only in the space of neutrality do we find harmonious relatedness. "Toxic masculinity" is far from a neutral assessment of the Masculine shadow, serving only to exacerbate the negative effects of its every articulation in its scornful disapproval. If you want to see more of the Masculine shadow unleashed in our world, then — by all means — go ahead and judge it as "toxic," while employing this phrase willy-nilly and often.

But I'm guessing that because you are holding this book in your hands, and have made it this far, that you're not angling for a less balanced, less loving, less tolerant, less harmonious planet, which is why I'm not actually lobbying for us to utilize this phrase at all, ever. Shaming, blaming and judging the Masculine shadow, along with all the men who have the potential to express it, only exacerbates this shadow's distortions. This is what intolerance does. It allows the things it modifies — and for which it refuses to hold space — to grow. Shaming men for their shadows does nothing to support them or any of us in coming into right relationship with these shadows. Instead, it otherizes, blames, shames and shit-talks, while fueling division and conflict amongst our human family.

Betterachical Upgrades for "Toxic Masculinity"

While the obvious betterarchical upgrade for "toxic masculinity" would be to simply call it what it is: the Masculine shadow, I am actually lobbying for us to do away with any iteration of this phrase altogether.

Shaming men for having shadows isn't a supportive means of encouraging a shift in how any of us relate to said shadows. This phrase is best replaced with a larger collective conversation around how we *all* relate to our shadows and how we can *all* take responsibility for coming into right relationship with them. Remember, we live in a reality forged of equal and opposite forces, which means that if the Masculine is indeed "toxic," then so too is the Feminine.

"Won't Let Me" / "Not Allowed To"

These super disempowering phrases reached peak popularity in the wowzer of a year that was 2020. Seemingly overnight, retailers were refusing to do business with people with exposed breathing holes, which inspired a slew of linguistic distortions and a veritable flurry of statements along the lines of, "I'm not allowed in without a mask," and "They won't let us sit inside." Luckily, it's not necessary to revisit global lockdown (and all the associated trauma and frustration embedded within it) to find examples of how this phrase is (mis)used to abdicate our sovereign authority and align us with the frequency bands of disempowerment and victimhood.

Some less charged examples include:

"We're not allowed to swim in the lake without our life jackets."

"He won't let me use the sauna without a note from my doctor."

"I'm not allowed to bring my tweezers on the plane."

Now, while these statements might accurately reference the dictates being imposed, their phrasing serves to fundamentally disempower us as sovereign individuals, while strengthening the construct that is hierarchy. Remember, complying with rules, restrictions and mandates is always a choice. To deny our choice is to willingly surrender our agency and our authority and to disempower ourselves in service to the enslavement construct that is hierarchy.

Every time we articulate the notion that we are "not allowed" or that some external entity "won't let" us to do something, say something, be something, go somewhere, etc., we are aligning ourselves with the frequencies of disempowerment; just as every time we sign onto an externally imposed limitation by way of our languaging, we are choosing to internalize hierarchy and all the wrong-use-of-will frequencies upon which it sustains itself.

When I say, "My husband won't let me wash his favorite scarf," I am attuning myself to the frequency bands of disempowerment and lack of agency, which will instruct my reality construct to configure to a sustained experience of disempowerment and lack of agency. It doesn't matter that the phrase is more of an unconscious throw-away than an accurate reflection of the situation, wherein my husband isn't physically restraining me from washing his scarf, but rather has vocalized a request (albeit a dozen times). The frequencies in the languaging remain consistent and program my reality construct accordingly. Hence, it would be far more accurate and empowering to say, "My husband has this thing about his favorite scarf and doesn't want me to wash it. So, I don't."

Syntax is Everything

When stating restrictions, it is most empowering to language those doing the restricting as the subject(s) of the sentence. The syntactical shift allows us to sidestep any quantum entanglements that would otherwise be forged between ourselves and the rules in question, instead bonding the restrictions with those doing the imposing. It's not that *we* are not allowed to do *thing X*, because *we* have nothing to do with any alleged rules or limitations. Others may choose to create rules and even attempt to impose them, while the choice to comply — or not — is ours.

Returning to the examples posited above, duly betterarchized,[48] we would re-language them as follows:

~~"We're not allowed to swim in the lake without our life jackets."~~
"They have a rule prohibiting swimming without life jackets."

~~"He won't let me use the sauna without a note from my doctor."~~
"The owner requires a doctor's note if we want to use the sauna."

~~"I'm not allowed to bring my tweezers on the plane."~~
"TSA has a 'No tweezers on the plane' rule."

Notice how these edits reposition the restrictions such that they belong to those attempting to impose them. There is no linguistic linking between said restrictions and ourselves. Communicated as such, we create detached

---

48 Yup, it functions as a verb, too!

distance between ourselves and these proposed constraints, while taking responsibility for our responses and pivots. The impositions are held at bay by the languaging. *We* have nothing to do with them. We speak to our awareness of them, while also languaging our choices to comply, or not, as precisely that: choices. This simple syntactical shift upends the enslavement coding embedded in the "not allowed"/"won't let" phrasing, shifting our frequencies from victimized bootlicker to empowered, betterarchical badass, instantly.

Ix-nay on the Personal Pronouns

Pairing personal pronouns with rules and limitations has this niggling tendency to create quantum entanglements, allowing folks to personalize the restrictions and self-police accordingly. For those of us less inclined to sign onto the limitations imposed by false authorities, personal pronouns trigger amygdala reactions, generating negative emotions and amplified pushback.

> One of the most misleading representational techniques in our language is the use of the word 'I.'"
> — *Ludwig Wittgenstein*

Employing impersonal pronouns that reference the rule or the imposition itself from a detached perspective allows us to sidestep any inclinations to merge said restrictions with ourselves or our reality constructs and thus hold any wrong-use-of-will frequencies at bay.

Notice how the betterarchical upgrades above have all been edited to shift the personal pronouns to the impersonal varieties. As inspired, I recommend taking a moment to read the wrong-use-of-will versions, as well as the upgrades aloud, so that you can feel the difference in the frequencies in your own body.

What Else Can We Do?

When articulating a limitation or a restriction, we are wise to include an alternative — something we *can* do instead. This programs the brain to be on the lookout for solutions, instead of acquiescing to imposed limitations, while shifting our attention from the frequencies of constraint to possibility.

Referring back to our restriction examples above, some betterarchical alternative upgrades include:

"They have a rule prohibiting swimming without life jackets. We can wade in the shallows or head to the river."

"The owner requires a doctor's note if we want to use the sauna. Let's figure out a different way to work up a sweat."

"TSA has a 'No tweezers on the plane' rule, so be sure to pack yours in your checked bag. Worst case scenario, we can pick up a pair when we land."

Do you feel the difference between these upgrades and the batch preceding them? Notice how the upgrades that came before — while held at bay — still left us languishing in the energies of restriction and disappointment, while these versions redirect our attention and our energy towards solutions and alternate possibilities.

I cannot underscore the value and impact of taking that extra step, honing in on potential pivots and giving voice to aligned alternatives. I liken the practice to caring for a toddler who's happened upon a sharp tool. We don't just take away the implement and trust that we've handled the situation; we replace the dangerous stabby thing with something safe and child-appropriate, thus redirecting her focus in the process. The same goes for the brain; instead of leaving it to languish in the frequencies of restriction and limitation, we program it with aligned alternatives that allow it to focus on what we *can* do, instead of what we (are being told we) can't.

Betterarchical Upgrades for "Won't Let Me"/"Not Allowed To"

- *Language those imposing the rules as the SUBJECT of the sentence.*
- *Use impersonal pronouns to communicate rules and restrictions.*
- *Take the extra step and propose a pivot or an alternative to the limitation.*

FIXITY

"What holds true for the individual holds true for a society. It is
never static; if it does not grow, it decays; if it does not transcend
the status quo for the better, it changes for the worse. Often we,
the individual or the people who make up a society have the illusion
we could stand still and not alter the given situation in the one or
the other direction. This is one of the most dangerous illusions. The
moment we stand still, we begin to decay."
— **Erich Fromm**

The projection of fixity is yet another hallmark of hierarchy, which aims
to keep us stuck, stagnant, immature and unevolved, such that we remain
dependent upon its structures and shenanigans. Growth and evolution fly
in the face of acquiescence to control mechanisms, as the deeper we know
ourselves and the more we expand our consciousness and our perspective,
the less willing we are to be told what to do, or where, when or how to do it.

The truth is that nothing, nothing, nothing in this reality construct is
permanent. Change is our only constant. Language that seeks to staple
fixity to our experience is a distorted falsehood as well as a trap that
functions to stunt our growth.

Betterarchy acknowledges the fundamental truth of our ever-evolving
nature and nourishes growth and development. Betterarchical languaging
fosters our evolution and supports us in the process of shifting,
transforming and quantum leaping into greater states of consciousness
and expansion.

Now, to be fair, not everyone is actively seeking growth and evolution. Some folks are comfy, cozy in their patterns, their Groundhog Days and their ever-so-predictable status quos. So, if the labels, identity constructs and reductive boxes that are allowing you to live small and limited are working for you — great! Keep rolling with it.

But for those of us who are walking conscious evolutionary paths and deliberately choosing to live great, big, empowered, impactful, abundant lives, we are wise to resist the urge to put pins in qualities, tendencies, expressions, circumstances and experiences, and to avoid languaging patterns that (attempt to) render these things permanent. Because in doing so, we are enslaving ourselves to their limits and their stigmas and locking ourselves in cages of our own forging.

THE LANGUAGE OF FIXITY

When we employ words and phrases coded with fixity, we are stunting our own growth and inviting stagnancy into our lives. The language of fixity programs our minds and our fields with the frequencies of status quo, verily commanding the forces of reality creation to keep on churning out the same ol'-same ol', while keeping change and evolutionary upgrades at bay.

Betterarchical reality creators are infinitely wiser to use language coded with evolutionary frequencies that acknowledge our creative power and our ever-changing, shifting, growing nature and that program reality to augment these processes of change as smoothly and gracefully as possible.

The Fixed, Forever-Clinging "My"

We've already examined personal pronouns as tools of identification and amplifiers of wrong-use-of-will. Now let's look at how they function as fixatives. When we tether the shadows, challenges and distortions from which our souls have been tasked to learn to personal pronouns, we are effectively stapling them to our identities, soldering them to our personhood and lending them an erroneous air of permanence.

Consider the following phrases: *My acne. My debt. My anxiety. My ex-husband. My arthritis. My attitude problem. My abandonment issues. My insomnia.*

In each instance, the personal pronoun functions not only to merge the speaker's identity with the issue in question but also to affix the issue to the speaker in perpetuity. "My" invites them to stick around and take up everlasting residence in our ongoing experience.

Sure, I might have an historical predilection towards manifesting depression-like symptoms. I might sometimes navigate psychic weather, dark moods and melancholy moments, but it's never "*my* depression," because I am not choosing to conflate a batch of symptoms with any disempowering identity constructs, nor am I inviting *more* psychic weather, *more* dark moods or *more* depression-like symptoms into my experience.

As I am authoring my own story, I choose to experience fewer and fewer extended bummer episodes, and that's certainly not going to happen when I am defining myself by an experience I have historically navigated and stapling it to my experience/identity.

Every time I say "*my* depression," I am inviting the symptoms of depression into my field and into my present moment and thus into my future. I am programming my reality with depressive symptoms and all the other tendrils of coding that come along with this declaration and this pathology. Let's be very clear: *I* am the one doing the programming. Not a shitty childhood. Not a batch of bum genes. Not some neurological predilection. *Me.* I am choosing to perpetuate depressive symptoms and seeding my future with depression.

The wiser choice is to language challenges and uncomfortable experiences with impersonal distance. It's not "my depression"; it's "*the* depression" or "*the* depressive symptoms" or "*the* psychic weather I sometimes experience." Duly depersonalized, there is no identification, no attachment and thus no coding that programs my subconscious mind — or the universal reality creation forces — with the idea that this is an experience to get too familiar with and thus perpetuate.

When we untether our identities from pathologies and other disempowering constructs, we open portals of possibility in the quantum field — cosmic doorways that lead to change and existential openings through which I am liberated from historic bouts of psychic weather. Or anxiety. Or debt. Or...or...or...

Betterarchical Upgrades for the Fixed, Forever-Clinging "My"

impersonal pronouns
articles (i.e. "the")

The Noun Trap

"Nothing ever is; everything is becoming."
— Plato

Nouns imply fixity. There is a solidity to nouns that lends itself to (the illusion of) permanence — a fallacy that hijacks the evolutionary process. Nouns attempt to pin things down, while purporting: *This is how it* is, instead of: *This is how it is expressing* now. Nouns conflate feelings, behaviors, symptoms and experiences with *IS*-ness, while implicitly denying the ever-shifting nature of reality.

To this end, I have embraced the practice of *de-gerunding* (aka: verbing nouns — especially nouns that squelch my joy and my confidence). Verbing nouns takes what was ostensibly solid and fixed and puts it in motion. When we language things in motion (especially experiences and circumstances we're not digging all that much), we acknowledge their transience, while directing them to keep on moving.

gerund, *n.*
a noun derived from a verb

de-gerund, *n.*
a verb derived from a noun; the act of verbing a noun

De-Gerunding: An Origin Story

I once texted a friend an apology for a reactive outburst. As I typed *I am taking responsibility for the emotions I leaked during our conversation*, I felt a flood of pressure spread across my chest and noticed my breathing becoming disrupted. There was a stagnancy to the word "emotions" that felt like a cage.

It was a pitch-perfect example of how the various layers of coding embedded in language program the human vessel. You see, there are collective codes, and there are personal codes. For me, the word "emotions" — as employed in this context — had become heavy with the shame and embarrassment that had historically plagued the flipside of so many volatile outbursts. For me, the word had become tainted and loaded, and it was anchoring me to a pattern I was ready to release.

I decided to innovate. As I deleted the stale, outdated noun and replaced it with "emotionalings" (as in, *I am taking responsibility for the emotionalings I leaked during our conversation*), I was instantly flooded with a palpable wave of relief. By acknowledging the transitory nature of said emotional weather, I felt liberated from its historic hold on me. All those otherwise tangled feels became less solid, less scary, less overwhelming and less likely to occur in the future. Mission accomplishing!

are we
- allowed
to do
that?

Of course we're allowed to do that! Like the Torah and the Cincinnati subway, our lexicon isn't a done deal. Our language — like our culture and our Selves — is always evolving. And no one person, entity or institution has the exclusive right to mind, manage, build or change it. We are all co-creating culture, in real-time, together.

Betterarchical Tips on De-Gerunding

There are no hard and fast rules when it comes to de-gerunding. It's all about flow and feels. What lands best in your body and feels most aligned slipping off your tongue? Sometimes, I'll simply de-gerund the noun (e.g., instead of eschewing "distractions," I prefer to sidestep "distractionings"). Other times, I'll change the noun to an adjective and go about de-gerunding from there, as I did in the case of "emotionalings." Utilizing this particular strategy, I'm not prone to "anxiety," though I have — in the past — noticed some "anxiousings" moving through my body.

Feeling some "grief" come up, again? Acknowledge that you're processing some "griefings" and be gentle while allowing yourself to feel all the feels. Noticing "inertia" around your writing session? Acknowledge the passing "inertiaings," and then strap yourself to your desk chair and write anyway. Starting to be pegged as "a woman of a certain" age (insert gags and eye rolls here)? You ain't no "crone," honey. You're "croning."

De-gerunding allows us to language ourselves in perpetual evolution, ever and always learning, growing and shifting. The process supports us in relinquishing any linguistic strongholds on what we are experiencing or expressing in the present moment, knowing that everything is in a constant state of flux and choosing to take refuge in the change that is ever unfolding.

Remember, betterarchical languaging is a transformational tool that fosters and accelerates our growth. When we language experiences as temporary states in motion, we are acknowledging the ever-shifting, ever-unfolding nature of our incarnations and availing ourselves to the evolution, upgrades and quantum leaps that pave our Earth walks.

Absolutes

For our intents and purposes, "absolutes" refer to hyperbolic words and phrases that double as temporal cages, eternal curses and definitive, non-negotiable obstructions. In this section, we are specifically examining the reckless and consistent mis-use of the words "always" and "never" and how they function to perpetuate and impose permanence onto our experiences.

Ubiquitous, though rarely accurate, "never" and "always" pepper the collective lexicon with grandiose theatrics that keep us stuck. As absolutes are employed in our current culture, things that happen frequently or repeatedly (or if you're a West Coast teenager, only once) are framed with "always" for dramatic effect, while those that occur less frequently are modified with "never," effectively seeing our quantum field with *lots* or *none* of whatever we are referencing.

When I say, "I can never remember my password," I am programming my brain to cooperate with this dictate and to hold password recollection at bay — *forever*. Similarly, when I say, "I always stutter when I'm nervous," I am directing my brain and my tongue and my nervous system to collaborate such that when the cute guy at the gym asks if he can call me, it takes me a good forty-four seconds to eke out the numbers between all the stuttering that will forever mortify me, as I've just seeded eternity with this distortion.

Given how language programs the subconscious mind and the morphic field at large, "never" and "always" operate as curses that doom us to repeat the patterns we are hyperbolically modifying, while programming our futures with more of them. While absolutes might be swell tools for drama queen theatrics, they're not effective when it comes to consciously crafting realities that aren't peppered with the repetitive patterns we're not digging.

Transmuting Absoluting

As we choose to transmute habitual patterns, while stepping into upgraded iterations of ourselves and expanded realms of experience, we are wise to ditch the dramatics, while speaking to the change we are claiming for ourselves and the world.

Instead of claiming, "I never remember my password," when the truth is that I have forgotten my password a bunch of times in the past, I say, "I am choosing to remember my password" or "Remembering my password is getting easier and easier."

If we are not feeling aligned with using expansive upgrades to transform our experience of password-remembering, we are still wise to language our past experiences as exactly that — past experiences — by utilizing more exacting language that doesn't program the future with *more* experiences of forgetting, as in the initial clarification, "I have forgotten my password many times in the past." This framing is infinitely more accurate than the "always" version, functioning to communicate our historical experience with neutrality, without seeding the quantum field with more of it.

Similarly, it's not that "I've never been to the Maldives," it's that "I haven't been to the Maldives *yet*." I might not (yet) feel confident or aligned in choosing to manifest the experience, but — at the very least — I can choose words that describe my experience honestly and accurately, without perving my morphic field with a perpetually Maldives-deprived experience.

Instead of giving voice to the negative pattern that isn't serving us, empowered, betterarchical reality creators language the up-leveled experience with as much present-moment confidence as we can muster, with whatever alchemical combination of words feels most aligned.

And so, instead of asserting that "Politicians always lie and sell out," I assert, "I look forward to electing an ethical, honest and integrous representative who honors the wellbeing of her constituents over corporate interests."

I don't infect the morphic field with the idea that "My boss never acknowledges all the extra hours I put in"; instead, I program it with the change I'm envisioning, in stating, "I am excited for my boss to honor my above-and-beyond efforts by taking me to lunch and offering me a raise."

The gist is to language past experiences with languaging that portends possibilities that "never" and "always" function to deny and drive away.

Betterarchical Upgrades for "Never"

"haven't yet"
"look forward to"
"excited to"
"calling in"

Betterarchical Upgrades for "Always"

"have, in the past"
"have, historically"
"used to"
"often"

"ALL" + "WAYS" = "ALWAYS"

While generally employed as a temporal reference, when we examine the components of the word, we see that "always" is actually spatial. It is a melding of two words — "all" + "ways" — meaning omnidirectional or in every manner possible.

How it came to connote a measure of time, I do not know. But I do know that it is yet another clusterfucky fiction embedded in our language that is doing little to streamline communication or reality creation.

Past-Tense the Shadows

You may have noticed how, in the previous fixity subsections, I proposed a handful of betterarchical upgrades that framed our hypothetical bummer patterns/experiences in the past. Past-tensing the shadows is a betterarchical communication strategy and an empowered reality creation technique I recommend employing on the regular.

The powers that were would like us to believe that the way things have been is not just the way they're supposed to be, but the way they will *always* be. This is false. The social engineers need to keep us trapped in the illusion of their same-ol'-same-ol' status quo to keep us driving their antiquated enslavement machines that hold us down while fattening their pockets. This means — rather, *has historically meant* — using language to (attempt to) keep us tethered to so many lackluster pasts.

Alas, we are not bound to our yesteryears, yesterdays or yester-five-minutes-agos. We are sovereign reality creators, which means we are free to make different choices and to establish new behaviors, new patterns and new ways of being in every now-moment.

The truth of the matter is that this now-moment is brand new. You have ~~never~~ *not yet* been here before, and neither have I. This now-moment is ours to craft however we wish. Sure, we can recycle our old thoughts, beliefs, behaviors and patterns. We can also switch it up, and transcend, transform and up-level as we choose.

For those of us leaning towards option B (the switch-it-up version), we are wise to utilize language that bolsters the process. So, instead of communicating with language that purports: *This is how it always **is***, betterarchical badassess utilize language that asserts: *This is how it **was*** or *This is how it **has been***.

The Intimacy of Sharing Shadows

Past-tensing our shadows fosters intimacy. The languaging technique allows others to glimpse the hiccups, roadblocks and challenges that have paved our paths. Instead of avoiding the shadows altogether, by bypassing and pretending they don't exist, we lean into the vulnerability of revealing our shadows and our challenges,[49] without invoking their vibrational voodoo in the present moment, and thus seeding our future with more of it.

With this in mind, I don't claim, "I have a terrible sense of direction"; rather, I say, "I used to get lost a lot," or "I have historically experienced some directional challenges," or "While I've been prone to getting lost in the past, I am in the process of cultivating a stronger, more aligned sense of direction." All of these options allow me to share the challenges I've historically experienced in an honest way, while simultaneously claiming the change I am choosing to live into.

Alas, it's not just a matter of our own personal shadows I recommend past-tensing; it's all shadows. It's why I consistently rewrite the phrase "the powers that be" as "the powers that *were*." In addition to rejecting the ruling elite's false authority in this now-moment, I am programming a future devoid of their tyranny.

As an empowered, betterarchical reality creator, I don't just past-tense the shadows and leave it at that. Rather, I take the extra step, or two, or twelve, and give voice to the preference, solution or upgrade I'm calling in, thus directing reality to begin the process of restructuring according to the directives I'm giving it, rather than simply languishing in the energies and experiences of the past.

It's why, instead of lamenting ocean pollution, I say, "I look forward to the Earth's waters rebalancing themselves."

Instead of complaining about a corrupt justice system, I choose to envision a jury selection process that defines "peers" by levels of consciousness,

---

49 aka: "opportunities"

rather than a handful of shallow identity markers that have little to do with shared values or worldviews.

I don't linger on what *isn't* working. Instead, I program the field with the improvements I am calling forth, while placing the bummer stuff behind me with past-tense languaging.

The act of past-tensing the shadows, while offering up-leveled alternatives, allows us to live *into* our language, instead of waiting for reality to magically change in some possibly, maybe future moment before earning the privilege of describing it as such.

Betterarchical Upgrades for Past-Tensing the Shadows

"historically"
"in the past"
"used to"
"have"
"was"
"did"
"powers that were"

Pathologizing

While we explored the detrimental downsides of pathologizing symptoms and temporary states of mind, mood, psyche and physiology back in our *Identity* chapter, let us remember that words function on multiple dimensions at once. Pathologies don't just operate as identity cages but as tools of fixity, effectively tethering us to the symptoms they describe and the trajectories they portend.

What's in a name?

The act of naming things doesn't just legitimize their existence; it sustains it. As such, pathologizing has this niggling habit of inviting otherwise passing symptoms to stick around longer than they would have, had we not given them a name. Pathologizing symptoms is akin to inviting a salesman knocking at the door to move into our guest bedroom. It is to hand him a key, clear space for him in the closet and the fridge and ask him to live with us...*forever* (or for as long as his coding tells us we should expect him to stick around).

Because the matrix aims to keep us disempowered, disconnected and dependent upon oh-so-many external fixes, we have been programmed to take comfort in the pathologies projected upon us. For many, having a name for the unknown ills that ail us quells the existential ache of so many of the dark, scary unknowns that necessarily come along with the process of incarnating in a mortal meat suit in a realm marked by contrast, extremes and uncertainty.

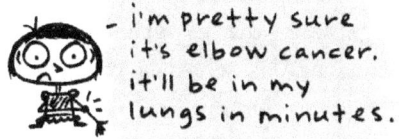

Pathologizing physical symptoms activates the coding embedded in the pathologies. Pathologies are portals to a Pandora's box of physiological possibility — implanting prognoses and probabilities and timelines that likely would not have found their way into our consciousnesses, had we not corralled them into the conceptual cages these diagnoses function to forge. Duly programmed with the pathologies' frequencies and narratives, the body/mind is infinitely more likely to express and unfold in accordance with the pathologies' stories than it would have, had it remained untainted by the labeling.

Symptoms = Neutral Communications

Pathologies victimize us to the symptoms they describe, effectively placing the diagnostic label in the hierarchical role of perpetrator. Alas, pain, disease, discomfort and imbalance are not our enemies. Nor are they the body/mind's way of punishing us. Rather, they are the body/mind's way of *communicating* with us.

Pathologies barrel over this process in their reductive stigmatizing of said symptoms, homogenizing our experience and victimizing us to the sensations they characterize. Alas, when we remove the victim/perpetrator mentality from the equation, we are free to perceive these expressions as neutral and to engage them with openness and curiosity. The process enables a deeper listening that empowers us to engage a cooperative relationship with our body/minds, instead of a contentious one, while learning to interpret what its various expressions are communicating.

Languaging Symptoms in Motion

Instead of pathologizing symptoms, tendencies and challenges, and thus victimizing ourselves to them, we are wise to relegate our descriptions and communications to the symptoms themselves, and to language said symptoms *in motion* as means of acknowledging and emphasizing their temporary nature.

Languaging physical (and all) challenges in motion empowers us to shift the relationship such that these symptoms don't hold power over us and that we are not victims to them. When we language symptoms in motion, we affirm their temporary nature and unhook ourselves from their negative implications. The reframe nudges the symptoms towards their accelerated conclusion, thus rebranding them as our teachers instead of our captors.

Instead of claiming possessive ownership of symptoms with "I have" or entangling them with our identities with "I am," I encourage us to distance ourselves from expressions of injury, dis-ease, discomfort and suckiness with verbs that render them fluid — that describe our experience of them as a temporary passing.

So I'm not "*having* an arthritis flare up"; I am "observing some pain and inflammation moving through my shoulder."

It's not a "Crohn's disease episode"; it's "a temporary bout of intestinal discomfort" that I am "noticing," or "learning from," or "inviting to pass."

I don't "*have* a migraine"; I am "experiencing some throbbing *moving* through my skull," or "*passing* behind my eye."

I'm not "*having* a bipolar episode," but rather I'm "*navigating* some psychological weather," or "*learning* to regulate my moods, which have been fluctuating of late."

The gist is to ditch any verbs that imply stasis and to instead move the symptoms along with "-ing" verbs that signal motion and onwards flow.

Healing Opportunities = Initiations

When we language our healing opportunities in motion, we are acknowledging their evolutionary function as thresholds and initiatory experiences through which we are walking on our ever-unfolding paths of awakening, expansion and optimization. The practice allows us to take back our power from challenges and discomforts and lay claim to the healing, growth and quantum leaps these initiations portend.

Remember, the hero's journey ain't no cakewalk. Crisis, challenge and seemingly insurmountable obstacles are necessarily baked into it. When we reframe ~~health challenges~~ healing opportunities as "initiations," we are claiming the evolutionary upgrades embedded in the mythical hero's journey, while fortifying ourselves with the courage, grit and mettle necessary to prevail.

BETTERARCHICAL BADASS REALITY CREATOR BONUS TIP

For accelerated miracle healing, I find it infinitely more effective to speak to the recovery I am living into, instead of lingering in the frequencies of the current challenge. So, I don't "have a cavity;" rather, "I am taking steps to strengthen and fortify my teeth." I'm not "dealing with methylation issues;" I am "up-leveling my body's detoxification functions."

Can you feel the difference in these subtle frameshifts?

The choice to shift our communication/framing from the paradigm of the symptoms or the "problem" to that of the healing or the solution is utterly epic in its programming and thus, in our lived experience. This betterarchical upgrade isn't just working on the levels of the micro, the quantum or the subconscious, these are palpable shifts that directly affect our mood, tone, timbre, pallor, posture and countenance, as well as all the other levels of reality creation upon which our words are always, always operating.

Betterarchical Upgrades for Un-Pathologizing/Describing Symptoms in Motion

"healing"
"transmuting"
"observing"
"navigating"
"engaging"
"noticing"
"clearing"
"learning from"
"dancing with"
"moving through"

FROM CLUMSY VICTIM TO (SLIGHTLY LESS CLUMSY) EVOLUTIONARY LEAPER

As a historically klutzy daredevil prone to large-scale wipe-outs, I've learned about the perpetuating problem of pathologizing the hard way.

Starting back when I was a tiny gymnast, brave beyond her abilities, I wore my casts, braces, crutches and bruises as medals of honor, delighting in the attention they garnered. When folks would inquire as to what was "wrong" and how my healing journey was going, I would take the opportunity to milk my misery, and stretch the diagnoses to their outermost limits, in order to collect maximum sympathy. In my mind, the formula was proportional: the worse my condition sounded, the more sympathy I received.

The problem with this strategy is that — while it was indeed an effective means of pity collection — it seriously slowed the healing process. Every time I described my situation as dire, I was directing my body to configure itself to dire frequencies. The wide-eyed sympathy combined with compassionate nods and words of concern functioned as a feedback loop for the stories I was telling and the frequencies encoded therein, thus confirming the narrative that alleged I was in bad shape and that others should be very, very worried about me. It was like adding fuel to an already blazing inferno, as these communications only affirmed my sorry state. And so it was that my body was continually being directed to drag out the injuries and stave off swift healing and continue to configure in sad, sorry ways.

At some point, I hit the wall on pity collection and decided to see what it would be like to prioritize my own lived experience of my body from the inside, instead of feeding off external reactions to my various expressions of mangled, broken and jacked-up, which — as I learned from decades of experience — did all of nothing to quell the pain, ease the aches or improve my body's functioning on any level whatsoever.

I did this by switching up my languaging. When people would ask me what happened to my foot, knee, finger or my anything, I would say: "I'm rocking a healing initiation," or "I'm clearing some karma, and resetting at warp speed." If I wasn't feeling quite as emboldened, I would offer variations of "I'm looking forward to feeling better," or "I'm excited to be off these crutches any day now."

What I didn't do was share any pathologies or offer any explanations that would tether me to present moment disruptions, slow my healing process or trigger the asker's pity or concern. My responses served to stave off any externally projected fear or worry and to affirm the ease and swiftness of my healing process.

While I am proud to say I have successfully switched up my communication strategies and the ways I go about programming my body and my subconscious mind, I am still unraveling those historically klutzy patterns, which means I have manifested plenty of opportunities to refine my languaging habits in this realm. Whereas the sprains, strains, breaks and bloodbaths used to trip me up for extended bouts of time, I have made great strides in learning to program my body to heal quickly and gracefully, easily transmuting what used to be dramatic-bobatic physiological nightmares into mere blips on an otherwise healthy, agile, embodied life.

"Woke"

"Woke" inserted itself into the collective lexicon alongside the phrase "fake news" when the American people suddenly found themselves deeply divided between wholly divergent narratives/reality constructs. Allegiances to one engineered "side" or the other were forged by way of identitarian ideology as well as a fat batch of propaganda, which was deployed upon the American people with a virulence and magnitude the likes of which the country had not ever experienced.[50]

Alas, this is not a history book — it is a languaging book — so I will resist the urge to go off on a lengthy propaganda diatribe[51] and resume our analysis of this "woke" word. According to the *Merriam-Webster Dictionary* editors, "woke" is defined as "aware of and actively attentive to important facts and issues (especially issues of racial and social justice)."

Let us sidestep the editorialized judgment embedded in Merriam-Webster's thoroughly unethical choice to take it upon themselves to deem the facts and issues with which *wokeness* occupies itself as "important."[52] Let us instead hone in on the growth-stunting, division-exacerbating arrogance that is coded inside this thoroughly weaponized word.

"Woke" attempts to take an ever-unfolding process, and stick a jagged, rusty stake in it, thereby declaring our evolution complete. *As if.* "Woke" is a trap that stunts our growth, as "woke" claims to be finished awakening and finished evolving. The "woke" have already *been there, done that* and can now check off that pesky "awakening" task that's taking up space on their bucket list. People who are "woke" have already handled that whole evolution thing and can proudly declare their consciousnesses just a little more expanded, a little more developed and a little more sparkly than everyone else's.

---

50 Thanks to the Smith-Mundt Modernization Act, which made it legal for the government to propagandize its own people.

51 While encouraging those who are interested to check out *Pop Propaganda: An Illustrated Guide*, written and illustrated by yours truly.

52 Because who doesn't love a little (okay, a whole, big bunch of) propaganda sprinkled into their reference materials?

The truth is that everyone incarnate in a meat suit in this third-dimensional construct is in the process of evolving, whether we are conscious of it or not. To declare ourselves *done* growing is to shoot ourselves in the feet, stunt our evolution and arrogantly claim ourselves perfected.

The implied finiteness of "woke" closes our minds. Since "woke" claims to have completed the waking process and (alleges that it) already knows everything there is to know about everything, "woke" isn't open to learning anything new or different than what it already (thinks it) knows. "Woke" boxes us into narrower and narrower cages of filtration, shutting us down to information that might challenge or expand our knowledge, understanding and perspectives.

While "woke" claims to be done growing, "awakening" speaks to our continued growth and evolution. When we acknowledge that we are in a perpetual process of awakening, then we remain open. "Awakening" people are infinitely more willing to avail themselves of new information and to different perspectives than our "woke" friends, who have apparently taken it upon themselves to close their minds, shut down their hearts and push away people or information that run counter to the ideologies and perspectives that define "woke-ness."

Betterarchical Upgrade for "Woke"

"awakening"

LACK + LIMITATION

Hierarchy sustains itself on illusions of lack and limitation. On scarcity and not-enoughness. On adjectives like "hard," and "challenging," and "impossible." The matrix force-feeds us fallacies of snags and obstacles, deficiencies and weakness in its ceaseless attempts to convince us that we are small, needy and powerless in the face of a cold, cruel, crumbling world.

Hierarchy's henchmen go the distance to program us with this fraudulent flimflam because if *as* we know ourselves as omniscopic creators existing in a fundamentally loving and abundant multiverse, we become *impossible* to control, divide and abuse. As we embrace ourselves as whole — as having enough, and being enough — we transmute the urge to seek outside ourselves for all the fixes, products, services, validation, recognition and acknowledgment we have been programmed to believe we must acquire to render us "enough." The reason we are dissuaded from knowing and embodying our enoughness is because it is our perpetual consuming and outward-reaching that drives the machinery of the matrix, which is what keeps hierarchy afloat.

Lack is woven into the very fabric of hierarchy. It is an illusion that is programmed into us from the get-go — the myth of scarcity that seeks to convince us that we must compete for a limited array of resources to survive on a depleted and dying planet. This is the fictional narrative that sustains the whole hierarchical construct.

As we come to know ourselves as co-creative allies sharing space on a fundamentally abundant and self-regulating planet, we aren't quite so willing to step on one another to climb our ways to the top, or lay claim to those stale, scanty pieces of that tired, old, genetically-modified pie. Mistrust is no longer the baseline frequency that defines our relationship to our fellow humans, and we aren't driven by the incessant comparison and competition vibes that have us thinking we need to constantly prove that we are better, smarter, sexier or *whatever*-er than everyone else is. As we know abundance as natural law, as well as our birthright, we are free from the lack vibes enslaving us, and we more readily cooperate with the brothers and sisters we are no longer being programmed to outdo, outshine, eclipse and dominate.

Abundance: The Real-Deal Skinny

Despite all programming and rap lyrics to the contrary, abundance has nothing to do with our net worth or our crypto holdings, the hundies stuffing our wallets or the commas gussying up our savings accounts. Abundance is a stream of energy in the quantum field–a frequency band to which we attune ourselves — rather than a dollar amount we amass. Abundance is not about how much we do or do not have; it is about our relationship to reality itself.

Abundance is our natural state, as we are living on a planet notably marked by the stuff. Have you wandered into a forest lately? Trees galore. Plant and nurture a single spinach seed and then watch it grow into a fluffy plant that gifts you exponentially more yummy, nutritious leaves every time you harvest it. Or water a bale of hay every day for a week, and then lift it up so you can marvel at the squirmy worm tribe that's made the damp Earth beneath it its home.

Nature knows nothing of the lack and scarcity programming that has infected the human species. The chipmunk doesn't panic about when she's going to scrounge her next acorn. The frog doesn't doubt his ability to find a fly to munch on. The river has no anxiety about the rainfall, nor does she hoard her flow because she heard rumors of impending draught on the nightly news. Nature is eternally abundant, as are we, because — despite any confusion to contrary—we are not separate from nature. We *are* nature.

When we are abundant, meaning when our internal vibration is attuned to the frequency of abundance, we manifest what we need, when we need it, and we naturally attract the things and experiences we ~~want~~ choose to have and experience. Abundance means trusting nature, trusting reality and trusting ourselves.

> *"The good news is that the moment you decide that what you know is more important than what you have been taught to believe, you will have shifted gears in your quest for abundance. Success comes from within, not from without."*
> — **Ralph Waldo Emerson**

The Lack Trap

Just as abundance is a frequency band in the quantum field, so too is lack. We calibrate ourselves to these energies with our words, thoughts and beliefs. Every time we speak lack into the field, we are attuning ourselves to the frequency band of lack. We are strengthening that connection and creating more lack.

Picture it like the old school bumper cars, with the pole that connects the car to the tracks in the ceiling. Our words function much like these poles, aligning us with different pathways in the collective field. Once we are duly attuned/hooked in, reality will configure according to the specific pathways these tracks delineate.

By the same token, every time we speak or think with language coded with the frequencies of abundance — every time we affirm an abundant belief through thought, word or deed — we are strengthening our connection to *those* frequency bands, and thus directing reality to configure to consistently affirm our abundance.

Hierarchy has a vested interest in our allegiance to lack, because lack is what keeps us small, and stuck, and limited, and dependent, which is why our language is verily lousy with the stuff.

Not-Enoughness

Not-enoughness is one of hierarchy's favorite enslavement programs. The mainstream media machine, combined with all the advertising that bankrolls it, snatches every possible opportunity it can to tell us we're not young enough, not thin enough, not smooth enough, not rich enough, not strong enough, not busty enough, not polished enough, not stylish enough, not smart enough, not cool enough and not loveable enough. According to the program and the incessant indoctrination propping it up, we don't have enough friends, followers, likes, shares, influence, melanin, muscles, hair, clout, collagen, money, mammary tissue, etc.

There is also the "too much" version of the *not enough* fiction, which programs us to believe we're too old, too fat, too thin, too flabby, too weird, too pimply, too bald, too hairy, too poor, too spotted, too stupid, too wrinkled or too rumpled. To make matters even worse, we drive the wrong car, wear the wrong shoes, drink the wrong coffee, use the wrong shampoo and eat the wrong cheese. You get the gist, yes?

Luckily, the altruistic oligarchs blasting out these messages, 24/7, just happen to have the just-right fix for all our too-muchness/not-enoughness — be it a product, a program, an idol, an ideology, a cause or a movement. Our belief in these fictions of lack and limitation is precisely the mechanism that drives the whole system, because it is the illusion of our not-enoughness that keeps us consistently reaching outside of ourselves for an ever-rotating array of "solutions" for our endless sea of purported "problems."

Alas, this lack and limitation are not restricted to just advertising and media programming; they have been embedded in our language itself. All day, every day, we speak words and phrases that are encoded with lack and limitation, thus harmonizing our frequencies with roadblocks and scarcity. The craziest part is that we don't even realize that *we* are the ones indoctrinating *ourselves* with these fictions with our every word.

The good news is that now we're onto the con. Duly informed, we can easily flip the script and course-correct by getting super clear on the insidious ways that lack and limitation have insinuated themselves into our lexicon, and switching it up with betterarchical upgrades that will resource us to speak abundance and omniscopic possibility into our lives and our world on the regular, thus shaping a reality forged in kind. Hurray!

LACK LANGUAGING

Lack languaging is an umbrella term for the languaging patterns that program us and our world with scarcity and not-enoughness. Remember, our reality constructs are amalgamated reflections of all the words, thoughts, beliefs and behaviors with which we are programming ourselves and the morphic field. The more lack we speak, the more lack we experience; just as the more abundance we speak, the more abundance we experience.

The following words and phrases are encoded with frequencies that direct reality to configure to lack.

"Need"/"Want"

I am combining "need" and "want" here because–despite subtle differences in the desperation and implied hysteria that "need" transmits, as compared to the ever-so-slightly less disempowered "want" — both words vibrate at similar frequencies of *not havingness*, which is the crux of their inclusion in this section.

Remember, ours is a world of vibration that conforms to frequency. When I claim that I "need" something or that I "want" something, I am affirming a state of lack, while programming my subconscious mind with the frequency of lack, and thus inviting the multiverse to continue to give me more lack.

"Need" is especially insidious, as it alleges that the forces of creation are withholding a necessity, verily accusing the multiverse of being a sadistic miser. "Want" is often mistaken for an empowered betterarchical upgrade, as it doesn't victimize itself to lack like its whiny, drama queen cousin "need" does. Still, as empowering as it is to hone in on our desires and lay claim to them, to employ the words "want" and "need" is to sustain the perceived distance between ourselves and said wants and needs and to (continue to) hold them at bay, as both "want" and "need" are encoded with the frequencies of *not havingness*.

Let's look at some examples:

"I need a new job."

Claiming "I need a new job" isn't a very empowering foundation from which to land a fabulous career opportunity. All it does is affirm the chasm between myself and gainful employment, while attuning my vibration to the frequencies of lack, desperation and disempowerment. Because lack, desperation and disempowerment are the primary frequencies embedded in the word "need," which — when articulated — is akin to a thousand tiny rodent claws scraping their way down a blackboard upon which a sad little mouse has scrawled *I am lack; I am disempowerment; I am victim* a thousand times.

Don't believe me? Try it for yourself. Say it out loud right now:

"Need."

*Neeeeeeeeeeeeed...*It's impossible to say the word without whining, because whining about what we don't have is quite often how the word operates.

"I want a new job" might sound like an empowered upgrade, because we've replaced "need's" simpering desperation with a declarative desire. Except that "want" is functioning in precisely the same manner that "need" was in affirming the very same *lack* of satisfactory employment.

Counterintuitive though it may be, when we are calling in an *anything* — be it an object, a being, an energy, emotion or sensation, or even a global evolutionary upgrade — our wisest and most effective means of bridging the perceived distance between ourselves and said *anything* is to claim it in the here and now, with definitive, present-moment languaging.

Now, because we have all been fed a fat load of convoluted fiction which has programmed us to thoroughly misunderstand the concept of time and how it functions here on planet Earth, it can be a major mindfuck to lay claim in the here and now to objects, energies and circumstances that have yet to materialize. I get it. When I say, "I love my new corner office" to a fellow waiter as I refill salt shakers in the bus station, my colleague may very well perceive me as delusional or schizophrenic. Not everyone is — as yet — hip to the power of present-tense, positive languaging when it comes to manifesting and materializing our visions.

Know Your Audience

Effective communication is bolstered by the maxim: *Know your audience.* While my nearest and dearest understand me well enough to go along with my "I love how the morning light bounces off my Pulitzer Prize while I'm writing in my penthouse corner office before my 10 am conference call with the Galactic Federation" spiel without writing me off as a total nut job, not everyone is — as yet — ready to roll with this level of linguistic magic.

When communicating to others about that which we are calling in, *excitement* is a fantastic tool to employ, as in, "I am excited to land a new job" or "I am excited to collaborate with fellow physics geniuses at a free energy lab in walking distance from my house." Excitement is expansive, inspiring sparkly, uplifting emotions and frequencies.

Still — as we've already discussed — expansive languaging isn't always authentic or aligned. Sometimes expansive languaging can be too much of a stretch for the subconscious mind to effectively lean into. When it comes to expanding our communication comfort zone, we don't want to push ourselves so far past our baseline frequency that the subconscious mind taps out, thinking we've gone completely bonkers.

So, if "excitement" doesn't feel appropriate when describing the new job/whatever it is we are calling in, neutral replacements for "want" and "need" are our best bet. A few options include "welcoming," "inviting," "magnetizing," "calling in" and "ready to receive," as in, "I am calling in a new job," "I am inviting the universe to bring me a career upgrade," "I am welcoming new employment opportunities" and "I am magnetizing a new gig."

Notice which upgrades feel resonant and which land sideways. There will be some trial and error as we hone in on the betterarchical sweet spots that align with us from moment-to-moment and situation-to-situation. Play. Experiment. Language the big betterarchical upgrade, notice how it feels and adjust accordingly.

Betterarchical Upgrades for "Need"/"Want"

"choose"

"invite"

"call in"

"claim"

"welcome"

"am excited to have/use/meet/engage"

"am grateful for"

"am blessed to have"

"am receiving/am ready to receive"

"am availing myself to"

"am open to receiving"

"am willing to receive"

THE WILLINGNESS WORD COUNT

Fun fact: The number of words we place between ourselves and the actions we are claiming to take reveals a direct correlation to our willingness to take said action.

Having familiarized myself with this procrastinatory languaging pattern over the past two decades of deep word nerdery, I don't need any additional information about the speaker or the action in question to assess the likelihood of the speaker taking said action, or the reticence the speaker is harboring towards taking said action. All I need to do is count the number of words a person places between themselves and the intention they are declaring — half-assed and self-deluding as it so often is.

Take, for example, the following statement:

"I'm thinking about starting to try to wean myself off of coffee.'"

Instead of simply stating, "I gave up coffee" or "I'm taking a break from coffee," I am inserting six extra words and three extraneous dilly-dally verbs between myself and the future-projected action in question (aka: relinquishing coffee), which is itself a weak proclamation, because the stated action — "weaning" — isn't actually about relinquishing; rather, it's about the process of relinquishing. Despite my alleged intention, all these extra words clue me in on the real-deal truth of the matter, which is that I drank a latté this morning, and I feel pretty crummy about it.

Extraneous dilly-dally words sabotage the progress we are deluding ourselves into thinking we're making. Sometimes. And sometimes, those extra words serve a valuable function, beyond mere bullshit.

TRANSITIONAL LANGUAGING

Did you notice how I included the following "need"/"want" upgrades in the previous section?

"I am *open to* receiving…"
"I am *willing* to receive…"

What's with the variations? Why dither with "being open to receive" and "being willing to receive," when we can just **receive**? Aren't all these words I am proposing we place between ourselves and the act of receiving just as half-assed and dishonest as claiming to "think about starting to try to wean myself off of coffee"?

Not exactly.

The words we use denote the programming and the belief systems that are running our subconscious minds. And so, while it is indeed infinitely more effective and empowering to simply "receive," "choose" or "call in" our desires, these actions and these languaging choices are not always authentic, aligned or appropriate for where we are in our present-moment ability to receive, choose or call in.

For folks who are still in the process of healing trauma around receiving (or whatever the action in question may be), "claiming" or "calling in" might be too much of a stretch for the unintegrated aspects of the Self to authentically sign onto. This is why when I presented the linguistic gunas in Part 2, I explained that expansive languaging — while a powerful communication/reality-creation tool — isn't always our most aligned choice, and that neutral languaging isn't always a cop-out, and does indeed have its time and place. This, my friend, is one of those times and places.

The truth is that we are not all ready to claim our abundance, or our dream job, or our soulmate partnership right this very moment. Some of us are still in the process of transmuting outdated belief systems that are inviting edits and rewrites before we are resourced to authentically claim the wonderfulness that is our birthright.

The language of betterarchy is an *evolutionary* communication tool/paradigm. Unlike hierarchical languaging, which aims to keep us stunted and stuck, the language of betterarchy is intended to support our evolutionary journeys with tools that promote, sustain and accelerate our life(times)-long process of growth and expansion.

> *"You cannot use butterfly language to communicate with caterpillars."*
> — **Timothy Leary**

When we upgrade our language, we upgrade our consciousness, which is to say we *evolve*. Evolution happens outside our comfort zones. This is why I encourage folks to step into that fluttery, low-grade agitation that betterarchical languaging upgrades so often inspire. Still, if we push too far or too fast — if, instead of low-grade agitation, we feel panic, terror or the sudden urge to burst into tears — then we've happened upon a wound that is beckoning healing and integrating, or an outdated belief structure that is inviting overhauling, before we are truly ready to quantum leap into the evolutionary upgrade we are languaging.

The language of betterarchy is a fundamentally compassionate communication system. Compassion means we don't push, and we don't force. And so, if the statement, *I am calling in my six-figure dream job offer by the end of the week*, has my eyes welling up as I choke back feelings of unworthiness, then that declaration is too much of a stretch for where I'm authentically at right now. Good to know.

It is yet another valuable function these languaging upgrades provide: They shine the light of awareness on the — as yet — unintegrated parts of ourselves that have been holding us back from embodying the totality of our wonderfulness. When employed consciously, and combined with the courage and willingness to do the work of acknowledging and integrating our traumas, the language of betterarchy accelerates our evolutionary processes by pointing our attention to the places where we are still holding onto hurt and remnants of the past.

And so, in the case of calling in our dream job, it's going to be infinitely more compassionate as well as effective for me to titrate into the upgrade with *transitional languaging*, as in:

"I am ready to call in my six-figure dream job."
"I am willing to step into my six-figure dream job."
"What would it feel like to call in my six-figure dream job?"

Willingness, readiness and curious inquiry are constructive, transitional baby steps that pave the way for our full-fledged receiving or *whatevering*. These words and their variations still move us towards the actions we are languaging, without perving the morphic field or our subconscious minds with lack or doubt or not-havingness.

Sabotage or Self-Love?

So, I can hear some of us wondering, *what's the difference between receiving something wonderful and giving up caffeine? How do we know which words to use, when?*

Great question, superstar. It's really a matter of self-honesty versus self-deception. The extraneous words I place between myself and my thoroughly half-assed coffee-quitting declaration are straight-up bullshit (as well as supremely common when dealing with addictive behaviors). We (claim we) want to give them up, but because our will and our commitment are half-assed, at best, we let ourselves off the hook by throwing in a bunch of non-committal, dilly-dally words, which only serve to undermine our intentions. This is sabotage, as well as self-deception.

In the case of calling in our dream jobs, the extraneous words *could* very well function as non-committal, dilly-dally verbiage that subvert our true intentions, *or* they could operate as a conscious, compassionate means of pendulating into expanded levels of self-worth with which we are still getting comfortable.

It's really a matter of deciphering *honesty* — which has us lovingly titrating into tender, new territory — from *delusion*, which has us sabotaging ourselves. I leave it to you to know the difference.

"I Can't Afford It."

If I could wave a magic wand and eradicate a single phrase from the collective lexicon, it would be "I can't afford it." I've yet to hear a single uttering of this thoroughly disempowering phrase that was aligned or appropriate and that didn't inspire me to wince in abject existential agony, because I find it rather excruciating to watch my fellow humans sabotage themselves.

To allege that "I can't afford" something is to victimize myself to the numbers in my bank statement, the cash in my handbag or the zeroes and ones in my crypto wallet. It is to thoroughly disempower myself to my finances, and to affirm lack and to invite reality to configure itself so as to perpetuate more lack. The phrase strengthens hierarchy, as it places me beneath my net worth and beneath the thing I allegedly "can't afford" on our imaginary hierarchical podium. And here's the kicker: It's rarely even true.

When I say "I can't afford" something, not only am I affirming lack, and victimizing myself to the (lack of) commas in my bank balance or the (lack of) bills in my wallet, I am denying my own agency in my financial dealings and declaring myself a fiscal victim. I am giving my power away to the (lack of) dollars in my savings account, while attuning myself to the frequencies of scarcity and victimhood. Even if those dollars aren't yet reflected in my bank account or net worth, to language them in this fashion serves only to keep them at bay.

For example, let's say I'm having lunch at a café. As I peruse the menu, a $12 glass of wine catches my eye.

I can't afford that, I think.

Except, I totally can. I have a fifty-dollar bill in my wallet, and the salad I ordered costs $15. My fifty bucks would more than cover it. To say "I can't afford" it is to allege that I don't have twelve dollars, which is an affront to all fifty of the dollars I have on me, let alone all the others hanging out in my bank/sock drawer. It is to deny the abundance I have and *am*, while feigning poverty and claiming victimhood. Not only that, it is to disempower myself to the notion of lack, while instructing reality to give me more of it.

Now, this isn't to allege that spending $12 on a Riesling is an intelligent or aligned allotment of my abundance. And I can tell you that — for me — it isn't, because I don't like wine, and I don't like being inebriated, and I don't like to disrupt the digestive process by imbibing liquids while I'm eating.

But to claim "I can't afford it" is to be dishonest and to play the victim, as well as to negate the abundance I have. The truth of the matter is that — when considered in light of my personal preferences, my financial commitments and my income stream — allotting twelve of my fifty dollars to an alcoholic beverage is not a wise or aligned choice. But it is a choice.

When I decide that spending twelve dollars on a glass of wine is not a wise choice for me in the grand scheme of my relationship with my abundance, that's not lack, and that's not poverty; that's discernment. That's me claiming my own agency and making a choice that is informed by my budget, my values and my priorities. That's wisdom. That's empowerment.

But what if I really don't *have the money?* I can hear a handful of readers asking through the ether.

Great question. Because we're not delusional, and weighing a glass of wine against the fifty dollars in our wallet is quite different from buying a four-acre stretch of riverfront property when we only have a thousand dollars in the bank. Very often there are real-deal (present moment) financial constraints that affect how we choose to allot our abundance. Still, it is important to remember how words function to create reality, and to keep in mind that the words we use to describe our present moment will determine how reality is going to configure in future moments. So, when I deny my own agency in my financial life, and I use lack languaging to describe my fiscal choices, all I am doing is ensuring that I will experience more lack.

In a case like this, I recommend employing the languaging upgrades from the "want"/"need" section and to stretch into greater and more expansive realms of abundance by "calling in," "receiving" and generating/claiming *excitement* for big-ticket investments that really, truly fetch more dollars than we can currently claim on this dimensional plane. The gist is to choose active words that move us *towards* that which we are wanting, and to be sure to language them definitively — as in, with absolute, unequivocal assurance that they are indeed happening, now.[53]

The language of havingness and abundance invites us to cultivate courage and confidence in ourselves as reality creators. It demands that we reconfigure our (mis)understanding of time, and that we lay claim to our abundance in this now-moment, regardless of how many commas are — as yet — marking our bank accounts.

It takes guts, and it takes grit *and* you wouldn't have read this far if you didn't have it in you.

Betterarchical Upgrades for "I Can't Afford It"

As we've already established, a life forged of *choice* is infinitely more empowering than one marked by victimization. And so it is that we are wise to language our financial choices as choices. Some empowering upgrades for "I can't afford it" include:

"It's not the wisest use of my abundance."
"I'm not budgeted for that."
"I'm not feeling aligned with this investment/purchase."
"I'm choosing to allot those dollars elsewhere."
"No, thank you."

---

53 On some dimension.

"NEVER COMPLAIN, NEVER EXPLAIN."

While this iconic quote is often attributed to Henry Ford, it was actually first put into the public discourse by British Prime Minister, Benjamin Disraeli.

The complaining part is fairly obvious at this point, yes? Complaining activates the frequencies of that which we are rejecting, thus seeding our realities with more of it, while activating the coding of the very thing(s) we're not digging in our own vessels and in the morphic field at large.

But what about the explaining part?

When we explain ourselves to others, we seek their approval. The act drops us beneath those to whom we are directing our explanations, as we unconsciously disempower ourselves and solicit their validation.

No one needs to know why we are choosing to eschew a $12 glass of wine, a weekend workshop or whatever it is we have concluded is not the wisest use of our omniscopic abundance. This is why the "No, thank you" option I offered above is so empowering.

"No, thank you" doesn't bend to peer pressure, and gives not a single whit what anyone else may or may not think of our choices. "No, thank you" stands in its dignity and its inner authority, while clearly communicating, without any extraneous hoop-jumping or people-pleasing.

"No, thank you" is empowered, betterarchical badass-speak.

"I Don't Have Time."

"Busy" has become the universal excuse for pretty much everything in our rush-rush, hustle-bustle, hierarchical culture. We have been fed the fallacy that if we're not busy, we're dropping the ball. Hierarchical programming has us thinking we need to be constantly doing, making, racing, producing, moving the needle or making shit happen to be worthy, relevant, successful and *not* a total loser. I mean, how else are we going to snag those dangling carrots the matrix taunts us to perpetually chase, so as to keep its slavey, sociopathic hamster wheel a-turnin'?

"I don't have time" has become the default *Get out of anything/everything free* card we play when we haven't done (or don't want to do) the thing we've been asked to do. When we say we "don't have time," we victimize ourselves to the illusion of *lack* of time, thus aligning our own individual frequencies with scarcity and directing the multiverse to configure reality accordingly. It is an incredibly disempowering allegation, which has the unfortunate effect of seeding lack and *not enoughness* into our realities, while victimizing us to the illusion of a perpetual time drought.

Remember those frequency bands in the collective field? Because "I don't have time" alleges *lack* of time, it attunes our internal vibration to that of lack, thus strengthening lack and empowering lack and inviting more lack into our lives. It doesn't matter that we're talking about time and not food or money or a conscious, high-vibe dating pool. Lack vibes are lack vibes, which — when activated — create more lack across the board.

As for this perpetual time-shortage that hierarchy loves to lord over us, it simply isn't true. It's not like there exists a time bank where the affluent and the privileged store all the extra hours and years that those less fortunate souls haven't amassed. All any of us have is the present moment, and we hedge our bets on future present moments that may or may not come. How we choose to allot our present moments is exactly that — a *choice*.

I can choose to allot my time cleaning my house instead of playing tennis with a friend, but I certainly don't "have to" clean my house. Alas, when I say, "I don't have time to play tennis, because I have to clean my house," I am empowering the hierarchical construct by playing victim to an alleged time deficiency while attuning my frequency to that of lack, thus creating more lack in my life. Also, I'm lying.

Again, I refer us back to the visual reference of our three-tiered competitors' podium. When I say "I don't have time," I am placing myself on the tier beneath time, and affirming time's authority over me. Except that time does not, in and of itself, have any authority over me. Time only has authority over me when I choose to deny my own agency and hand over this erroneous authority of my own volition. When we choose to make ourselves time's proverbial bitch by languaging ourselves as subordinates to the present moments we are claiming to lack, we are — again — doing hierarchy's bidding for it by giving our power away to the (mis)perceived superiority of time.

On the flipside, when I take my power back from time and language my choices as to how to allot my temporal increments as exactly that — *choices* — then I am aligning myself with the frequency of empowerment; I am strengthening those frequency bands and those neural networks, while directing reality to configure according to the frequency of empowerment.

The ubiquitous uttering, thinking and inking of "I don't have time" is a self-sabotaging practice in disempowerment. Every time we say, "I don't have time," we disempower ourselves and strengthen those aforementioned frequency bands, grooves and neural networks. And every time we language our time allotments as choices by utilizing phrases such as, "I'm already scheduled. How about we do it next Thursday?" we are affirming that we are empowered beings with agency over our lives and our present moments and attuning our frequencies to those of empowerment, agency and choice.

The Power of Choice

When I take my power back from time by languaging my present moment allotments as *choices*, I am sidestepping the hierarchical trap and removing my consent from the control matrix. I am rescinding my endorsement of hierarchy by choosing not to language my reality according to status or to the illusion of any kind of external authority acting upon me.

Languaging my time allotments — and *all* my behaviors and actions — as choices evens out the status imbalance that is hierarchy, placing us all on an even playing field: me, you, time, money, our tasks, to-dos and commitments, along with every other human on the planet.

Betterarchical Upgrades for "I Don't Have Time"

"I'm already scheduled."

"My schedule is full."

"I've already allotted my bandwidth units elsewhere."

"That doesn't work for me. How about _____ [insert alternative here]?"

"I'm not feeling aligned with that. How about _____ [insert alternative here]?"

LIMITATION LANGUAGING

Limitation languaging functions to impose imaginary external authority upon us. It programs us to deny our power, to give away our power and to surrender our power to so many lackluster status quos, as well as to sucky, suffocating, contracted situations we'd really rather not endure, but over which we (have been programmed to) believe — consciously or unconsciously — we have no choice.

Alas, limitation languaging isn't just about words and phrases that allow us to defer to external authority. Limitation languaging aims to squelch potential and possibility in its unspoken devotion to fallacies like "impossible," while enabling/pandering to underdeveloped imaginations.

The matrix is clever this way. It doesn't even need to impose limitations upon us by way of its false authority when we, ourselves, ~~are~~ have been doing its bidding for it all day, every day, by way of our unconscious languaging patterns. And so it is that the swiftest, easiest way for us to liberate ourselves from these ersatz limitations is to eradicate them from our lexicon altogether.

The Limiting "Can't"

While we've already covered the victim vibes embedded in this little contraction, "can't" is a world-class multi-tasker that functions to disempower us on multiple levels. And so it is that I am including it here, so that we can examine how it operates as a tool of limitation.

Because words have multiple meanings and functions, there are indeed exceptions to some of these betterarchical precepts. As such, there are instances wherein the word "can't" is totally appropriate, as in "I can't fly that helicopter."

This is a germane use of the word "can't," when we consider that I haven't taken any lessons, and I know nothing about how the vehicle operates.

In this case, "can't" is not a distortion of hierarchy, nor is it a means of disempowering myself. It's simply a fact.

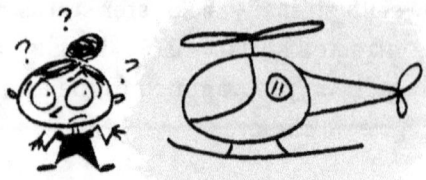

"Can't," as in "I'm not comfortable"

Except what if I actually *can* fly that helicopter, but my pilot's license has expired? Would it be accurate to say, "I can't fly that helicopter," then? Heck, no! Because I absolutely *can* fly that helicopter; I'd simply rather not get into any hot water with the FAA over the whole license situation. So, it's not that "I can't fly that helicopter"; it's that "I am *choosing* not to pilot that helicopter, because I don't feel comfortable flying with an expired license."

Do you feel the difference between these two statements? In taking responsibility for my feelings and my choices, I am not giving away my agency to the situation, or the FAA, or the powers that were, or hierarchy. I am maintaining my sovereignty while still operating within the parameters that feel most aligned for me. I am asserting my choice to adhere to standard industry rules, instead of claiming that I have no choice and that I am a victim to the limits being imposed upon me.

"Can't, Yet"

Let's look at another variation of "can't," wherein flying a helicopter is a dream of mine and a goal I hold for myself. In this instance, articulating the statement, "I can't fly that helicopter" is not actually an empowered, betterarchical languaging choice, because in denying my ability to fly the helicopter, I am pushing the skills and knowledge necessary to do so even farther away from me than they already are. I am limiting myself.

In this instance, it is infinitely more empowering to speak to the mastery I am calling in by saying, "I look forward to being able to fly that helicopter," or "I am still learning to fly," or "I am excited to fly that helicopter next August."

When languaging goals and visions, we are wise to eschew the urge to affirm perceived limitations and to speak instead to the skills, mastery and competence we are cultivating and calling in. Empowered, betterarchical reality creators frame reality in terms of the skills, mastery and competence we are fostering, instead of pushing them away with language that limits us.

This applies, not just for the "can'ts" employed to limit ourselves, but for those we may erroneously/unconsciously project upon others. To impose limitations onto other folks is wrong-use-of-will and bad form, as the act is tantamount to cursing them. Let us resist the urge to project low-vibe voodoo onto others just because we, ourselves, are still relinquishing fallacies of "can't," and instead gift them our faith and our trust in their own omniscopic experience.

Betterarchical Upgrades for the Limiting "Can't"

"excited to"
"look forward to"
"calling in"
"cultivating"
"learning"
"mastering"
"am getting better every day"

The Doubting "If"

"If" is a non-committal lollygagger of a word. "If" lounges upon the airy, cloud-perched fields of possibility, entertaining half-assed notions of this and that, while evading commitment and taking zero responsibility for the dreams, visions, plans and potential it's not really all that invested in actualizing.

"If" is an effective way of staving off realization, because "if" calls into question the likelihood of the realization of that which it is modifying. "If" is encoded with the frequencies of doubt and failure, thus seeding doubt and failure into the situations it's kinda, sorta thinking about possibly, maybe realizing.

Consider the following phrases:

"If my book gets published"
"If we raise enough money to fund the launch"
"If anyone signs up for my workshop"
"If we see each other again"
"If I get promoted"
"If humanity awakens to our multidimensional awesomeness"

Are you convinced that any of these things is actually going to happen? Because the speakers sure aren't. Where's the conviction? Where's the confidence? Where's the agency? In each of these instances, the speaker is giving away her power to an imaginary authority, or a string of theoretical circumstances that may arbitrarily allow the scenarios the corresponding "ifs" are modifying permission to be. Or not. *Whatevs.*

All these "ifs" are hanging out in an old paradigm forged of linear time, external authority and 3D disempowerment. Except we're not here to acquiesce to old-paradigm, linear lies, or to continue to feed an outdated status quo. We incarnated to help quantum leap our species and our world into multidimensional, co-creative awesomeness, which is why our courage is now being called upon to help language a betterarchical reality into being. Our task is to summon the chutzpah to claim the scenarios that "if" is too timid to declare. It is to language them in the definitive here and now, knowing that the coding in this here-and-now languaging is precisely the magic X-factor that "if" passively hopes will sweep in to render things so and that *will* materialize the visions in question.

Feel the difference between the "if" statements listed above, and the following upgrades:

"When my book gets published"
"As we raise enough money to fund the launch"
"As my workshop is filling quickly"
"When we see each other again"
"When I get promoted"
"As humanity awakens to their multidimensional awesomeness"

The upside of "when," utilized as a replacement for "if," is that it confidently claims how the future will configure itself, thus rendering it infinitely more likely that our tomorrows will follow suit. "When" transmits the frequencies of confidence and triumph, assured as it is in the scenarios it modifies.

Present > Future

While "when" is indeed an effective and appropriate upgrade for "if," it's still future-reliant. "When" describes what will happen in a coming tomorrow, while "as" collapses (the illusion of) time and brings the actualization and success of our visions into the present moment, thus accelerating our realization and aligning us with the frequencies of that which we are describing in the here and now.

"When" transmits the frequencies of stasis, hedging its bets on future-based forward motion, which — while certain — still allows for present-moment lollygagging. Modifying our actions with "when" heralds their absence in affirming that they are not here, now. "As" collapses this gap by transporting the actions it modifies into our present moment and moving us into the stated action, now.

Consider the following phrases:

"When I give up caffeine"
"When I clean out my closet"
"When I get into the practice of exercising every day"

While there is a certainty to the declaration, there is also a glaring gap between these claims and these nebulous, future-based moments wherein I will actually begin to execute the actions in question. These "whens" transmit the frequencies of present-moment *not*-doing, despite their alleged certitude.

Feel into the following betterarchical upgrades:

"As I am giving up caffeine"
"As I am cleaning out my closet"
"As I am exercising every day"

Do you feel the difference? "As" takes these future-based pledges and draws them into this now-moment. This collapsing of time eradicates any anticipation/commitment anxiety embedded in the "when"-statements above. Duly modified, these are no longer scary commitments looming in the future; they are tasks we are accomplishing in this now-moment. Languaged accordingly, we are infinitely more likely to follow through, as the subconscious mind is programmed to believe it is already doing, rather than waiting for that just-right moment to possibly, maybe begin to follow through.

Betterarchical Upgrades for "If"

"when"
"as"

"Impossible"

"Impossible" is a judgment we place on ideas, circumstances and experiences that may very well be possible. It's just that we, ourselves, have yet to tap into the possibility or to the *how* that activates it, and then we employ "impossible" as a means of projecting our ignorance and imaginal deficiencies onto whatever the word is modifying.

"Impossible" doubles as an absolute, as it alleges to ascribe a fixed "never gonna happen" notion onto what may be a very real possibility, attempting to shut every forever door on its manifestation by way of its fixed denial and contracted vision.

It wasn't all that long ago that we thought it was "impossible" to reach the top of Mt. Everest. To fly across an ocean. To run a mile in under 4 minutes. To tumble a triple somersault. To convince half of 21st century America that censorship and segregation are awesome. The powers that were go the distance to get us to forget that we are an ever-evolving species, consistently expanding the boundaries and obliterating the notions of what we had previously believed was — or was not — possible.

To project limitations like "impossible" upon situations our imaginations have yet to figure out how to sign onto is the ultimate in arrogance. It is to smear our imaginal deficiencies onto empirical reality and convince ourselves that our own personal limitations reflect objective truth. Alas, just because we haven't *yet* developed the capacity to imagine something, or haven't *yet* seen it accomplished doesn't necessarily mean it's "impossible."

Again, I remind us that we are an ever-evolving/expanding species, living in an ever-evolving/expanding reality construct, within an eternally evolving/expanding multiverse. As such, our wisest, most truthful and most supportive move is to language that which we have yet to conceive or witness as possibilities that have simply "yet" to manifest.

It's not that it's "impossible" to breathe under water; it's just that I haven't done it or heard of anyone else doing it, *yet*. It's not that it is "impossible" to bilocate; it's simply a phenomenon I'm *still learning* to execute. It's not "impossible" to fall in love with a jellyfish; it's just that I've *yet* to meet one that tickles my fancy.

The more possibilities we speak into our world and hold space for in our world, the more "impossibilities" we will accomplish and bear witness to. Ours is a reality forged of intention, vibration and belief. As we stop speaking "impossible" into our collective field, the more otherwise unimagined possibilities we begin to witness and experience. To this end, I encourage you to take a moment to imagine all the possibilities awaiting us once we remove the fallacy of "impossible" from our lexicon and our discourse.

Betterarchical Upgrades for "Impossible"

"haven't yet"
"look forward to"
"haven't seen that"
"don't have a reference for"
"am excited to witness"

"Unlimited/Limitless"

The "un-/-less" sham is comparable to the "anti-" version, wherein we state a concept, invoke a frequency and then delude ourselves into thinking we haven't just stated what we've stated or invoked what we've invoked, because we tacked on a little prefix or suffix that tells us we didn't.

Except we did. And every creative force in the multiverse knows that we did.

While there are myriad erroneous applications of the "un-/-less" scam, let's narrow our examination to the words "unlimited" and "limitless," which allege to remove limitations from the conversation at hand by invoking the frequencies of limitation in their uttering and then purporting to cancel them out with the linguistic circle/slash that is "un-" or "-less."

It's one of the larger meta scams those engineering the language have — to date — pulled upon the populace, because it alleges to eradicate any and all notions of omniscopic possibility, instead tethering us to a realm hampered by every which way limitation.

"Omniscopic"

And so it is that our liberation lies in novelty, in our choice to claim our sovereign authority to continue to build the lexicon by creating new words to help liberate humanity from illusions of limitation and whatever else is alleging to hold us back.

I encourage us to utilize "omniscopic" as a means of replacing the contractive, limitation frequencies necessarily embedded in the words "unlimited" and "limitless" as a means of liberating ourselves and our species from fallacies of limitation. Duly untethered from these energies, I am excited to see what humanity accomplishes and what otherwise mislabeled limitations are shattered in the face of the mass unshackling the lexicon upgrade portends.

Betterarchical Upgrade for "Unlimited/Limitless"

"omniscopic"

FEAR

Hierarchy goes the distance to keep us focused on doom, gloom and terror — on worst-case scenarios and a perpetual stream of apocalyptic possibilities they loudly and consistently proclaim are threatening our safety, survival and freedom. That's why our media is flooded with the stuff. The news is a veritable 24/7 barrage of war, crime, murder, disease, disruption and climate crisis. Hollywood is no better, putting out evermore graphic, violent and disturbing programming that's seeped its way into pop music, gaming and "activism."

But it's not just apocalyptic news cycles or entertainment; it's also the advertising industry, which loves to tell us about all the horrible things we're definitely in for — be it wrinkles, rashes, rape, cellulite, cancer, bankruptcy, loneliness or what have you — *unless* we buy Product or Service X or vote for Policy or Candidate Y, that is.

Here's how it works: The social engineers shilling for the matrix collaborate closely with the mainstream media machine to generate an incessant stream of programming and propaganda intended to keep the populace in a near-constant state of amygdala hijack. When the amygdala registers fear, it sends a flurry of hormones into the bloodstream. These hormones disrupt our immune systems and our emotional regulatory systems, as well as our perceptions of reality. As rational brain functions are dialed down, emotional reactivity is dialed up. Negative input is emphasized. Perceived threats become bigger and more menacing than they really are. The world becomes distorted, as through a fun house mirror, rendering us infinitely easier to manipulate and control. Duly drenched in fear hormones, we willingly give away our power, while reaching for hierarchy's ever-expanding array of hook-laden life rafts, which wouldn't appeal to us were our systems not flooded with cortisol and our minds not programmed by an incessant barrage of worst-case scenarios.

Some examples I scrounged from a handful of real-deal "news" headlines:

> *Look Out West Coast, Here Comes Meat Allergy Tick*
> *There's Another Woman Waiting for Every Man. Including Yours.*
> *Neo-Nazi Opens Fire on Local Pre-School. Is Your Child Next?*
> *If Roe is Overturned, Women Will Die*
> *Climate Crisis Points to Imminent Economic Collapse. Recovery Unlikely.*
> *These Are the Ticking Time Bombs of US Infrastructure*

The through line coming out of all this fearmongering, across all the industries flooding the media space with the stuff, is the definitive languaging bolstering these ideas. The framing is intended to eradicate any notions of potential or possibility, instead seeking to establish these narratives as unequivocal facts. It's standard issue propaganda/mass manipulation, as the matrix machine consistently projects worst-case scenarios presented as inevitabilities, which are stated often and repeatedly, and thus programmed into the collective consciousness as unavoidable catastrophes that will positively — for surely — happen, and ruin everything.

But not to worry, little plebes, because hierarchy has our every solution — be it a cream, a salve, an app, a meme, a gadget, a prescription, a payment plan, an insurance policy, an ideology, an emergency order or a stimulus check — which just so happens to be the only thing we can really lean on as this inevitable emergency, disaster or atrocity unfolds and threatens our safety, existence and the world as we know it.

THE LANGUAGE OF FEAR

Fear is future-based. Fear is about what may or may not happen at a point that has yet to materialize. It's also generative, which means the more fear we effectuate, the more likelihood there is of these potential bummer futures manifesting. This means that when we feel fear and we think and loop and speak and transmit fear, we abandon the present moment, while programming our realities with the very scenarios whose potential manifestation is causing our distress.

The language of fear is marked by future-based projections, which are often framed with definitive languaging that denies other possibilities and outcomes. When it comes to transmuting the language of fear, notice the inclination to frame possibilities as inevitabilities. Notice how you feel after watching the news or that latest dystopian blockbuster or the new season of that Nazi werewolf series. Unless you genuinely dig the feeling of cortisol flooding your bloodstream, compromising your immune system and chipping away at your physiological/psycho-emotional integrity, I recommend stepping away from the kinds of media that inspire these feelings, while creating boundaries around relationship dynamics steeped in these vibrations (aka: that friend who is always talking about that horrific thing her favorite social media influencer told her is going to happen).

When dealing with fear, we are well served by the practice of reframing the situation in question in terms of solutions and best-case scenarios, while rooting ourselves in radical presence. Because fear is future-based, it's really slippery territory when it comes to reality creation. The more life and legitimacy we give to future-projected bummer scenarios, the more likely they are to manifest.

Some fear languaging to steer clear of...

"Worry"

Worrying is — essentially — praying for what we don't want. When we worry, we give life to unpleasant scenarios by way of our attention and our emotions. The act of worrying only empowers the circumstances we don't want to manifest, thus increasing our likelihood of manifesting them.

The Erroneous "Worry"

Oftentimes, the frequencies of worry are tossed into our collective communications by default, given how frequently this word is misused. For example, my yoga teacher is fond of offering instructions along the lines of, "You don't need to worry about how high your leg is; just worry about how steady you're breathing." It's maddening, as I witness him — class after class — programming his students to worry.

The English word "worry" comes from the Middle English "to strangle" — hardly an action we want connected to our breath or our *anything*. Today it is translated to mean, "to cause mental distress, anxiety and trouble." Again, not a practice that serves our highest joy and wellbeing.

You don't have to take his instructions so literally, I can hear some folks protest, while completely discounting the role the subconscious mind plays in organizing our realities. Because, of course, we all understand what my yoga teacher means. His "worry" spiel is just his cheeky way of urging his students to focus our attention on our breath. We know he isn't intentionally encouraging us to cultivate a state of mental anxiety.

Still, the subconscious mind is having a very different experience. The subconscious mind doesn't translate, doesn't infer, doesn't adjust for nuance, sarcasm or metaphor. It's literal *af*. So, while his students aren't likely *consciously* tripping on their breathing patterns, the instructions are still being received by the subconscious mind, which most certainly is.

The frequencies encoded in this word — *choke, strangle, mindfuck, freak-out* — are absolutely distorting the experience and creating disruptions in the body-mind, which would otherwise be avoided by simply replacing the word "worry" with the instructions "focus on," or "direct your attention to," or any number of options that are infinitely more precise, while far less sabotagey.

The Ruminating "Worry"

Like most words, "worry" has multiple meanings and applications. And while my yoga teacher has been in the practice of (mis)using it to guide his students to direct their attention in specific ways, plenty of folks use it as a means of mindfucking themselves into contracted states of fear, panic and overwhelm.

The human mind is tricky, sticky territory, vulnerable as it is to looping on thoughts that aren't serving our joy, health, wellbeing or sanity, and that may or may not even be our own. And so it is that a whole big bunch of us have fallen into the deleterious habit of worrying, as in causing ourselves "mental distress, anxiety and trouble," by way of runaway thought patterns that function to make us miserable, while programming reality to configure in the exact ways we don't want it to.

From this perspective, we empowered, betterarchical reality creators are wise to eschew both the word "worry," as well as the practice of looping on fears and worst-case scenarios themselves, while cultivating mindfulness and redirecting our attention towards the outcomes we would prefer to experience.

Betterarchical Upgrades for "Worry"

The erroneous version:
"focus on"
"point your attention to"
"be mindful of"

The ruminating variety:
"creating a story"
"noticing some concerns/anxiety"
"honing in on solutions for"
"inviting solutions/pivots for"

"Afraid"

Much like its trouble-maker buddies "worry" and "argue," "afraid" is fallaciously tossed about in casual (and not so casual) conversations, where it inadvertently smears its sticky fear vibes all over our exchanges and our world at large.

"I'm afraid we're fully booked, ma'am," says the front desk attendant at my favorite hot spring.

"I'm afraid the chef doesn't do substitutions," the waiter tells me, denying my request to hold the cheese and the nightshades and to replace the chicken with tempeh.

Except, neither case is cause for fear. Unless we're talking about the speakers' implied fear of the customers freaking out because their requests are being denied. In both instances, the speakers are employing the word "afraid" as a means of softening the negations and inferring something akin to regret for being the bearer of bad news. Fair enough. But there are more precise words that can be employed here — words that don't perv the exchange or the morphic field with unnecessary fear vibes, like "I regret to inform you," which — while formal and fussy-sounding — is infinitely more accurate in both of these contexts.

"I'm afraid ski season has already passed," says the travel agent to the eager downhill enthusiast.

A pattern is emerging, yes? It seems that the erroneous "afraid" is often employed when one delivers news that might disappoint the person he is addressing. And so, to a certain extent, the phrase is technically correct, in a codependent, *Please don't be mad at me* kind of way.

Still, given what we know about reality creation and how words function to program the subconscious mind and the morphic field, do we really want to go smearing fear atop otherwise neutral exchanges when there's no real threat involved? When we're not actually navigating cortisol surges or amygdala activations? When we can just hold the people we are addressing in the light of their self-responsible emotional intelligence and trust that they can handle a little disappointment without completely losing their shit?

"I'm afraid we'll never know how the Egyptians built the pyramids," the archeology professor tells her students.

Except the professor isn't afraid at all. The professor is *disappointed* and possibly even *frustrated*. But fear is not an appropriate emotional response to the mystery she is communicating. Alas, the subconscious mind isn't hip to the mis-use, and so it goes about responding to the command, "I'm afraid," and thus directing reality and the professor's physiology, accordingly.

It happens on subtle levels, and likely, isn't anything of which we are consciously aware as it is occurring. Still, it *is* occurring. The fear vibes being transmitted through this oft-misused word program flood our reality construct with fear, while normalizing the state itself, such that it quietly morphs into our default setting.

In case you have any doubt as to just how deleterious erroneous fear languaging can be to a culture when it comes to normalizing the fear state, I invite you to consider every person you see wearing a mask while alone in their car.

Fear language creates a reality construct forged of fear, which is why I am inviting you and me and all of us to switch it up, and ditch the fear and the "afraid" and the all of it.

Betterarchical Upgrades for "Afraid"

The extraneous "afraid" is a throw-away lead-in, and so our move, as betterarchical badass reality creators, is less about attuning to any specific betterarchical upgrades, than it is about letting go of fear altogether. The erroneous "afraid" adds nothing to the communication in question, while perving the reality creation mechanisms that will take its careless misuse as instructions. Our most empowered move is to ditch the faulty "afraid" altogether, and to own our statements without this otherwise unconscious, co-dependent crutch.

"Terribly"

I have a friend who is in the habit of using "terribly" to modify otherwise benign statements, as in, "I wasn't terribly impressed by his dancing," or "I didn't think the pakoras were terribly tasty."

Obviously, he is using the word to mean "to a great extent," which — upon flipping through my ancient, oversized, unabridged dictionary — is a valid definition for the word. Still, every time he says it, I am acutely aware of the *terrible* coding he is activating in the morphic field, as well as our shared dynamic.

Clear, cancel, delete, I think, when this judgy-pants adverb slips through his lips, as I'm not signing onto the activation of any terrible vibes in my reality construct.

When we dive into the etymology, "terribly" originated in the mid-15th century, when it was coined to mean "dreadfully, so as to cause terror, in a horrible manner."

Can we take a moment to let that sink in? Because "terribly" — in its most raw, roots form — doesn't *just mean* "dreadfully," and doesn't *just* hold the intention of "causing terror," but it does both "in a horrible manner." It's like extreme fear jacked up on some sort of hyper-concentrated, liquid rabies supplement. As if the intention of *causing terror* isn't freaky enough, it's being executed by way of the frequencies of horror. Personally, I'm amazed those 15th century linguists could squeeze so much fear into a single adverb. Respect. And still: no, thank you.

It's colorful, and it's not linguistically inaccurate, given that "extremely; very much; to a great extent" are included among "terribly's" modern-day definitions. Still, knowing what we now know about its roots and all the dreadful horror embedded therein, is it really our wisest move to continue to employ this adverb in this manner?

Free will rocks, so I leave it to each of us to decide for ourselves, while encouraging us to dial down the fear when it comes to that whole reality seeding function our every word is performing.

Betterarchical Upgrades for "Terribly"

"very"
"all that"
"super"
"massively"
"notably"

Absolutes: The Fear-Mongering Kind

As we established in our *Fixity* chapter, *absolutes* function as sweeping generalizations that program our futures with experiences from the past. This is fine and dandy when we're seeding our future nows with wonderfulness we are excited to manifest. But when it comes to sucky bummer scenarios, absolutes are not our friend.

Absolutes allege to guarantee the outcomes and experiences they modify. This can be fortuitous when the outcomes and experiences they modify are positive, such as: "I always have more than enough money," or "I am never going to forget how blessed I am to have full use of my senses, limbs and neurological faculties." But when these linguistic tools are used to modify scenarios that generate fear or other negative emotions, they function as curses, and are thus wise to eschew.

Take the following examples:

"I never have enough money to pay my rent AND my cell phone bill at the end of the month."

"Politicians always lie."

"You'll never find a job with that attitude."

"I always date sociopaths."

"We're never going to solve the Israel/Palestine conflict."

"My hair always falls out when I get stressed."[54]

None of these absolutes are accurate assessments of what *is*; rather they are projections scavenged from the past, balled up into giant, sweeping assessments of our limited experience, and then twisted into crummy, bummer commands we are giving the universal reality creation mechanisms

---

54 Author's note: My sincere apologies for this barrage of crumminess. Thank you for shaking it off in service to the lesson at hand.

that craft our nows and our futures. They are instructions that say, *Hey, Universe. You know that thing that's happened a few times in the past, or maybe even only once? Yeah, keep doing that. Perpetuate that pattern, exactly as it is FOREVER.*

I don't know about you, but when I'm on the receiving end of an absolute that alleges to curse my future with repetitive suckiness, I contract, while fearing and resisting said future scenarios. It bodes supremely unwell for reality creation, because why bother showing up in my fully empowered awesomeness for a future that's clearly going to blow?

When referencing less-than-stellar situations or experiences, we are wise to put them behind us by languaging them in the past, where they belong. This means pulling back on the urge to exaggerate the experiences we are describing with absolutes that invoke eternal repetition, while languaging them in such a way that allows space for a different experience in our ever-unfolding futures.

With this in mind, I've taken it upon myself to rewrite our fear-infused absolutes/curses as follows:

"I look forward to having more than enough money to easily pay both my rent and my cell phone bill at the end of every month."

"Historically, politicians have been prone to lying."

"Perhaps an attitude adjustment would make it easier to find a nanny gig."

"While I've dated a handful of sociopaths in the past, I am availing myself to a new type."

"It's going to take some next-level creativity to solve the Israel/Palestine conflict."

"I used to lose my hair when I was stressed out."

Betterarchical Upgrades for Fear-Mongering Absolutes

The betterarchical upgrade remains the same for our every absolute varietal: employ precise languaging that allows our past experiences to remain in the past, where they rightfully belong, while being brave and choosing to language the change we are calling in, instead of languishing in experiences we would prefer not to re-experience.

Disasterbation

Disasterbation is the act of looping on worst-case scenarios, thus programming our morphic field with the most horrific possibilities we can imagine. The vast majority of media being put out these days — either as "news" or entertainment — functions as disasterbation.

Disasterbating takes one of several (if not infinite) potentials and blows it up to epic proportions, while presenting it as an inevitable likelihood, playing it out to its various extremes and looping on, or repeating the idea, over and over and over again.

The media does this by taking vague, far-fetched or erroneous statistical possibilities (compiled by a handful of academic institutions controlled by the very same groups) and projecting them onto our collective future as conclusive catastrophic nightmares that will absolutely, positively come true — unless we adhere to their dictates, that is. It's a control strategy that works astonishingly well, and has convinced the populace — time and time again — to surrender their civil liberties (as well as their critical thinking capacities) in exchange for "protection" from so many nebulous, big, bad boogie men in the guise of terrorists, pathogens and extreme weather.

Disasterbation tells us we are barreling towards extinction on a swiftly dying planet, whose resources are depleting at a breakneck pace. Disasterbation tells us that we, humans, are a blight upon the Earth and are ruining everything — yes, everything.

Disasterbation is the mechanism that obsesses on that mole on our chest and tells us that it is definitely, *for surely* cancerous, and has probably metastasized, and that we should get our estate in order, given that we will likely be dead by spring.

Disasterbation has us certain that the whole of humanity will be injected with murder and surveillance technology, duly microchipped and enslaved, as meat, free speech and petroleum-powered cars are outlawed, transforming us into a society of mind-controlled, transhumanist slaves subsisting on a steady diet of bugs, lab-grown meat-like products and fear.

There's a certain kind of cultural caché that comes along with disasterbating. It's pure ego, and still, it's there. Disasterbation is a way of telling others: *I'm informed. I know what's going on, and I know what's going to happen, and trust me, it's going to be terrible!* These inferred proclamations garner gasps, furrowed brows and freak-outs, along with wide-eyed looks of disbelief, which feed the disasterbater, in an energetically vampiric kind of way.

There are no betterarchical languaging upgrades for disasterbating. It's simply a matter of resisting the urge to allow our minds to run wild in these realms or to feed off the attention and the reactions this kind of cataclysmic showboating can garner. Talking about creepy shit we don't want to happen is a great way of directing reality to configure in the shape of creepy shit we don't want to happen.

Let us be mindful of the stories we are telling and the realities upon which we are looping. By the same token, let us be discerning when it comes to what kind of programming we allow into our consciousnesses — be it by way of conversations shared with friends or information we digest through our screens. Instead of disasterbating, we are wiser to turn our attention onto solutions, best case scenarios and optimal outcomes, and — if we're going to ruminate on anything — ruminate on those. Our collective reality construct thanks you for your service.

STATUS

As we've already learned, hierarchy is, by definition, fundamentally steeped in status. Status is the very basis of the entire structure, which organizes people, elements and groups according to rank — each one either higher or lower in status than the other.

This organizational strategy, which serves to foment mistrust, resentment, inequality and disempowerment, is embedded in our language, which has us — as language exchangers — inadvertently doing hierarchy's bidding for it.

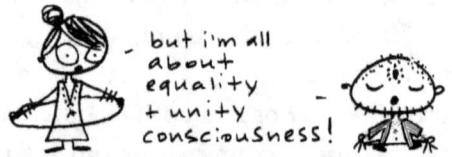

And, while we may claim commitment to equality and inclusion, as far as how our values align, the fact remains that our language is verily lousy with hierarchy and all the lack, limitation and separation coding that comes along with it. Unless we illuminate the hierarchical programs infusing our language and make a concerted effort to change our communication patterns, we are all complicit in hierarchy's detrimental effects on society and humanity at large, because we are the ones enabling it with our words.

Remember, the subconscious mind is ever and always listening and responding to our directives, even when the conscious mind is doing its darndest to adjust for tone, context, metaphor and intention. So, when we are on the receiving end of hierarchical languaging that alleges status, the brain releases hormones that signal danger, alerting our bodies to the (perceived) peril of the (alleged) enemy that is (supposedly) threatening our survival and/or challenging our sovereign authority.

It's an ineffective communication strategy, given that status-based languaging inspires contraction, putting those we are addressing on the defensive, while inspiring a host of negative emotions, reactions and implications in the process.

STATUS-SPEAK

When we speak status, we effectively claim the superior/inferior position, placing those we are addressing/referencing onto the opposing pole, whether by default or intention. Unconscious though this communication pattern so often is, it seeds subliminal power dynamics into our relationships, thus inspiring opposition and defensiveness, while creating more dissonance, resentment and separation amongst our human family.

I see this a lot in my consulting practice, wherein I guide organizations to up-level their communications culture in service to greater efficiency, impact, innovation and profit. Oftentimes, leadership will push back on invitations to avoid status-based, hierarchical languaging, while doubling down on their ranks within the organization. Alas, just because someone is operating in a "higher" position within a hierarchical structure doesn't meant that speaking to and from these differentials in status is going to be *effective* in terms of generating optimal performance or cultivating team morale. In fact, the results are usually the polar opposite, functioning to cultivate feelings of resentment and ill will amongst those serving in positions deemed "lower" on the hierarchical totem pole.

We explored this in Part 1, wherein I referenced my own struggle to understand organic hierarchy versus the artificially imposed version. Hierarchies exist; there's no getting around that. Still, exacerbating organic status delineations with communication patterns that impose and emphasize power differentials is a surefire way to shut folks down and piss them way off, while fomenting all the negative emotions and consequences associated with hierarchy.

Let's take a look at some examples of the ways hierarchy seeps into our everyday language by way of words encoded with status, shall we?

"Just"

"Just" is a master multi-tasker, meaning any number of things, from "honorable and fair in one's dealings," to "precisely, exactly," and even "just now" or "very soon." When employed in any of these capacities, "just" is both benign and appropriate, as in:

Q: "Will you please feed the cat?"
A: "I *just* did."

Or:

"I agree that the choice to expel Molly was a *just* decision, given that she set the gymnasium on fire."

Still, there are the oodles of instances wherein we unconsciously employ "just" as a preemptive strategy to avoid potential conflict and ingratiate ourselves onto another's good side, thereby diminishing ourselves and placing ourselves in a lower status position than the person or entity we are addressing. Because "just" — master multi-tasker that it is — is also defined as "only, or simply."

Imagine a dog that has *just* been caught chewing up your favorite cashmere sweater. She cowers as you reprimand her: head down, tail between her legs, as her little doggie brain rationalizes that if she looks small and pathetic, then you won't be quite as angry with her. This behavior is the equivalent of using the word "just" to make ourselves smaller and less intimidating.

"Jimmy, this stew is amazing!"
"Oh, it's just a leftover mash-up."

"Your movie is brilliant!"
"I was just the production designer."

"What do you do for work, Emma?"
"I'm just a waitress."

When we utilize "just" to diminish our efforts, our value, our rank or our importance, we willingly place ourselves on a lower rung of the hierarchical tier. As far as social acceptance strategies go, "just" is low-hanging fruit. It may seem harmless, but when employed in this manner, this linguistic tic is as degenerative as it is masochistic, functioning to erode our confidence as well as our sense of Self.

Every time we use "just" to claim lower status — whether we are doing it consciously or unconsciously — we shrink. We disempower ourselves. We diminish our worth, and we allow ourselves to be less-than. The kicker is that it's not just self-defeating sabotage; it's selfishness.

When we make ourselves small, we withhold our light and shroud our gifts from the world. The last thing this world needs is more disempowered people willingly taking short shrift. The world is not well-served by anyone playing small, meek, weak or powerless. The world needs our greatness. How do you think we're going to turn this Earth ship of ours around? By playing small? By cowering in that proverbial corner, shirking our gifts, and our talents, and our light, so as not to offend anyone? Please. The world needs us shining big, and bold, and bright, owning our gifts and embodying our genius. When we hold back, and dim our light, and shrink to fit in, we are dropping the ball on our responsibility as custodians of this beautiful planet that is all of ours to mind and manage.

Betterarchical Upgrades for "Just"

Ditch 'em.[55]

---

55 See also: "only."

"JUST": AN INVITATION TO UP-LEVEL OUR RECEIVING ABILITIES

Take another look at those first two "just" examples above. Notice how the word isn't just functioning as a means of making ourselves small; it's also serving to push away the compliments being offered.

This is yet another expression of the Masculine/Feminine imbalance the language of betterarchy is swiftly redressing. Remember, the Masculine gives, and the Feminine receives. This is one of the primary delineations between the two polarities. Think of Lakshmi, Green Tara, or your favorite Asian goddess. These iconic images consistently feature a beatific woman sitting in meditative repose, with one of her palms open and facing upwards, in the universal symbol of receiving.

Receiving is a quintessentially Feminine undertaking, one that we in the West have (historically) sucked at. Part of the Masculine/Feminine imbalance that has shaped our culture places undue emphasis on giving, doing and hustling, while placing little value on the practice of receiving, which is why so many of us are now being called to strengthen that muscle and increase our competency here.

To this end, let us be mindful of the "justs" peppering our lexicon, and take note when we are using them to push away compliments, and to dodge the opportunity to flex our receiving muscles. And then let's switch it up. Up-leveling our receiving competency is a crucial step in bringing our Masculine/Feminine polarities into balance, as well as attuning us to the frequencies of abundance, thus allowing us to benefit from the infinite blessings the multiverse is jonesing to bestow upon us.

"But"

For anyone who's dipped a toe into the wily world of improv comedy, we know that "Yes, and..." is the cardinal precept of the artform. The principle requires all improvisors to accept their fellow players' ideas and choices, and to roll with them, instead of contracting and rejecting them with the opposite polarity, "No, but..."

"But" invalidates the idea(s) that came before it, putting an abrupt halt to the creative process. As well, "but" unconsciously claims superior validity, relevance and status, verily deriding the ideas it opposes. There is nothing *not* hierarchical about "but," as its very function is to step on top of whatever it follows/denies, allowing the idea with which it is allied to claw its way to the rung above it.

Not only does "but" invalidate the ideas that precede it, it negates them. When my gymnastics coach says, "Your dismount was beautiful, but the landing really needs some work," the subconscious mind dismisses the compliment, while placing its focus on the critique. I will have little to no recollection of the praise I was given for the dismount, while overemphasizing the feedback about the landing. This isn't me being oversensitive or hard on myself; this is how the word "but" programs the subconscious mind.

Our BFF "And"

As the conjunction's polar opposite, "and" makes for a consistently effective "but" upgrade. Whereas "but" discounts and separates, "and" acknowledges and includes. Still, sometimes replacing "but" with "and" can be a bit awkward, because while we are offering an alternative to something, we are introducing this alternative with a word that has historically been used to suggest agreement. To this end, I find it supremely effective to add a little extra enunciative *oomph* to the "and"-as-"but" alternative, which goes a long way in service to clear communication, as in, "Your dismount was beautiful, **and** the landing could use some work."

When replacing the dismissive "but," I recommend leaning into words that acknowledge and include, thus creating space for the ideas preceding it to coexist with those that follow. While the shadowy Masculine "but" divides and dismisses, "and" — along with "still" and "yet" — expand the landscape, carving out Feminine spaciousness for coexistence and multiplicity.

Betterarchical Upgrades for "But"

"and"
"still"
"yet"

"Sorry"

"Sorry" is a recklessly misused word, often blurted compulsively, unnecessarily and inappropriately, when the person doing the uttering is startled, caught off guard or — yet, again — laying claim to lower status as an unconscious social strategy. This word, once employed as an apology, is now offered as a way of preemptively avoiding conflict, thus performing double duty as both disempowering shrinking mechanism and global sorrow-smearer.

"Sorry" is derived from Middle English, meaning "full of sorrow." So, when I exit the public restroom at my favorite café, only to see two people standing in the hallway, waiting to use the facilities, and I chirp "Sorry!" — even though I've done nothing wrong, and owe no one my sorrow — I am nevertheless activating the frequencies of sorrow in the field, verily sprinkling the stuff all over the sneakers of the people waiting to use the bathroom, as well as the entire planet.

Beyond smearing our world in the frequencies of sorrow, the misused "sorry" takes any and all mojo out of the appropriately utilized, apologetic version. If I say "sorry" when asking the cashier if she can break a hundred, then does the "sorry" I offer after dropping an insensitive comment and hurting a friend's feelings really mean anything? I clearly don't know what the word signifies when I so readily hurl it, willy-nilly-like, to establish my non-threatening nature while fueling hierarchy, instead of consciously employing it as a means of acknowledging and taking responsibility for the consequences of my actions.

"Sorry" = Acknowledgment Technology

Despite its deleterious coding, "sorry" is primarily employed as a means of acknowledgement. Whether used erroneously or appropriately, our every "sorry" aims to acknowledge a hurt, a hold-up, an inconvenience or a disappointment. It is to say, *I am aware that this happened, and I wish you no ill-will or undue suffering because of this thing that happened.*

Still, when it comes to acknowledging, we have plenty of other options. My personal favorite is to replace the hierarchical "sorry" with "thank you," as in, "Thank you for your patience in receiving my response," when there is a lag in my email reply; or "Thank you for giving me an opportunity to see where I can refine my communication," instead of "Sorry I was so bitchy" or "Thank you for your listening," instead of "Sorry I keep blathering on about this."

One of my coaching clients was born and raised in Russia and is still transmuting some lingering self-consciousness about his English language skills. Whereas he used to begin his email communications with an apology (e.g., *Sorry if my English is not up to speed. It is not my first language),* he has now embraced the upgrade: *Thank you for your understanding in reading my words, as I am still mastering English as a second language.*

And then there are the times when it's not about us or the inconveniences for which we perceive ourselves responsible; it's about the discomfort we — as compassionate beings — witness others enduring. In those instances, we are wise to communicate our understanding and empathy without taking responsibility for the discomfort or adding unnecessary sorrow to the situation.

So, instead of saying, "I'm sorry you broke your arm," I say, "Bone breaks suck. Are you in pain? Is there anything I can do to support you while you're healing?"

Similarly, I'm not in the practice of apologizing when folks die. I don't offer the standard issue, "I'm sorry you lost your uncle"-spiel. Instead, I say something along the lines of, "Letting go of our loved ones is so painful. How did he die? What did you love most about him?" Rather than spreading more sorrow atop an already sucky situation, I offer a clear indication of my empathy and understanding, while stepping *into* the experience with whomever is dealing with the hardship, instead of offering a stock, scripted, sorrow-smeared response.

Again, this is not to dissuade the genuine, appropriate apology. It is to invite us to examine our own unique relationship with this word and to start to observe when and how we use it. And in those moments when we hone in on an inappropriate or status-laden "sorry," to quickly clear the field with "Clear, cancel, delete," and then go about switching it up.

Betterarchical Upgrades for "Sorry"

"Thank you"
"Surprise!"
"That just happened!"
"My apologies" (when authentically appropriate)

"Privilege"

The word "privilege" has taken on a particularly polarizing position in the collective lexicon, as it is currently being hurled at folks for such egregious atrocities as being born with penises, functioning limbs, heteronormative inclinations and (perceived) melanin deficiencies.

Shaming and berating people for their perceived/projected "privilege" is violent, sadistic and pointless. All it does is legitimize and empower the very system that is doing the privileging. It reinforces inequality by naming and claiming the perceived/projected inequality, while sustaining the issues it alleges to call out, and seeding more of them into our future.

Let's take a moment to define what "privilege" actually means, given that the word has been so weaponized, and has become so dangerously loaded that it now functions to project an epic array of programmed assumptions onto folks based on superficial optics that don't accurately speak to anyone's lived experience, only to the stereotypes we have been indoctrinated to hurl upon one another.

privilege, n.
"a right or benefit given to some people and not to others"

It's true that some folks are bestowed with benefits that others are not. Some folks are born into broken homes, while others incarnate into tightly bonded family units. Some inherit disabilities or neurological distortions, while others are blessed with exceptional gifts and talents. Plenty of folks endure a combination of these factors, as is the case with Stephen Hawkins, Vincent Van Gogh and Daniel Johnston, among countless others whose names we will likely never know. Some folks undergo traumatic experiences that will scar them for life, while others are blessed with safe, incident-free childhoods that allow them to preserve their innocence and skate through their formative years without PTSD. Some are born into peaceful, resource-rich geographies, while others are born into impoverished, war-torn environments. Some folks benefit from family connections and esteemed bloodlines, while others are left to figure it out on their own, without these kinds of support structures already in place. When it comes to privilege, it's really a mixed bag.

Alas, the matrix has thoroughly mangled the true meaning of this word to now connote a reductive checklist of stereotypes and externalities that we have been manipulated into associating with a deeply unfair, unchecked advantage, which is now being mislabeled as "privilege." According to this paradigm, every person with white skin has more "privilege" than anyone with dark skin, just as anyone with a penis has more privilege than anyone with a vagina. This is supposed to apply even if the Black person was born into a loving family of wealth, and the "white" person was born to an abusive crack whore who sold him into child slavery when he was four; or if the male was born with a rare blood disease that forced him to endure several painful operations throughout the childhood he spent in isolation, while the female was born healthy and excelled at sports at an early age, ultimately earning a full ride to an ivy league university and two Division One championship titles.

Do you see how this word has been maligned and weaponized?

The cancel culture blood sport of hurling the word "privilege" only serves to direct our attention towards the perception of inequality or unfairness.[56] And for some, that's the point, as we have been lead to believe that there is value in compulsively calling out disparity. Alas, there is acknowledging, and there is wallowing. This is not to deny the legitimacy of the descriptive,[57] or the pain that hierarchy's trademark inequity foments. It is simply to explain how this word is functioning as a means of reality-creation technology, and to understand the frequencies it is seeding into the morphic field, as well as the minds of our fellow humans.

Acknowledgment happens in a moment. We illuminate a shadow. We slip off the blindfold, look at what we've done, take stock of how it's affected ourselves and others, acknowledge our responsibility, glean the lessons and move forward — all the wiser, more humble and integrated for the experience and the lessons it afforded us.

"Privilege" — as it's being wielded these days — is akin to a bludgeon, driving the oftentimes misguided and erroneous point home, again, and again, and again, and again, rendering the top tier higher and the lower tier lower, verily expanding the distance between the levels of hierarchy. It makes separation *separater* — moving us further and further away from each other.

Being positioned on a higher status rung than another doesn't mean that someone is bad, has done something wrong or is deserving of punishment/ societal disfavor. To judge someone for his position is to fuel the construct that is doing the positioning. Because that construct is reliant upon our distraction and our obsession with the task of blaming each other for the

---

56 Which only serves to sustain and exacerbate inequality and unfairness.
57 Except when it's completely unwarranted and thus merits denial.

THE LANGUAGE OF BETTERARCHY

inequities between us, which keeps us from addressing the actual problem, which is the meta-structural overlord that is manipulating the positioning and is trying to convince us that we need positions in the first place.

Labeling folks "privileged" is disempowering sour grapes. Not only does it do all of nothing to equalize the playing field, it puts down those folks who are being placed in the "unprivileged" category. When we hurl the "privilege" label, we place those who fall outside the boundaries of this classification on a lower tier of the hierarchical scale. In this way, the modern-day use of this word does the exact opposite of what those who wield it claim to intend.

Projecting "privilege" onto folks isn't just reductive and divisive, it is to maintain the very inequities we are claiming to critique. Only when we speak equality will we pave the way for an equal society. And, by "equal," I mean one forged of equal opportunity, not equality of outcome, which is an idealistic fairy tale incompatible with the natural order of life here on planet Earth.

There are no betterarchical languaging upgrades for "privilege" as the word is currently being wielded. Because it is not a matter of a better word or phrase; it's a matter of shifting the focus of our attention onto the empowerment and equality we are choosing to live into, instead of harping on the inequities that piss us off. To this end, we are wise to examine the urge to hurl the "privilege" label, and to instead turn our attention inwards, and to get real with the parts of ourselves that are feeling inadequate, or left out, or less-than, and to take responsibility, heal and integrate in service to our wholeness and our evolution.

YOU SAY YOU WANT
(A R)EVOLUTION

> *"You never change things by fighting the existing reality. To change something, build a new model that makes the existing model obsolete."*
> **— R. Buckminster Fuller**

Now that we understand some of the various ways that language functions, we can turn our attention towards utilizing it to transform, evolve and quantum leap our culture in every possible way.

For some, the idea of revamping our entire culture/planet from hierarchy to betterarchy may seem intimidating or overwhelming, if not downright impossible, what with all the moving parts, which are themselves being held in dysfunctional place by several centuries' worth of old paradigm entropy and control constructs. When we catalog all the systems clawing for an upgrade — justice, energy, finance, healthcare, infrastructure, education, academia, media, social services — it's easy to get overwhelmed, tap out and capitulate to our lackluster same ol' — same ol', thinking that widescale systemic renovation is simply too hard to pull off.

Except, this iteration of global (r)evolution is actually slated to be smooth, quick and graceful, provided enough of us get on the same page and start utilizing these evolutionary tools, consistently and tenaciously, on the sooner side of later (aka: now).

Global (R)Evolution: An Aquatic Metaphor

Let us consider the ocean — the Pacific, the Atlantic, the Indian, the Arctic — any ocean will do. Imagine that something toxic spills into said ocean — say, an offshore power plant springs a leak, and a whole big bunch of icky, sticky poison is now spilling into the water.

The contamination is affecting all the different species of marine life differently. The seahorses are depressed, the whales' gums are bleeding, the angler fish are experiencing vertigo, the flounders are gassy and bloated and the octopi are juggling joint pain and blotchy rashes.

Now, one way to deal with the situation is to attempt to treat each ocean creature individually, to call in a team of various specialists to treat each case of isolated symptoms, one-by-one. We bring in a periodontist for the whales and a psychedelic facilitator for the seahorses (because they didn't respond well to the SSRIs they were initially prescribed). We consult with a polarity therapist for the anglers, while putting the flounders on an anti-inflammatory diet, topped off with probiotics. We treat the octopi rashes topically with aloe and lavender, along with a full-spectrum CBD for their many aching protrusions.

Problem solved, right?

Nope. Not by a long shot.

Not only is this strategy costly and inefficient, it's ineffective, as the primary issue has neither been addressed, nor corrected. Because the primary issue has been duly sidestepped, the creatures' symptoms will persist, regardless of all their spendy, alternative, individualized treatments.

The smarter, swifter, more efficient way to solve the issue is to simply purify the water. Because the water is the meta structure in which every species of marine life is contained, as well as the actual *source* of the imbalance. If the water is out of balance, the beings immersed in it will necessarily embody and express those imbalances as well. Once the water has been purified, the animals' systems will naturally rebalance themselves, without needing their own individual treatment protocols, because nature is self-regulating.

It's called homeostasis — a natural process which allows biological systems to continually adjust for optimal survival. Life is programmed to self-regulate and to course-correct itself, as long as the life in question is functioning in a healthy environment.

Like the toxic ocean water, the language of hierarchy has created a noxious environment for the humans living within it. This environment is fundamentally divisive and disproportionate, fomenting fear, lack, greed, conflict and disempowerment the world over. As the container for our entire societal structure, its deleterious vibratory frequencies program every aspect of our culture — be it government, media, education, economics, psychology, relationships, you name it. To attempt to revamp all the structures and elements comprising hierarchy, one-by-one, is ludicrous and doomed to accomplish all of diddly squat, while wasting exorbitant amounts of energy and resources in the process.

The way we transform our culture and all the elements comprising it — for the infinitely more equal, inclusive, empowered and free — is by evolving our language. Because language is the meta structure containing and programming our *everything*. It is the water in which we humans, and the world we have created, are all swimming.

Hierarchy, while real, is an abstraction. It has no material weight or mass. It is a conceptual structure crafted and sustained with language — with *its* language. Every time we utilize the language of hierarchy, we give hierarchy more life and more legitimacy, empowering its frequencies and its influence over our realities.

As we stop speaking hierarchy, we remove our consent from its influence, and we starve it out. As we replace the language of hierarchy with the language of betterarchy, we shift the whole paradigm. Because now we are reprogramming the morphic field and our subconscious minds with a language that consistently vibrates at the frequencies of unity, trust, equality, abundance, cooperation, empowerment and agency, and that programs us and the morphic field accordingly. Now, we are flipping the whole script.

It doesn't matter that we (think we) don't know how to fix all the world's problems, or how this next iteration of our evolution looks, functions or rolls itself out. All that matters is that we are harmonizing our vibrations with the frequencies of the qualities with which we are choosing to seed our reality construct. As we consistently and tenaciously program the morphic field with a language that vibrates at the frequencies of peace, unity, trust, equality, inclusivity, abundance, cooperation, empowerment and sovereign agency, then the reality that emerges from our words will necessarily express those same qualities.

Given that language is our A#1 all-purpose reality-programming tool, the quickest, easiest and most graceful way to evolve our realities for the more sustainable, humane, abundant and delightful is to stop speaking hierarchy, and to speak betterarchy — consistently and in unison, with a twinkle in our eye and a smile on our face.

Our task, as duly educated, empowered reality creators, is to share these betterarchical codes and upgrades far and wide, such that our friends, family and colleagues are all speaking betterarchy into our field, our world and our reality constructs, thus (r)evolutionizing our planet with our every word.

Thank you for joining us on the frontlines of reality-shifting, superstar, and doing your part to disseminate these tools near and far, swiftly and joyfully, while we speak a new world into being and live into a betterarchical reality together.

We got this.